Praise for

Police Wife, 1st edition

WINNER OF THESE INTERNATIONAL BOOK AWARDS:

- American Society of Journalists and Authors' Arlene Book Award for Writing that Makes a Difference
- Hollywood Book Festival non-fiction book award (runner-up)
- eLit Book Awards (silver medal)
- INDIEFAB Book of the Year Awards (bronze)
- Next Generation Indie Book Awards (finalist)

Praise for

Police Wife, 2nd edition

"I LOVED YOUR BOOK.... THIS IS A BOOK THAT SHOULD BE GIVEN TO THE WIFE OR GIRLFRIEND OF EVERY SINGLE MALE POLICE OFFICER.... These women have no place to turn.... It is very apparent that neither the police nor the courts are willing to deal with the problem."

– *SGT. AMY L. RAMSAY, PhD, Ontario, senior police policy analyst, former president, International Association of Women Police, founding president, Ontario Women in Law Enforcement*

"KUDOS AND GRATITUDE TO ALEX ROSLIN for speaking on behalf of the too-often silenced voices in abusive police families. This book needs to be widely circulated.... [It] transforms the police wife's private agony into a public issue, provides a plethora of recommendations for effecting change and powerfully concludes that both private and public players share responsibility in liberating and empowering victims."

– *LEANOR JOHNSON, sociologist, Arizona State University, founder of ASU's African and African American Studies Department, former member of FBI advisory board on police stress and family violence*

"AMY'S STORY MIRRORS MINE IN SO MANY WAYS. Like her, I lived in fear for my personal safety and my life for years. Like her, I experienced violence at the hands of a police officer who was my intimate partner. Like her, I felt trapped in a system that would protect the perpetrator because of the badge he carried…. Batterers are attracted to professions in which they can have power and control over others…. All of us associated with this profession must make it clear domestic violence will not be tolerated in our ranks."

– Deputy Chief Dottie Davis, Retired, Fort Wayne Police Department, Indiana, former chair, Governor's Council for the Prevention and Treatment of Family Violence, Indiana

"ROSLIN HAS DONE AN EXCELLENT JOB in *Police Wife*, painting an accurate picture of domestic violence in the police family. The average citizen is unaware of the issue that has been well known for years to the men wearing a badge and their agencies. Roslin's years of research reveal the heartbreaking violence that many officers inflict on their wives and children. *Police Wife* is an important read for any police officer's spouse, but is also recommended to anyone interested in a significant issue in today's society."

– Det. Albert F. Seng, PhD, Retired, Tucson Police Department, Arizona

"ALEX ROSLIN HAS THOROUGHLY DOCUMENTED the pervasiveness of woman abuse perpetrated by male police officers and also the seemingly universal tendency of these officers' peers and superiors to close ranks around them, protect their careers and shield the bureaucratic evidence from the possibility of public scrutiny.

"Roslin has brought to the surface a mostly hidden social issue that should matter greatly to every adult. His book is a must-read for anyone who has ever experienced—or known or worked with someone who has experienced—the misery of domestic violence."

– Deborah Harrison, sociologist, University of New Brunswick, author of The First Casualty: Violence Against Women in Canadian Military Communities, *former member of the Canadian Forces Advisory Council to the federal Department of Veterans Affairs*

"I APPRECIATED MS. MORRISON'S CANDOUR. It is clear that it has taken a great deal of courage to open herself and her story to the public. One real treasure in this story is the people in her circles who helped. Their actions often took great courage in the face of daunting challenges. For me this speaks to each officer who comes into contact with a possible domestic violence situation: Never accept the story on face value, and always remain open to the possibility of unexpected moments where small kindnesses may do great good.

"Different people form their opinions from different types of information. For some, it is emotional resonance that hooks them. For others it may be an evidence-based engagement that convinces them of the value of what they are reading. *Police Wife* delivers on both accounts."

– *STAFF SGT. MARGARET SHORTER, Retired, RCMP, president, International Association of Women Police*

POLICE

WIFE

The Secret Epidemic of
Police Domestic Violence

Alex Roslin

Library and Archives Canada Cataloguing in Publication

Roslin, Alex, author
    Police wife : the secret epidemic of police domestic
violence / Alex Roslin. -- 2nd edition.

First edition by Susanna Hope and Alex Roslin. Published
    by: Knowlton, Québec: Alex Roslin, 2015.
Issued in print and electronic formats.
ISBN 978-0-9948617-6-4 (paperback).--ISBN 978-0-9948617-8-8 (kindle).--
ISBN 978-0-9948617-9-5 (pdf).--ISBN 978-0-9948617-7-1 (epub)

    1. Police spouses--Violence against--Canada. 2. Wife abuse--Canada.
3. Family violence--Canada. 4. Abused wives--Canada--Anecdotes. 5. Police
spouses--Canada--Anecdotes. I. Hope, Susanna Police wife. II. Title.

HV6626.23.C3R69 2017   362.82'92092   C2016-906976-1
                                                    C2016-906977-X

We acknowledge the support of the Canada Council for the Arts, which last year invested $153 million to bring the arts to Canadians throughout the country.

Nous remercions le Conseil des arts du Canada de son soutien. L'an dernier, le Conseil a investi 153 millions de dollars pour mettre de l'art dans la vie des Canadiennes et des Canadiens de tout le pays.

 Canada Council   Conseil des arts
for the Arts   du Canada

Published by Sugar Hill Books

Cover photo credit: A derivative of a photo by Jason Ralston, http://tinyurl.com/p8gfscp, cropped with colours modified from the original, used under Creative Commons Attribution 2.0 Generic License, https://creativecommons.org/licenses/by/2.0/.

Note that website addresses listed in this book may change after publication. Their inclusion doesn't imply the author's endorsement.

ABOUT THE AUTHOR

Alex Roslin is an award-winning journalist who was president of the board of the Canadian Centre for Investigative Reporting. He co-authored the first edition of *Police Wife*, which won the American Society of Journalists and Authors' Arlene Book Award for Writing that Makes a Difference and was the runner-up for the Hollywood Book Festival non-fiction book award.

It also won silver in the eLit Book Awards and bronze in the INDIEFAB Book of the Year Awards and was a finalist in the Next Generation Indie Book Awards. Roslin is the author of the updated and revised second edition of *Police Wife*.

Roslin has also won three Canadian Association of Journalists prizes for investigative reporting, a gold prize in Canada's National Magazine Awards and nine nominations for CAJ awards and NMAs, including one for his story "Killer Cop" about RCMP Constable Jocelyn Hotte's murder of his ex-girlfriend Lucie Gélinas.

He has worked as an associate producer for the CBC-TV investigative programs *the fifth estate* and *Disclosure* and has written for *The Montreal Gazette, The Financial Post, The Globe and Mail, The Toronto Star, Maclean's, L'Actualité, The Georgia Straight, Zoomer, Canadian Geographic, Today's Parent* and many others.

He lives in Quebec with his wife and two daughters, whom he homeschools.

Connect with Roslin at his blog <u>PoliceDomesticViolence.Blogspot.com</u>.

To Rhonda, Odessa and Sasha, with all my love

CONTENTS

FOREWORD

BY LANE AND PATTY JUDSON

Assaulting a spouse is a crime regardless of who does it, but when the perpetrator is a law enforcement officer it is especially heinous.

One of the most notorious cases happened to our daughter, Crystal Judson-Brame. She was murdered by her estranged husband, Police Chief David Brame of Tacoma, Washington, in a shopping center parking lot with their two young children just feet away from this horrific tragedy.

Our whole family is affected daily by this murder. The kids go to the gravesite and lie down on their mother's grave and cry as they miss her. They see their Mom up in the clouds and blow her kisses—and they say to Gramma, "She caught them." What will they say and what can we do when it comes time for their first date or prom night? When they get married and have their own children, what will we say when the children ask about their Gramma Crystal and Grandpa Brame?

We grieve every day. How we all miss Crystal during the holidays. There are no more phone calls, just to talk. Crystal will never become a Gramma. Everything taken for granted daily is forever lost to Crystal and her children. The effect of domestic violence will always be there.

Since Crystal's murder in 2003, we have worked to educate cities and states in the U.S. as well as others in the UK and Australia about officer-involved domestic violence.

The stories of police domestic violence in this book are not an anomaly. Countless women and children have suffered brutality at the hands of police officers. Some have lost their lives trying to protect themselves or their children. Studies have found that up to 40 percent of police officers commit domestic violence. That is shocking.

We would like to ask politicians and other public servants: What, if anything, is your administration doing to protect those who are abused in a relationship with a law enforcement officer? And what can be done to correct the judicial system's handling of such crimes? That goes from top to bottom—from judges to prosecutors, chiefs of police and sheriffs, on down to newly hired personnel.

Officer-involved domestic violence is in our opinion a greater threat than many other crimes because the abused feel they have nowhere to turn for help. Why is that? Someone says, "Call the police." But in this case, the perpetrators are the police. A friend or former partner of the officer may answer the domestic violence call and too often is said to side with the accused. They rationalize their inaction by saying the accused could lose their badge and gun or be put on administrative leave.

Protection of a fellow law enforcement officer is often paramount in police culture. They usually investigate their own via internal affairs. Law enforcement agencies rarely have specific rules covering domestic violence committed by their employees. Internal affairs departments too often appear to follow the course of inaction.

Prosecutors tend to side with officers accused of offending because they can't believe police lie. Charges against law enforcement officers are plea-bargained away because "they may lose their job."

The abuse can continue and get worse. It may end up in a murder or murder-suicide with civil-rights litigation pursued for wrongful death. Governments and taxpayers face huge liabilities, especially when they involve law-breaking public servants who are in the profession of protecting citizens. We encourage those who are suffering from officer-involved domestic violence or whose loved ones were murdered by a police officer to file civil litigation.

We filed a \$75-million[1] lawsuit against the city of Tacoma for wrongful death in the case of our daughter. The suit was settled out of court for the benefit of our daughter's children. The city also agreed to change police procedures.

We launched a campaign that convinced the state of Washington to adopt legislation requiring police agencies to have a policy on officer-involved domestic violence. Our campaign also led Congress to pass an amendment to the Violence Against Women Act under our daughter's name, which President George W. Bush signed into law in 2006. It gave law enforcement agencies access to millions of dollars in annual grants for domestic violence training for officers.

---

[1] All dollar amounts in this book are in the funds of the country in question.

Other jurisdictions do not need this to happen to them. Officer-involved domestic violence tarnishes the image, badge and credibility of outstanding law enforcement personnel who lay their lives on the line every day to protect their communities. Citizens look up to these agencies as the ones to call for help.

Those of you reading this powerful book have an opportunity to stand up and get laws and policies in place for your law enforcement agencies and to protect your cities from unwanted lawsuits.

As the majority of domestic violence is committed by men, we need to do all we can to get men involved in helping to solve this epidemic—not only at the community level, but also nationwide. Men should hold other men who choose to abuse their families accountable. Let us not be silent, but instead acknowledge that a personable co-worker next to us can be an abuser.

Stop and think how adults and children can be scarred for life by this terrible crime. Its effect on young boys and girls can lead them to commit domestic violence when they grow up. They may feel it's "okay" to hit mommy or girls, as they learned it from the man or woman in the house. And girls learn it is okay for them to be hit and controlled by boyfriends in school.

It takes a strong person to walk the other way, and we can do this by developing attitudes and actions to support healthy families. Awareness of domestic violence is one of the key factors in accomplishing this, and knowing where to go and get proper training and professional help is critical. The news media is essential in helping to get the word out. Young people need to see and learn the warning signs of domestic abuse early in their life.

Our website lanejudson.com identifies more than 200 law enforcement personnel around the U.S. who committed suicide and/or murder targeting their spouse, children, girlfriend, family, friends and even their dogs.

Please listen to the voices of those who have lost their lives to domestic violence. They are calling out for your help.

POLICE

WIFE

INTRODUCTION

BY ALEX ROSLIN

T he mood in the car was festive. It was the evening of June 23, 2001—the night before St. Jean Baptiste Day, Quebec's version of the Fourth of July or Canada Day.

Lucie Gélinas was driving with three friends to the Boite à Marius tavern in Montreal's east end, where traditional Québécois *chansonniers* would lead the crowd in French Canadian folk songs as part of "La Fête Nationale," as the holiday is known in Quebec.

A cool drizzle fell as Lucie headed south on Montreal's Autoroute 13 highway in her Hyundai Accent, when an SUV suddenly rammed her from behind and everyone went flying. At the wheel of the SUV was her ex-boyfriend Jocelyn Hotte, a constable in the fabled Royal Canadian Mounted Police, Canada's iconic police force and also its largest. Their six-year relationship had ended less than a month before, and he was angry about the breakup and jealous of Lucie's new boyfriend.[2]

The SUV smashed into her car two more times. Lucie, 37, a mother of three, started to panic. "What do I do? What do I do?" she cried out.

Lucie tried to steady the wheel as she dialed 911 on her cell phone. "We are on the 13 south, the 13 south," she shouted to a Sûreté du Québec provincial police dispatcher. "Hurry up! Hurry up!"

---

[2] A version of the account here and in Chapter 2 appeared in Alex Roslin, "Killer Cop," *This Magazine*, November/December 2004, accessed March 18, 2015, http://albloggedup.blogspot.com/2007/09/police-family-violence-officer-involved-domestic-violence.html. This story was nominated for a National Magazine Award. See Chapter 2 for complete references.

As she turned onto congested Autoroute 40—Montreal's busiest high-way—the windows came apart on both sides of the car. Glass flew every-where. In the passenger seat, Lucie's downstairs neighbour Hugues felt as if an iron bar had hit him in the mouth. A bullet entered his left jaw, smashed through his teeth and shredded his tongue, exiting the right side of his face.

Another friend David, who sat in the rear behind Lucie, raised his left arm to shield his head. Two bullets struck his forearm, fracturing it. "He's shoot-ing at us! He's shooting at us!" Lucie said. "Get down!"

Hugues' cousin Pierre, sitting in the back beside David, was too stunned to react. Lucie turned and pushed his head down with her hand. "Get down," she said. Pierre and David crouched as low as they could in the cramped rear of the car.

Chilly rain now sprayed in through the shattered windows. Pierre realized Lucie was struggling to drive as she talked to the police dispatcher, so he took the phone from her hand. He shouted into it, trying to make himself heard over the screams of his friends and the noise of rain and traffic.

"Hey, listen, we are being shot at! We are being shot at, *tabarnak*.[3] There are two injured people in the car," Pierre said.

"You are being shot at by who?" asked the dispatcher.

Pierre asked the others in the car: "What's his name?"

"Jocelyn Hotte!" Lucie screamed. "Jocelyn Hotte! Jocelyn Hotte!"

"Jocelyn Hotte! A guy from the RCMP," Pierre said. "He is just behind us. What do we do, *ostie*?"[4]

Dense traffic on the highway forced Lucie to slow down. She continued to shout her ex-boyfriend's name as she passed office buildings, car dealerships and highway billboards. "Jocelyn Hotte! Jocelyn Hotte!"

She made her way to the highway's juncture with the Décarie Expressway, which heads south toward downtown. Here the dispatcher heard her piercing shriek over the phone. A bullet had passed through the car door and hit Lucie in the thigh, cutting through muscle and lodging in her knee. She sideswiped other vehicles as she struggled to get away from the SUV.

But Jocelyn Hotte was a 17-year veteran of the RCMP—a crack shot on the force's VIP-protection squad trained in advanced driving tactics. He easily kept pace. He collided with Lucie's car again and again, reloaded his 9 mm Smith & Wesson police pistol and kept peppering her car with bullets.

Six days before that night, Lucie had called 911 in tears to report that Hotte had threatened to kill her. Two police officers from the Montreal

---

[3] As used here, the Quebec French slang word "*tabarnak*" can be translated as "for fuck's sake."

[4] "*Ostie*" roughly translates in this case as "dammit."

suburb of Laval had visited her home, but after a half-hour visit they had dismissed her complaint as "unfounded."

Now here was Hotte acting out his "unfounded" threat.

"Hurry up," Pierre shouted to the SQ dispatcher.

"Is he still shooting at you?" asked the voice on the phone.

"Yes, yes," said Pierre. "He is just behind us."

The dispatcher seemed confused. "Who are you? Jocelyn?" he asked.

Exasperated, Pierre replied, "No, no! I am not Jocelyn! He is Jocelyn—Christ, the guy shooting at us! Hurry up, man."

"Still on the 40, sir?"

"Hey, we are being shot at," Pierre answered. "Do you understand?"

Pierre had still not dared to look back. As Lucie dodged the traffic, he lifted his head to peek to the rear. He felt a sudden jolt and screamed, then lost his breath. It felt as if he had fallen hard onto his back. He dropped the cell phone and slumped onto his left side.

When he could breathe again, Pierre told David, "I think I was hit in the back."

"No, I don't think so," David said. But when he put his hand on Pierre's back and pulled it back, it was covered in blood.

"You're right. Don't move," he told Pierre.

"Sir? Sir? Answer me, sir," the SQ dispatcher said. "They got him."

Lucie had to slow to 50 kilometres an hour (30 miles per hour) in the heavy traffic around the Décarie Interchange. The RCMP officer pulled up parallel to the left side of her car and opened fire at virtually point-blank range.

Hugues, seated in front and already shot in the face, was hit three more times. He felt his arm jerk as one bullet sectioned two nerves in his hand and severed an artery. A second bullet ripped into his hip. A third tore through his left shoulder and into his chest, cleaving apart his left lung. He heard bullets whistling all around.[5]

Lucie was shot again, too. One bullet broke apart as it passed through the rear car window. The projectiles ripped through her headrest and hit her left jaw. Another bullet penetrated her upper left arm and chest. A third chopped into her left shoulder. It splintered her shoulder blade and spine and lodged in the back of her neck. The fourth, fatal bullet struck her behind her left ear, passed through her brain and exited three centimetres above her right ear.

The car, its inside sprayed with blood, slowed as it arced toward a concrete barrier. "Brake, brake, brake!" David shouted. The Hyundai hit the

---

[5] Christiane Desjardins, "Procès de Jocelyn Hotte; 'Un policier, ça tire pas sur du bon monde,' se disait Pierre Mainville," *La Presse*, November 22, 2002, A5.

barrier and veered back into the middle lanes, rolling several car lengths before it stopped amid the traffic—13 kilometres (8 miles) from where the chase had started.

David lay on top of Pierre. Neither man budged as they heard the SUV stop by the driver's side of the car. They heard its engine rev almost within touching distance. They couldn't hear Lucie or Hugues in front or see what had happened to them.

The SQ dispatcher's voice came through again on the cell phone. "Hello? I can't hear you. Hello, sir?"

The dispatcher heard a gunshot. Then a man's voice: "Help." Another gunshot. "Help." Another shot. "Help, help."

"Hello?" asked the dispatcher.

Several minutes passed before the dispatcher heard someone speak again. "Help, help, help!"

Pierre and David were looking for the phone but couldn't find it. The dispatcher heard Pierre pleading: "Hurry up. There are a lot of hurt people. Quick. Quick. Quick."

Jocelyn Hotte had sped away.

When we think of domestic violence, we usually think of the police as the ones breaking it up, not committing it. Watch a TV show or movie about police—the most depicted profession in entertainment—and you'll often see stories about abusive men, while the police are generally the heroes.

But what happens when the camera is gone and a real-life police officer goes home to his wife and kids? This is where the Hollywood version ends and a darker story emerges. Jocelyn Hotte's murder of Lucie Gélinas was not an isolated tragedy. It was unusual only because it was so public and so bloody. In the vast majority of cases, cops who hurt a family member do so in utter secrecy, while their spouses and children live in desperate isolation with very little hope of help.

A staggering amount of domestic violence rages behind the walls of cops' homes, while most police departments do little about it, research shows.[6]

- **Abuse at epidemic levels**—An astonishing 40 percent of cops acknowledged in one U.S. survey that they were violent with their spouse or children in the previous six months. A second survey had remarkably similar results—40 percent of officers admitted there

---

[6] References for the information in these bullet points are given later in this book.

was violence in their relationship in the previous year. The cops' abuse rate was up to 15 times that of the public.

Younger officers, narcotics cops, those on the night shift and cops who were divorced or separated reported even higher rates of violence at home—up to 66 percent. Eight percent of cops reported "severe" violence—strangulation, beating up their spouse, using a knife or gun.

- **Discipline is startlingly lax**—A U.S. study found that only 6 percent of police departments normally terminated an officer after a sustained domestic violence complaint. In the Los Angeles Police Department, a cop is nearly three times more likely to lose his job if he is involved in an off-duty altercation than for domestic violence and six times more likely if he makes a false statement.

  An investigation of the Puerto Rico Police Department found that 86 percent of cops with two or more arrests for domestic violence still remained on active duty.

- **The abuse epidemic is ignored worldwide**—Canadians and Europeans like to think they're socially more progressive than the U.S., but they have little to be proud of when it comes to police domestic violence. I surveyed dozens of police forces in 10 countries—the first international survey ever done on the problem—and found that the inaction is a worldwide phenomenon. Only about one in five departments typically fires an officer even after a second domestic violence conviction or sustained complaint.

  In Canada, a civilian is seven times more likely to be sentenced to prison time than a cop when convicted of domestic violence. The RCMP disciplines Mounties more harshly if they steal or lie than if they assault an intimate partner.

Amy Morrison lived the consequences of such inaction. She tells the chilling story of her marriage to a police officer in Chapter 1 of this book. I met her after several years of investigating domestic violence in police homes. I started looking into the problem after a friend told me a curious story. She attended a support group for abused women in Montreal. Many of the women in the group were partners of bikers, but she was surprised to learn that just as many were spouses of cops. Intrigued, I started calling women's shelters, counsellors, cops and academics. It took only a few conversations to see my friend had stumbled on a massive, little-known problem.

My research led to an investigative story in 2000 for the Canadian current-affairs magazine *Saturday Night* (now sadly defunct) and a feature article in *The Montreal Gazette* daily newspaper. I found that some of my best information came from cops and ex-cops who were outraged about domestic abuse in their ranks and the challenges of stopping it.

My inquiries took an unusual turn when I learned of a group of eight policewomen in Toronto who had themselves been abused in relationships with fellow cops. Even they faced enormous obstacles when they tried to get help and justice. The women said investigations into their cases were bungled and that they were ostracized and faced career blowback for complaining. "The common theme is that all of our careers are affected, while most of the men didn't suffer any career repercussions. Some got promoted," one of the women officers told me.

I wondered just what kind of a horror show I had come across. If even a cop couldn't get a fair hearing from her own department, what hope did a civilian woman have? It seemed incredible that a crime wave of such magnitude and far-reaching social consequences could be so unknown to the public and yet at the same time an open secret in a mostly indifferent law enforcement community. It was surely one of the most surreal crime epidemics of our time—at once disavowed, generalized and virtually unchecked.

Aptly summing up the bizarre disconnect, retired Lieutenant Detective Mark Wynn of the Nashville Metropolitan Police Department in Tennessee told PBS in a story on the issue: "What's amazing to me is we're having this conversation at all. I mean, could you imagine us sitting here talking about this and saying, how do you feel about officers using crack before they go to work, or how do you feel about the officer who every once in a while just robs a bank, or every once in a while decides to go in and steal a car from a dealership? We wouldn't have this conversation. Why is it that we've taken violence against women and separated that from other crimes?"[7]

Wynn also made another disturbing point: "You teach them [cops] all these skills, and then you add all of that to someone who is violent, you've got a lethal combination on your hands."

It also dawned on me that the implications went far beyond police families. Without realizing it, we all pay a steep price for the abuse epidemic. How

---

[7] Mark Wynn, interview, "How to Combat Officer-Involved Domestic Violence," PBS *Frontline*, November 23, 2013, accessed July 14, 2015, http://www.pbs.org/wgbh/pages/frontline/criminal-justice/death-in-st-augustine/how-to-combat-officer-involved-domestic-violence/. Wynn served in his department's domestic violence division and SWAT team. He has spoken about domestic violence at the White House and before Congress.

does a wife-beating cop act on the job? Domestic violence is the single most common reason the public contacts the police in the U.S., accounting for up to 50 percent of all calls in some areas.[8] Yet, a battered woman who calls 911 may have a two-in-five chance of an abuser coming to her door. Whose side do you suppose he is more likely to take? Official investigations have found law enforcement departments that tolerate abuse in officers' homes also mishandle violence against women in other homes. We all pay as taxpayers for this bungling when governments have to settle multi-million-dollar lawsuits with survivors of police abuse or negligence.

Cops who batter at home are also more prone to other misconduct, such as brutality against civilians and even violence against fellow officers. Here was a hidden clue to understanding all kinds of abuses of police power, including the police shootings of African Americans that have rocked the U.S. and sparked the Black Lives Matter movement. Police domestic violence also has close connections to other abuses, such as police sexual harassment of young female drivers at traffic stops and women cops, and broader questions, such as mass shootings, the militarization of police and growing inequality in our society.

What goes on in police homes clearly has an intimate connection to police relations with the public. Understanding police domestic violence can show us why those relations are getting worse, how those relations are a barometer for our society's health and what we must do to turn the situation around.

And as some of the abused women I spoke with emphasized, police officers themselves are victims, too. Even though our society calls cops heroes, we give them little support to cope with the pressure of police work. A big part of the job is to wield power to control other people. As a result, policing attracts people who are good at controlling others or may have a craving for that kind of power—and then trains them to use their power better. Wanting control over a spouse is, as it happens, also the main cause of domestic violence. Is it a surprise then that so many cops are violent at home?

---

[8] U.S. Department of Justice, *Practical Implications of Current Domestic Violence Research*, 1. See also Paul C. Friday et al., "Evaluating the Impact of a Specialized Domestic Violence Police Unit" (report submitted to the U.S. Department of Justice, May 2006), 9, 12, accessed May 19, 2015, https://www.ncjrs.gov/pdffiles1/nij/grants/215916.pdf; and Dave Vieser, "Police hire 2 to investigate domestic violence in Statesville," *The Charlotte Observer*, August 4, 2015, accessed August 23, 2015, http://www.charlotteobserver.com/news/local/community/lake-norman-mooresville/article29958798.html.

At the heart of all this is the police wife or girlfriend. Even finding women to interview is a major challenge. They live a nightmare so intense that many of the ones I contacted weren't willing to talk, even anonymously. Some still live in terror years after leaving the relationship. Others have experienced such severe trauma, they are physically sick when they speak about their past.

My reporting eventually convinced some abused ex-police spouses to talk to me. Most were frantic for help and felt they had nowhere to turn. They had exhausted all other avenues such as calling police, filing complaints or speaking with counsellors and advocates.

One such woman is Amy Morrison, a journalist who shares her dramatic story of marriage to a police officer in Chapter 1 of this book. Amy Morrison is a pseudonym. Her actual name and other identifying details have been omitted for security and privacy reasons. Despite the pain of reliving her experiences, Amy tells her story because she wants to help other police family members. Like many of the other accounts I heard, Amy's story is remarkable and inspiring—on par with any of the most astonishing examples of human survival in extreme conditions. Her challenge wasn't drifting far at sea or living through a plane crash in remote mountains, but escaping with her children from the police state that was their home.

Amy and the other police spouses I spoke with are unsung heroes of the law enforcement community. Their stories are a tribute to human courage, the determination to survive and help others, and the meaning of hope. (This book focuses chiefly on male-on-female abuse because research shows women are the target of most intimate-partner violence, especially severe forms, and since the vast majority of cops are men.[9] But regardless of who

---

[9] Women aged 15 and up accounted for 81 percent of spousal violence victims in Canada, according to Maire Sinha, *Family violence in Canada: A statistical profile, 2010* (Ottawa: Statistics Canada, 2012), 13, accessed March 18, 2015, http://www.statcan.gc.ca/pub/85-002-x/2012001/article/11643-eng.pdf. In the U.S., men account for 81 to 92 percent of domestic violence perpetrators who come to the attention of the court system, depending on the jurisdiction. See U.S. Department of Justice, Office of Justice Programs, National Institute of Justice, *Practical Implications of Current Domestic Violence Research: For Law Enforcement, Prosecutors and Judges*, (Washington, D.C.: June 2009), 15, accessed May 28, 2015, https://www.ncjrs.gov/pdffiles1/nij/225722.pdf. Women also experience far more severe abuse than men. In the U.S., 42 percent of abused women suffered an injury (versus 14 percent of abused men) and 22 percent needed medical care (versus 5.5 percent of men), according to Michele C. Black et al., *The National Intimate Partner and Sexual Violence Survey: 2010 Summary Report* (Atlanta, Georgia: Centers for Disease Control and Prevention, 2011), 56-7, accessed March 18, 2015, http://www.cdc.gov/violenceprevention/pdf/nisvs_report2010-a.pdf. See data on the portion of women in police forces in Chapter 5.

the target is, abuse in a police home usually poses extra challenges, including for children, men, same-sex partners and racialized people.[10])

Police spouses who are being abused face unimaginable barriers to finding help, safety and justice. They rarely complain to police, criminal charges are rarer still, and an abusive officer's chances of losing his badge and gun are virtually nil.

Domestic violence is bad enough for any woman to deal with. Shelters, many of them chronically underfunded, regularly turn away abused women because they are full, while only about one in four incidents in the wider population ever get reported to police. Hundreds of U.S. communities have adopted "nuisance property" laws that pressure landlords to evict tenants if police are repeatedly called to their home for domestic abuse or other issues, further dissuading survivors from seeking help.[11]

But abuse at home is far worse for the wife or girlfriend of a cop. Who will she call—911? What if a co-worker or friend of her husband responds? Police officers are trained to use physical force and know how to hurt someone without leaving a trace. They have guns and often bring them home.

And if a cop's wife runs, where will she hide? He usually knows where the women's shelters are. Shelter staff admit they are often powerless to protect abused police spouses. Amazingly, some shelters even reportedly turn police spouses away.[12] Cops who abuse often have training and tools to track their spouse's phone calls, travels and web use to find out if she is researching how to get help or, if she has fled, where she went.

The counsellors available to help other abuse survivors are often clueless about how to help police spouses. "Victims of police officer batterers typically report that advocates do not appreciate how different their situation is because the abuser is in law enforcement," writes Diane Wetendorf, a retired Chicago-area domestic violence counsellor who has helped hundreds of

---

[10] Some groups face unique hurdles. For example, police spouses with children may fear for their children's safety as well as their own and, in a separation, can face highly abusive legal battles over custody, family assets and child support. Female officers in a relationship with a fellow cop may face career repercussions and ostracism from colleagues if they report abuse. Same-sex intimate partners of a cop have the added problem of police homophobia toward them or their partner if they disclose abuse. And partners of racialized officers may struggle with the extra burden of not wanting to expose the officer to a justice system that could discriminate against them.

[11] See Chapter 5 for more details and references.

[12] Diane Wetendorf, *When the Batterer Is a Law Enforcement Officer: A Guide for Advocates* (Battered Women's Justice Project, 2004), 28, accessed March 27, 2015, http://www.bwjp.org/assets/documents/pdfs/batterer_officer_guide_for_advocates.pdf.

abused police spouses and is author of *Police Domestic Violence: A Handbook for Victims*. "It is disappointing and frustrating for a victim to have to educate the very people who she had hoped would be able to inform her."[13]

Even the usual safety tips offered to domestic violence survivors often don't work for police spouses. For example, other abused women are typically advised to open a bank account in their name to create financial independence when planning to leave the relationship. But police officers may be able to track financial information and could have contacts at local banks. Instead, Wetendorf advises police spouses to set aside cash. Other women can call anonymous domestic violence hotlines to get information or help, but a cop's significant other has to be careful about that, too. A counsellor who believes a woman or her children are at risk of harm is often required to pass the caller's information on to law enforcement—the very last thing a police spouse may want.

In the rare case where the woman works up the nerve to complain, the police department and justice system often victimize her again. She must take on the infamous "blue code of silence"—the strict unwritten rule of cops protecting each other in investigations. The police have their own name for it—extending "professional courtesy." In the words of Anthony Bouza, a one-time commander in the New York Police Department and former police chief of Minneapolis, "The Mafia never enforced its code of blood-sworn omerta with the ferocity, efficacy and enthusiasm the police bring to the Blue Code of Silence."[14]

Police departments often try to steer complaints into closed-door disciplinary hearings instead of the criminal proceedings that civilians face. The internal hearings usually result in no more than a token slap on the wrist for the officer—for example, a reprimand or brief suspension. Despite the high number of abusive officers, charges are laid in only a tiny number of cases—often, it seems, only those too extreme to ignore. In court, the officer has major advantages, too. He is usually at ease with courtroom procedures and testifying on the stand. He may have worked in the past with the prosecutor or judge. Officers called to testify are notorious for covering for each other. In police lingo, it's known as "testilying."[15]

---

[13] Wetendorf, *When the Batterer Is a Law Enforcement Officer*, 14. See also Diane Wetendorf, *Police Domestic Violence: A Handbook for Victims* (2013), accessed March 27, 2015, http://www.abuseofpower.info/Book_Index.htm; and Diane Wetendorf, "Annotated Safety Plan for OIDV Survivors" (2014), accessed April 2, 2015, http://www.abuseofpower.info/Tool_AnnotatedSafety.htm.
[14] Anthony V. Bouza, *Police Unbound: Corruption, Abuse, and Heroism by the Boys in Blue* (Amherst, New York: Prometheus Books, 2001), 18.
[15] Ibid., 24-25.

"A batterer is a master manipulator and makes the victim look like it's all her fault. A batterer who is a police officer is a master manipulator who has a PhD—an in-depth knowledge of the law and how to work the law so as not to be held accountable," said David Thomas, a retired police officer who helped create the first domestic violence unit in the Montgomery County Police Department in Maryland. Thomas has toured the U.S. educating cops on police domestic violence on behalf of the International Association of Chiefs of Police.

"I'd put up a picture of the Three Stooges in police uniform and say, 'This is the way this individual looks at you. They have worked you like a tool,'" Thomas told me.

Unsurprisingly, convictions are highly unusual. In the rare exceptions, the sentence is often a discharge, which can mean no criminal record if certain conditions are met for a period of time. It is exceedingly rare for a convicted police officer to be sentenced to prison time, except in some cases of extreme violence. He isn't even likely to lose his job. I was surprised to learn that virtually no U.S. or Canadian police departments have a policy of automatically firing officers with a criminal conviction for domestic abuse.

And both countries have huge loopholes in their gun-control laws that let cops hang on to firearms even when convicted of domestic violence. (As an example of how many countries are slow to act on the issue, Canada is about 20 years behind the U.S. in keeping guns out of cop abusers' hands—this, despite Canada's reputation for far stricter gun laws and an overhaul of its firearms legislation in 2015.)

It all adds up to the police having a de facto licence to abuse their spouses and children. The families live in silent terror—cut off, forsaken by those who are supposed to help them, fearing for their safety or their very lives. Insofar as the abuse epidemic is perpetrated by government employees whose actions are intimately connected to their service and tacitly condoned by authorities, the epidemic effectively amounts to state-supported domestic terrorism. And it's a worldwide phenomenon that police families struggle with everywhere from Montreal to Los Angeles, Puerto Rico, the UK, Australia and South Africa.

Unsurprisingly, police departments are incredibly tight-lipped about the crime spree in their ranks and unreceptive to questions about it. Some departments refuse to say how many cops they punish for abuse or don't even know. Others, like the Vancouver Police Department, actually insist that none of their cops are abusive. When I filed freedom-of-information requests for data on the problem, the Toronto Police Service simply ignored my letter.

Meanwhile, the RCMP demanded a fee of over $29,000 to search for data that I later discovered was largely available for free online.

Little wonder then that the torrent of abuse is virtually unknown to the public.

Not long after I wrote my *Saturday Night* story, RCMP Constable Jocelyn Hotte murdered Lucie Gélinas in Montreal in 2001. I continued my reporting with a feature article about the tragedy in *This Magazine*, a current-affairs magazine in Toronto. At Hotte's murder trial, every side (including Hotte's own lawyers and Hotte himself) agreed that if police had taken Gélinas's 911 call before the shooting more seriously, there's a good chance she'd be alive today. The article, titled "Killer Cop," was nominated for a National Magazine Award in Canada. I also proposed and helped research a program on the issue for the CBC-TV investigative show *Disclosure* and wrote feature articles for *The Georgia Straight* weekly of Vancouver and others.

As I worked on these stories, I found disappointingly few other journalists or academics were looking into the problems or aware of them. When occasional cases came to light, reporters usually covered them as one-off crime stories—and then moved on without following up on the obvious questions that such incidents raise. Academics have done only a tiny handful of studies. The main U.S. research on the extent of the problem is over 20 years old. And no studies have ever been done on the prevalence in other countries. Yet, cops in Canada, for example, told me the problem is just as widespread north of the border.

My reporting eventually evolved into the book *Police Wife*, which I co-authored in 2015. The first edition won the American Society of Journalists and Authors' Arlene Book Award for Writing that Makes a Difference, silver in the eLit Book Awards and bronze in the INDIEFAB Book of the Year Awards. It was also the runner-up for the Hollywood Book Festival non-fiction book award and a finalist in the Next Generation Indie Book Awards.

The book you're now reading is my updated and revised second edition of *Police Wife*. The new material includes the memoir of former police wife Amy Morrison. This edition also reports for the first time the results of a survey I sent to 178 police forces in 10 countries, including the U.S., Canada, the UK and France, to gauge the police response to the abuse. I also write about documents I obtained from four of Canada's largest police forces showing that not a single abusive police officer had been terminated at any of these departments in recent years. (See Chapter 8 and Appendix E for details on the survey and documents.)

The new edition also has updated appendices, including contributions from police officers with 96 years of collective experience on the job; advice and resources for survivors, friends and family; recommendations for police agencies, governments, advocates, the public, journalists and academics; and selected statistics.

During 16 years of researching and reporting on police domestic violence and over 10 years of work on this book, I kept coming back to a few basic questions:

- How many ticking bombs like Jocelyn Hotte are there in uniform waiting to explode? What are police forces and governments doing about the mounting toll of injuries and deaths?
- What is behind the abuse epidemic? How much is domestic violence an inevitable job hazard for law enforcement families, like black lung disease for a coal miner? Apart from police families, what are the impacts on other people, such as other abused women, African Americans, young women drivers, female cops and Native Americans?
- How does society fuel police domestic violence by giving officers massive, largely unchecked coercive power and then mostly ignoring the inevitable consequences? How is the abuse driven by an increasingly unequal society that gives police a tacit mandate to keep marginalized groups in check? And what are the solutions?

These questions are relevant to everyone, not just cops and their families. The surprising answers lay bare some critical, yet uncomfortable truths that go far beyond the world of the police—touching us all and the way we live.

PART I

Amy's Story

By Amy Morrison

CHAPTER 1

Everything Seemed Perfect

I was only 22 when I met the man of my dreams.[16] Tom was nearly 30. He was a police officer, fearless but also gentle. As a journalist, I had been assigned to go to the police station every day at 5:30 p.m. for a briefing on the latest crime developments. I didn't know Tom, but he apparently noticed me at these briefings. He tracked me down on the Internet and sent me a few messages praising my reporting, then eventually asked me out.

We soon became a couple. We went out to restaurants, movies, bars. He gave me flowers and was protective. Tom liked to tell me he had decided to become a police officer to serve and protect people. Everything seemed perfect. I thought we'd be together for the rest of our lives.

Early on in our relationship, Tom told me about his ex-wife and how she had left him and taken their son. The way he described her, she sounded like a monster. He told me she had cheated on him and tried to commit suicide. He said he didn't know why he had loved her and that she had ruined his credit rating with all her unpaid bills. The more he talked about her, the more I was inclined to agree with him. His ex-wife really was a nut job.

Tom kept a very close eye on her. He often parked in front of her house and would sometimes even bring me along. He regularly checked her driver and vehicle records to see if she had gotten a ticket or changed cars. I was

---

[16] Amy Morrison is a pseudonym. The writer's actual name and other identifying details have been omitted for security and privacy reasons.

very uncomfortable when he told me this, but he justified it by saying he just wanted to make sure his son was okay. "One day you'll know what it's like to worry about your own kid," he said.

He kept an eye on me too. If he saw me out in the city while he was on patrol, he'd follow me. When I saw him doing this, he said he wanted me to feel protected. I told him it felt overbearing. "I love you, and I want to make sure you're safe," he replied.

Tom was clearly unhappy. Not only did he complain a lot about his ex-wife and his financial situation, but also about his incompetent co-workers and superiors. During our first few dates, Tom talked so much about his ex-wife and so little about himself that I sometimes felt like a third wheel. When he did talk about himself, it was usually to point out what a brave and outstanding police officer he was.

He also clearly enjoyed the power he had as a cop. He knew when and where all the police traffic stops were and liked to show me how he could get away with speeding and drunk driving because he wouldn't get caught. He didn't drink excessively, but neither did he watch how much he drank when we were out, and he always drove very fast. He acted as if the law didn't apply to him.

I often asked him to slow down, especially later on when one of our kids was in the car. "I know how to drive," he'd snap.

He loved to talk about his dangerous and heroic deeds, like the time he walked into a room where a man had just shot himself in the head. He went into great detail about seeing the man's skull half blown off and having to pick up chunks of brain, and then console the man's family. He told me the other cops couldn't handle the call. They didn't want to go into the room or examine the scene and couldn't bring themselves to talk to the family. He had to do everything.

Another of Tom's favorite stories was the time he responded to a call involving a car accident. The way he told it, he alone saved a child's life. Of course, cops don't usually respond to car accidents alone. Two other police officers were on the scene along with firefighters and paramedics. But in Tom's telling, he was the sole hero.

He also liked to boast about his athletic prowess on the job. Whenever he had to chase small-time drug dealers on foot, the other cops could never keep up or anticipate which way the fleeing perp would turn. It was always Tom who caught the bad guys.

To be honest, I never tried to verify these stories. I believed Tom. But even if I had wanted to ask someone about them, I wouldn't have been able to. His stories always seemed to take place in a different jurisdiction, never the one he was working in.

I really didn't know what I was doing with Tom, but I stayed. He just had this indescribable charm. I felt an intense need to console him and do little things for him. He liked that. He also liked to tell me that even though I had my flaws, I was the "perfect woman." My friends thought we were living the perfect love story. Admittedly, Tom and his life were a bit unusual, but I chalked up my qualms to the getting-to-know-each-another phase. There was certainly a lot of passion... and suffering.

Our relationship felt like it became official when Tom invited me to meet his police buddies for the first time. Even though I had already met some of them through my work as a journalist, Tom and I never went to any bars where his co-workers might hang out. They all knew about our relationship, but Tom waited a few weeks to make it official. He took me to a party for cops and their families.

Tom briefed me beforehand. "People will tell you I'm a real womanizer and sexist, but it's not true. If anyone says any crap about me, just tell them that I'll tell you the truth," he said. Sure enough, Tom's co-workers told me he was a womanizer and sexist, but I didn't believe them because Tom had warned me.

Despite these comments, I had a good time at the party and felt like I was part of the group. But they made it very clear to me that whatever happened in the department stayed in the department and that journalists weren't necessarily welcome in their world. They told me they'd decided to let me in because I had proven to be trustworthy. (I had written an article on 24 hours in the life of a cop, and they were happy with the story.) Now that I had been officially introduced and Tom's colleagues were reminded of my line of work and my willingness to speak well of the police, I was deemed "fit for service."

And Tom made it very clear that it was time for me to act like it. We had been together a few weeks by this point, and he was becoming sexually impatient. His caresses and kisses were increasingly urgent. I let him take me into his bed one night, and he tried to force me to have sex. When I told him I wasn't ready, he accused me of being uptight and told me I should be willing to prove my love for him.

I felt guilty about my first "failure" in our budding relationship and didn't sleep a wink that night. Instead, I lay there listening to him snore, waiting for him to wake up and tell me to get out. I was disoriented by his strange mix of charm and oppression. But I wanted to believe that I was in love and just needed to learn how to be a better girlfriend. Again and again, he told me he had a lot to teach me because he knew much better than me how relationships were supposed to work, having been with his wife for seven years.

A few months after we met, Tom asked me to move in with him. At the time, I was working on a month-long contract in another city 100 miles away and was staying with a friend who lived there. After that, I'd be unemployed. Tom said I could live with him afterward instead of worrying about finding other work. He made the suggestion even though he saw my income as a major bonus because he had a lot of debts. (He wouldn't go into detail about those, except to regularly complain about them.)

Tom felt my job as a journalist put me in too much contact with the outside world, and he hated the fact that I had male work colleagues and regularly interviewed men. He didn't like not being able to control my schedule. During our month apart, I found myself constantly having to justify where I had been, what I had been doing and with whom.

When my contract ended, I moved in with Tom. I didn't have a new journalism assignment lined up, but I knew one could come my way at a moment's notice. Sure enough, less than a month later, I got another assignment. Even though it was a dream job, I wasn't excited about it. Once again, it was in a different city, a 90-minute drive away. The distance and 12-hour workdays meant having to rent an apartment there. And this time, the contract was for a year—possibly longer if it turned into a permanent position. Still, the opportunity was too good to refuse.

Tom was obviously less than thrilled. In order to prove that I loved him, he insisted that I should plan all my time off around his schedule. He wanted me to be available to take care of his son when Tom had visitation on weekends and school holidays. Tom had better things to do, like going to football games with his buddies.

Tom didn't seem to notice how hard it was for me to keep up the hectic pace of constantly travelling back and forth between both cities or that I had to fight with my boss and colleagues to get the days off that Tom insisted I take. He didn't care that his son was sick of seeing his father's girlfriend instead of his own father. What mattered most was his own freedom and comfort. And because he seemed to be so unhappy, I gave in to his demands. So I took care of his apartment and son.

But Tom also made it clear I was to butt out of his son's upbringing. "You don't have kids," he said. "You don't know anything about it." In other words, I had to accept any and all behavior from this boy. Caring for Tom's son was not easy. He virtually never actually spoke to me. For example, instead of asking me for bread, he would say, "She should give me some bread."

I was expected to give in to the boy's every whim and craving—even things I don't do for my own children today. If he asked for candy or chocolate at the supermarket, I bought it. If he had new shoes or clothes, it was because I paid for them.

On the weekends when Tom had his son, I had to cook only what the boy said he ate at his mother's house. He systematically refused to eat anything else I made, even though he'd accept the same meal if his father made it. Once, when he threw up his vegetables all over my plate, I stood up and said enough was enough. Tom quickly put me back in my place, saying, "It was obviously no good!"

By the time Tom's son was 5, he started to insult me to my face. I wasn't allowed to ask for an explanation or apology. I couldn't say a word.

Tom's apartment was mostly empty because, he claimed, his wife had stolen all his furniture. But it was filled with photos of Tom. The living room had a huge painting of him on one wall. Photos of him in uniform were in the bedroom. There were no photos of his son.

I once teased him about it. "Do you think you might be a little self-centered?" I asked. "Bullshit," he snapped.

But the heart has funny ways. I was deeply in love and only 23. Tom was intelligent, charming and attractive—always very attentive. He showed a pride in his work that seemed to be a prerequisite for the authority he represented. But he also showed humility and seemed to try his best to be a good father. He made time for us as a couple and introduced me to his family as the perfect partner. He was a man who needed love, and I had a lot of love to give. At the same time, I had a lot to learn, and he seemed to have a lot to teach me.

Only later on did I realize that many of the traits I saw as admirable or excusable were actually warning signs for what was to come. One of his traits was jealousy, which was getting worse. I figured he just needed extra reassurance because his ex-wife had cheated on him. I was still living and working in the other city and commuting back and forth regularly. When I was away for work, I had to give Tom my schedule, answer several texts a day from him and be on Facebook daily after work.

One night my boss and his wife invited me out to see a movie, so I told Tom I wouldn't be on Facebook. "Who are you going out with?" Tom texted.

"Naomi and John," I wrote back. "We're going to the movies. They're picking me up and bringing me back home."

"So it's a threesome?"

"I'm spending the evening with co-workers. They're here. Talk to you later."

"You're the love of my life and you're leaving me all alone with my computer," Tom said. "I want to kill myself."

I read this last message when I was in the car with my friends and must have reacted strongly because Naomi asked if I was okay. Once we got to the movie theatre and sat down, I read them his message. They both just laughed and told me not to write back because it was obviously a joke. I didn't answer until I got back home.

"Back home now. You okay?" I asked.

"What if I really had killed myself?" Tom asked. "My ex left me. Don't be like her."

"I'm sorry. I won't go out anymore. I love you."

I spent a sleepless night imagining the man I loved putting a bullet in his head. When I told some friends, they said I should leave him. Instead, I decided I didn't have to go out anymore.

Tom asked me to marry him on Valentine's Day. We got engaged during a romantic dinner where, as usual, he spent the entire time talking about his work, his extraordinary skills as a cop and how the entire world was out to get him. And how everyone around him was completely incompetent. When I announced my engagement at work, everyone told me not to go through with it. I ignored them.

Meanwhile, Tom continued to track my every step. He now expected me to be on Facebook during the day, too, so I wouldn't be able to take coffee breaks with my work friends. "Journalists are all bastards and liars," he said. "Your magazine is a rag. You're better off spending your breaks talking with your fiancé." I gave in.

Not long after, I told him I had joined an online police wives' forum and that we were planning to meet in person because we all got along and understood what it was like to be married to a cop. Not only was he not surprised, he told me he knew I was talking about myself on the site, even though the forum was completely private. I asked the forum administrator to do a search for Tom's email addresses. It turned out Tom had signed up on the forum shortly after me, using a female pseudonym. When I asked Tom about this, he said he wanted to monitor when I was online and what I was saying to make sure I wasn't cheating on him. I forgave him and quit the forum.

Nine months after I started my new job, Tom sprained his ankle playing sports and had to take 10 days off work. He told me he was completely immobile and asked me to make the round trip every day from the other city so I could take care of him. When the 10 days were over, I went with him to see his doctor. Tom wanted a three-week extension to his work leave. The doctor said Tom could still get around as long as he didn't put any weight on his foot and refused Tom's request for an MRI because it was just a simple sprain. But Tom was constantly complaining about the pain and taking a lot of painkillers. He said he couldn't move.

Again, I believed him. I kept making the exhausting daily round trips by car. I often showed up late for work and had to leave early. I was exhausted and irritable. Eventually, my boss had enough and reassigned me to a job in my own city in hope that this would make life easier for me. But things actually got worse. Tom constantly belittled my profession, my colleagues and the company I worked for.

Everything I did was "shit," he told me in a text. "Your newspaper is trash! If you write for it, you're trash. Don't you realize the crap you're writing?"

"Journalists are all leftists and sell-outs!" he texted another time. "I left a comment on your site because your stories are full of shit, especially when you talk about cops!" One work colleague was "a big cunt," a "liar" and a "cheat." My boss John was a "lazy manipulator." And Tom added, "You're becoming just like him!"

In rereading his texts today, I notice Tom used a lot of exclamation points, which is very different from how he spoke, especially at work. He usually talked in a very monotonous, emotionless tone.

What Tom wrote about John reminds me of another incident. One night, I was working late, so Tom decided to make the long drive to pick me up at the office. He sent me a text saying he was on his way. "I'm coming to pick you up. We're going out for dinner."

I told John and asked if I could give Tom a tour of the office. John naturally said yes and, as a joke, wrote on the whiteboard: "Police everywhere, justice nowhere." It was just a silly joke. But Tom talked about it for years. He said it was "injurious" and "defamatory." (He liked to use legal jargon whenever he criticized journalists.)

I stopped paying attention to compliments from my editors because Tom said they were only praising me in order to get in my pants. I was miserable.

By the summer, I had no social life and my budding career was starting to collapse. Whenever I talked with friends and colleagues about my relationship with Tom, I rarely talked about myself. Instead, I told them all about how my fiancé was this perfect police officer and how I was going to give him what he hadn't found with his unfaithful wife. I rarely talked about what I wanted or needed. I didn't listen to my friends' warnings. I was in love.

And blind. Or powerless. Tom always satisfied his sexual desires without my consent. I woke up one night with him holding my hand on his penis. "See, you turn me on even when you're asleep. I've found the woman of my dreams," he said.

I started to hate my body because it didn't want enough sex to satisfy Tom. He knew how much sex I should want because he had more experience, and he always reminded me of this. I stopped ballet dancing, which I had been doing since I was four, because I couldn't bear to see myself in the mirror or even to touch my body to correct my postures.

Early that summer, I found out I was pregnant. I was 23. I decided to keep the baby. I also bought a car with my own money. Tom quickly confiscated the keys, claiming he had left them in his uniform at work. But from that moment on, he would only give them to me after I told him when I was leaving, when I'd be back, where I was going and whom I'd see. At the time, I didn't think anything was wrong with that, even though I sometimes wondered why he needed to know every little detail. I chalked it up to him being a caring spouse who was concerned about the woman carrying his child. And from the outside, we did seem to be a perfect and inseparable couple.

I lost my job when I was three months pregnant. For Tom, this was good news. Now I could take care of his son and our future baby and have home-cooked meals waiting for him when he got home from work. I also no longer had an excuse to go out for a coffee with my work friends. I no longer went out at all.

Tom also cleaned up my Facebook account. I was no longer allowed to have any contact with men. Tom memorized the names of my friends and where they lived. He created a Twitter account so he could see what I was doing with my account and so he could follow all the people I talked with. Whenever I sent or got a text or phone call, I had to tell him why. Tom regularly looked through my cellphone, and when I saw him, he said he was surprised I didn't do the same with his phone.

He finalized his divorce during my pregnancy. I asked him to stop signing up for phone and TV plans he wouldn't pay for and to stop spending a fortune on scratch-and-win tickets. He wouldn't tell me how much he was spending, but he insisted it wasn't a lot. Credit agencies were harassing him, but he explained that it was because they were "lying thieves." Everyone from his ex-wife to the banks was plotting against him—even his own family, who he said had always rejected him (though they had helped him a lot when his wife left).

I believed everything he told me. Tom convinced me that because of the decent income I had enjoyed until I lost my job, I didn't understand what life was like for the average working person. But despite the excuses, Tom promised to stop the unnecessary spending. I agreed to marry him the summer after our baby was born.

Our daughter Zoe was born just a few days after my 24th birthday. Tom helped out at first, but I had to deal with her at night because he had to work. I encouraged him to have time alone with her—just the two of them—to make up for the fact that I was breastfeeding, but he never offered to help.

From the moment our daughter was born, Tom constantly compared me to his ex-wife. I was breastfeeding; she bottle-fed. I was a hippie who liked cloth diapers; she didn't worry about chemicals and used store-bought. I guess he thought I was a better mother and wife because he always went out of his way to point out her every little flaw. Unlike his ex with her "degenerate" lifestyle—for example, she insisted on having a girls' night out every month—I was "safe" because I no longer had any contact with the outside world.

I was 24 and already had a four-month-old baby when we got married. I paid for the entire $11,000 wedding bill out of my savings and took care of all of the planning. I justified this by telling myself that my husband's job was so demanding. My in-laws were less than thrilled with the marriage. They still hadn't accepted me because I was wife number two and because we hadn't joined their church. Tom's brother hated me so much that we almost had to force him to read a few words at the ceremony. To make matters worse, my in-laws were insulted that I wanted to hyphenate my last name (adding salt to the wound I had already inflicted by having done the same with our daughter's last name).

For our wedding night, I booked a beautiful suite for two nights at a very nice hotel not too far from where we were married. We had a bedroom for us, another bedroom for Zoe and a bathroom with a large tub. The hotel was in the middle of the woods, with lots of walking trails. It was the perfect spot to spend a quiet first weekend as newlyweds.

We arrived at the hotel in the middle of the night after all of the guests had left the party. I took off my dress and quickly put Zoe to bed, figuring that after such a busy and exhausting day, we would go to bed too. But Tom had other plans.

"We have to consummate the marriage," he said, smiling, when I climbed into bed with him. I smiled too and suggested we wait until the next day since it was 3 a.m. "No, go take a bath. I'll sleep a little. Wake me up with a little massage. Newlyweds have to make love. It's now your duty as my wife."

I don't know why, but I gave in. Maybe it was out of a sense of duty, or because he was always the one giving orders. Maybe I just didn't want to fight on our wedding night.

I took a long bath, and when I got out I woke him up like he had asked. He asked me if I wanted to have sex, and I said no.

"Wrong answer," he said.

He asked me if I wanted to give him a blow job, and I said no.

"Wrong again."

I don't have a good memory of what happened next. But I do remember very clearly that he raped me, and then stayed mad at me the entire the weekend because I refused to give him a blow job.

Not long after, Tom decided to apply for a new job in another city where he thought being a police officer would be less stressful. So at the end of the summer, we moved to the other end of the country. I was still unemployed, but I paid for all the costs of moving and furnishing our new apartment since most of Tom's old furniture didn't survive the trip. After settling in, Tom made a point of telling everyone we met that it was me who forced him to move. I almost found it cute that he wanted people to think that he was willing to make such a big change out of love for me. I let it slide.

I never saw my family anymore after we moved because we were too far away. Tom regularly went to see his family and son on every vacation, but he refused to consider visiting my family. Even though my family was no further away than his, Tom said visiting my folks would cost too much. In any case, I would have been the one to pay. But by that point my savings were running out and I had very little money left. And Tom insisted that I spend what was left on our daily expenses.

I didn't always have access to the bank accounts, but Tom insisted I pay for necessities like groceries and gas. Despite his high salary and his promise to stop unnecessary spending, he never had any money. We soon started getting collection notices. Tom had written bad checks at the supermarket, and the utility company almost cut us off for unpaid bills. (I later discovered he had signed up for a TV plan under my name, but never paid for it.)

I started to question my marriage when our daughter was nine months old. We had an argument over the fact that Tom never defended me when his mother insulted me. His mother had written him a letter calling me a "lazy bitch" who was using him for his money. She also asked him to focus more on his son rather than his daughter and wife because he was already doing so much for us, like providing us with a home. I wanted him to defend me. Even though he had a steady income and I was unemployed, I was the one who paid for most of our household expenses. But he never said a word to his mother about that.

That night, I told him our relationship didn't seem fair. He got upset and said that if he had to choose between me and his mother, he would choose his mother. "There are plenty of women out there who want me," he said. He said no one else would put up with me and that I should be grateful he was still with me. "I'm doing you a favour by living with you," he said.

That was when it dawned on me that he never defended me—and that sometimes he was the one calling me names, like "piece of shit," "whiny," "little woman," "blow-up doll," "loudmouth."

I found it unbearable to constantly give in to his sexual demands just to keep the peace (or because he insisted he needed it). Our arguments were also becoming more verbally violent—only in his words, though, never in his tone, which remained perfectly calm. Our fights increasingly ended the same way. He would calmly remind me that his gun was in the closet. He always left his gun in the belt and kept it at the top of the closet. Whenever he wanted to remind me it was in easy reach, he would open the closet door and turn the belt so the gun grip was facing the front of the shelf, ready to be grabbed.

"You know police officers take their guns home," he would say. Or: "I know how to use a gun." At these times, I would lock myself in the bathroom, terrified and crying. He'd then gently knock on the door, and I'd ask him to stop.

Some of the neighbors in our apartment building complained that I made too much noise. At it happens, a couple of other police officers lived in the same building. One lived next door with his wife. He never said a word to me, but his wife often complained about "all the door-slamming." One day I left our apartment in tears with my daughter in the baby carrier. I bumped into her, and she said: "Going for a walk? Don't get too much sun. But at least it's better than screaming."

Upstairs lived another cop who had been disciplined because of alcohol-related incidents. He complained if I made any noise after 8 p.m. He also couldn't stand hearing our daughter cry. Everyone in the building knew he was a violent alcoholic with impulsive tendencies. He threatened me one night when my husband was on patrol and I was alone. "Keep it up, and I'll kill you," he told me. "We'll settle it in the basement with a knife, just me and you." None of the neighbors ever asked what was going on or if we were okay. They just asked me to be quiet.

When we moved to another apartment in the same building, our new neighbors complained about me making noise and waking up their son. "You're so hysterical. He's brave to put up with you." "Your kids must be terrified of you." Sometimes my husband would get a text and show it to me: "Your wife is making too much noise. Shut her up." "She needs a little lesson."

I'd still often give in to Tom's sexual blackmail; when he didn't get what he wanted, he'd harass me all day, saying, "When are you finally going to give me a blow job?" He'd even ask me in front of our daughter or during meals.

I tried to leave Tom for the first time just before my 25th birthday. I grabbed my bag and our daughter and drove over 100 miles to the home of a friend who was waiting for us.

Tom texted me on the third day. "Where are you? Who are you with?"

"Abigail," I replied.

"Are you coming back? Are you cheating on me?"

"I'm not cheating on you."

"When are you coming back?"

"Zoe is good. Thanks for asking," I replied.

"Come back. You don't know what you're doing," Tom said. "If you stopped acting like a child, things would be better between us."

On the sixth day, he texted again: "When are you coming back?"

"I don't know," I replied.

"Don't tell me you're scared of me. You don't know what you're doing."

"I need some time away," I said.

"Time away from what? You don't do anything! I'm here all alone like an idiot, taking care of everything at home."

I gave in on the seventh day. "I'm taking the train and will be home soon," I texted Tom.

"It's about time. You always take things too far. Do you know how you're making me look? I'm a cop. I have a reputation and career to protect!"

"We'll be home soon."

"You hurt me this week. I love you, and you just left."

When I got back home, he looked through my bag and found a brochure for an apartment-hotel I had considered staying at. He called me a "whore" because he thought it was one of those "pay-by-the-hour" hotels.

I told myself that Tom loved and respected me, that he loved our daughter and that I couldn't deprive her of her father. I convinced myself I had blown everything out of proportion and that I was damaging his career. He blamed me for fanning his jealousy and said that his jealousy only proved he loved me. I hated myself for hurting him. To defuse the situation, I offered to use what was left of my savings to take the three of us on a beach holiday.

By summer's end, I was pregnant again. Tom wasn't very happy about it, but as long as his intense sexual needs were being met, he said he'd accept it. He knew perfectly well that I didn't have contraception. (Tom refused to wear a condom, and for medical reasons, I couldn't use birth control pills or intrauterine devices.) His family accused me of getting pregnant behind his back so I could keep taking advantage of him financially. I didn't bother telling them the baby was probably conceived during yet another night of nonconsensual sex.

Tom was becoming more violent, but I couldn't see it. The constant insults, the rapes, being humiliated in front of his co-workers—it was all becoming routine. My friends started telling me I had to leave him, that I shouldn't be forced to have sex and that he treated me like garbage. I couldn't accept that my perfect police officer husband was the man they said he was.

Our second daughter was born a few weeks after my 26th birthday—in my car in the hospital parking lot. Tom told me he was terrified by how "awful" the labor had been. It was a natural childbirth, and I had screamed loudly. But what had bothered him even more was all the amniotic fluid and blood. "Your pussy is a butcher shop," he said.

From that night on, he slept in another room. At first, it was under the pretext of letting me get my sleep when he took the baby for feedings. Later, it was because he only wanted to sleep in the same bed when I let him "come" (as he put it). He told me all his police friends hated me because I was "hysterical." He was tired of the neighbors complaining about me screaming.

Many times, I ran out of our apartment crying—sometimes with the kids, sometimes without them. He sometimes stopped me from going into their rooms to get them. When that happened, I never stayed away long because I was afraid he'd take revenge on them or tell them I had abandoned them.

Many times, I locked myself in the bathroom, screaming for him to leave me alone. He'd criticize me for making noise, especially at night when people were trying to sleep.

Meanwhile, Tom continued to insult me calmly. He continued to rape me calmly. He did everything calmly. It was his job to remain calm at all times. And he was very good at it, even during sex.

Whenever Tom felt the need to grab me, he did it just like he learned on the job, leaving no marks. He would often change the spot where he held my arm so his fingers wouldn't leave marks or he would use his palm to cover a larger area so I wouldn't get a bruise.

From his police training, he also knew how to do joint-locking techniques on my wrists, elbows and knees. That never left bruises and didn't require much strength. They're techniques that completely immobilize a person, and it's extremely painful to try to break free of the grip. Or he would just lie on top of me. I couldn't get away, and it never left any marks. By the end of our relationship, Tom's favorite saying was: "I won't be stupid enough to leave any marks."

But one day, he did accidentally leave finger marks on my arm. When I told him I was going to file a police complaint, he bit his forearm and said, "If you file a complaint, so will I." The next day he showed everyone his bite mark. After that, he was very careful about how he held me and repeatedly told me that he wasn't stupid enough to hit me in a way that would leave marks.

He told me that no one would believe me because he was a cop and all the neighbors would testify that I was crazy, while he was a model of perfect behavior. He told me I couldn't leave because I had used up all my savings and didn't have a job. He told me I had two young children and that without the food and shelter he provided, I had nothing.

I was completely trapped. I was married to a man with a perfect reputation, the perfect job and the perfect co-workers to ensure I could never be protected. He had all the power.

When I was 26, I made a second attempt to leave. A friend secretly came to see me while Tom was away on holiday and told me I couldn't continue this way—that Tom would eventually kill me. I started planning to stay again with the same friend I went to the first time I tried to leave.

It would be easy to get there, but it still seemed far enough away from Tom's network of contacts. But Tom heard about my plans from a mutual acquaintance. Tom told the acquaintance that our marriage was in trouble because I wasn't good enough in bed. He promised me that he'd change, but he also threatened to accuse me of kidnapping our girls if I left, which made me worry about losing custody of them.

"I won't let you take the kids. You'll never get custody! I'm a cop. You're nothing!" he texted.

"The judge will take my side. You know very well that if I ask for custody, I'll win. I'll take everything from you, even the kids."

I cancelled my plans and accepted the fact that I'd never get out of our relationship. My sleep was constantly being interrupted by my baby, who needed a lot of attention. Tom, always dressed in uniform, took our oldest daughter to day care in the morning because I was so exhausted and he worried someone might notice how badly I was doing and offer to help me.

"If you tell the school anything, how will that make me look?" he said. "I'd rather take Zoe so that you won't tell the other moms your nonsense."

My days were spent confined to our apartment. The only place I was allowed to go was a nearby café where Tom knew the managers. They reported my every move back to him. Tom constantly told me I was good for nothing, that the house was filthy and that the meals were too plain. He often texted me late in the evening, when I was giving the baby her last feeding before bed.

"You don't even clean the house. You don't do anything," he once wrote. "You think I don't do anything, but you're good for nothing." Another time: "I'd rather eat anything than your crap."

Late at night, while he watched TV and I breastfed our baby, he'd criticize me for not having mopped the living room floor or put away the dishes. He would only do housework if I gave him what he wanted sexually. He told me that he was becoming less interested in me, but that he was "obliged" to meet his needs and had to "come" somewhere. Sometimes he chose my vagina because he didn't like using the toilet. "I'm not going to jerk off with toilet paper in the bathroom all the time," he said.

By the time I turned 27, I was a complete wreck and visibly on the brink of exhaustion. Everyone started telling Tom that he should care for me and help out more. Instead, he left on vacation. He couldn't stand me anymore, and for good reason.

I was doing virtually no housework and little cooking and was no longer his sex slave. I refused all sexual relations. Tom constantly asked me for blow jobs, even when we met for lunch. He often criticized me in front of the kids for not having sex with him.

One night I was sick with the flu and had dozed off on the sofa. I woke up because he was stroking my thighs. I told him to stop, and he hit his fist close to my face. "Cunt. No one could put up with you." From that night on until I left several months later, I slept in the office with the door locked.

We frequently argued. When I would finally break down and cry, he would look at me coldly and tell our girls, "Mommy doesn't want to take care of you and isn't nice to daddy."

When a number of mutual acquaintances warned him I was looking really unwell, he told me to stop putting on a show for everyone. He said he treated me like a queen and I didn't even thank him in return. Three of my friends tried to maintain contact with me even though Tom forbade it and spied on me (digging through my Internet accounts, purse and phone). All three of them talked to me about the violence and psychological abuse. (They didn't know about everything Tom did to me.) They lived hundreds of miles away.

One was a doctor who went to great lengths to try to get me to leave my husband during the last year of our relationship. She felt I was in real danger. Tom intercepted one of our text exchanges.

"He demeans you and insults you," Cynthia said. "You don't even have the right to think for yourself. You're not allowed to work. Leave. He will eventually kill you."

"We fight sometimes but I can't leave," I replied. "No money, no place to live, no work."

Cynthia: "You'll have help."

"The girls need stability," I said.

"Your children will be better off when you're safe. What are you waiting for? For him to hit you? Shoot you?" Cynthia replied.

Tom read the last text and told me Cynthia was a bad doctor because she had supposedly encouraged him to hit me and a bad friend because she had encouraged me to leave. "No one will ever want you," he said.

I asked Cynthia to stop contacting me. Shortly after, I received a package from these three friends. And my husband received messages:

"Your wife is exhausted and you demand too much of her."

"Why can't you see your wife is unwell? She was not like this before."

"You're acting like a dictator, not like a husband."

Tom was enraged. He blocked these three friends so I could no longer have any contact with them. He threw away the package they sent, and for the first time he lost his cool. He paced the apartment while I was feeding our daughter her baby food, screaming that I was going to destroy his career. When my daughter finished her meal, I went to her room with her because I think he could have hit me that day.

Tom tried to stop me from having any more contact with these friends, but I managed to communicate with them by creating a private Twitter account, which ended up saving my life. I used the account like a journal to keep a record of what Tom did and said to me. My friends took turns monitoring my tweets and sending me messages of support. This account for a while was my only lifeline to the outside world. I changed my password every two days to keep it hidden from Tom.

By this point, I was spending my evenings trying to steer clear of my husband. After putting the kids to bed, I would leave the apartment and wander the empty streets. I'd often walk to a bridge to see if I was able to free myself from him through death since I hadn't been able to in any other way.

Every night, when I came back from my walks, there he was on the balcony, waiting for me. Waiting to attack me—first with questions and then physically. He used a technique the police have for making someone in custody crack. He walked right up to me and without making any contact prevented me from moving. He stayed at least a foot and a half away and never touched me, but he got in my personal space.

Whenever I returned to the apartment, that's how he'd greet me at the door. I'd take off my jacket and shoes with him standing a foot and a half in front of me. He followed me like that wherever I went in the apartment, even going up the stairs to my office on the second floor, where I slept with the door locked. It was next to the kids' room. I rarely left. I lived in a space of 80 square feet.

I was at the breaking point. I finally understood why his first wife did what she did. She wasn't crazy at all. A few weeks went by and he left again, alone, to visit his mother, promising to come back a new man. While he was away, he didn't contact us once to see how we were doing, although I did find out that he had gotten some of his police friends to track my comings and goings.

He also created a fake Twitter account using a woman's name and pretending to be me. The account was supposedly that of a woman who was coming out of a seven-year relationship with a "narcissistic pervert." The profile picture was a pair of ballet slippers. (Ballet was my lifelong passion, and I had used a photo of ballet slippers for my own Twitter account.) He used his fake account to contact anyone he thought was likely to help me, especially those who followed my Twitter account. He claimed to be "some one [sic] you know under another pseudonym." In one message, he wrote (with original spelling mistakes), "Im trying to protect my self from my husband who has a lot of influence."

When people responded, they got another message saying, "I have two daughters! Im a mess! Im unable to leave!" "You know me. My first name starts with A!" "I cant say too much because I dont know who to trust."

If they continued the conversation, they soon realized it wasn't me because of all the spelling mistakes and exclamation marks. That's how I found out about it. His account was reported to Twitter.

But before he deleted the account, he tried to contact me directly, pretending to be this same woman. "I think your in the same boat as me. I can help you." He also posted a few tweets: "Im still feeling the consequences." "I need support." "We need to stick together."

While Tom was gone visiting his mother, I finally decided to take my girls to see my family. So that I couldn't be accused of kidnapping the kids, I told him in advance that I was leaving and what our route would be. As we drove, Tom started to send harassing text messages.

Twenty-one texts arrived by noon asking, "Where are you?" (He knew I was driving and wouldn't be able to answer.)

Just after noon, I wrote back: "I'm at Abigail's. We're eating and then we'll be driving together. The girls are fine." More than a dozen more texts arrived by mid-afternoon, again asking, "Where are you?"

Later in the afternoon came another text: "How's the car? Giving you any problems?"

He had taken the car in for a checkup the month before and told me the car was fine. But his text scared me. I called his boss to see what I should do. I stopped at a highway rest area and turned the car around to go back home.

He was still away on his trip when I returned, but he left me a voice message (which he normally never did). "Why did you come back?" he demanded. "Why aren't you answering your phone? Answer me at least! You were taking the girls to visit your parents. Why did you turn around? You were halfway there! Leave. I don't want to see you when I get home. I'm not throwing you out but I want you and the girls to leave. Why did you come back? Why aren't you answering my calls?" That night he texted me 12 times saying the same thing as his voice message.

I took advantage of his absence to meet with the bank to clear up the bills. Our account balance didn't add up. Tom had agreed to pay the utilities and health insurance, while he used my savings for groceries because he said he didn't have anything left over. But after deducting the bills from his salary, I saw he had more than $1,000 left over each month.

Because he was away, he hadn't collected the mail. I saw we had gotten bank notices about bounced checks for the kids' doctor appointments because the account was empty. I also found bailiff's letters for debts of $4,500 and $8,000 that I knew nothing about. I went through the account statements to see why he didn't have any money. I discovered he had plenty of money. The account manager told me, "He emptied his account. For professional reasons I can't say more than that, but I can tell you one thing, ma'am: Take your little girls and leave."

I called my doctor for help. I couldn't sleep and hadn't eaten for nine days. I couldn't even stand up. I needed someone to talk to. The day I made the appointment, I told the secretary, "I need help," and when I got to the doctor's office I cried so hard I couldn't speak. He understood I was having serious problems, but I refused to let him write down the word "violence" in his notes. He gave me a medical certificate attesting to my "mental distress" and "psychological abuse through means of communication because the husband is away." He asked me to come back the next morning and every morning until I left the house.

My doctor wanted me to meet a psychologist who worked in the local social services office. I told her a few things about what was happening with my husband, and she decided to refer me to a victim support group. A social worker drove me there (it was 25 miles away), and the group took me on as an emergency case. I saw a psychologist there who specialized in victimology and domestic violence. She issued a certificate noting "a state of total psychological domination," "visible and obvious" psychological trauma and "an imminent danger" requiring immediate, personalized and close care.

After a week, Tom still hadn't come back and refused to tell me when he would. I spoke with one of Tom's supervisors. I told him I was afraid to stay at home because I didn't know when Tom would return from his vacation and that I had to divorce him. I explained that every time I had left or tried to leave, I came back or never even managed to leave, and that I felt incapable of leaving. But I also couldn't stay. He said it didn't surprise him and that he would do whatever he could to help me.

I couldn't sleep or eat, and my condition was getting worse. I didn't know when Tom planned to come back. I was terrified because he was so furious and I didn't know what he would do. The wife of Tom's boss was very supportive and invited me to their home every day.

I saw another social worker and told her that about the insults, the rapes and the fact that I didn't have the means to feed my children. It was only when she said she would get us out of there that I burst into tears. That same evening I got a text from Tom: "What were you doing talking to social workers?" He always found out about everything. I decided to leave all my important papers with the social worker because Tom often searched my purse and phone and I had no idea when he would come back. I refused to take the social worker's card or put her number in my phone.

Tom's boss finally told me when my husband was scheduled to return to work, so we were able to guess when he'd be back home. I was absolutely terrified. My doctor offered to issue a certificate saying that my psychological state required some time away before my husband returned, but I refused.

My doctor and social services contacted the psychologist from the victim support group for her opinion. She told them she was worried I would commit suicide to escape my husband. I told my doctor that was an option. So I had to leave.

We planned for me to stay with my family across the country. We would make it look like the tickets for our trip were being paid for by my family, not social services. I was asked to take all the original copies of nonreplaceable documents with me and to photocopy all my other important documents. I couldn't take too much luggage so it wouldn't look like I was moving out. I had to tell the children we were going on a holiday. Despite the intense stress, I managed to get everything ready and pull off the lie we had prepared. I was also advised to see a lawyer to initiate divorce proceedings right away so I wouldn't be tempted to go back to Tom. To be on the safe side, the divorce request would be sent to Tom only after I was gone.

We left before Tom returned, which was a big relief. That's when I told him I was taking the girls on vacation. I sent him a text, based on the advice of my lawyer and Tom's boss: "We're finally going. Beth [my aunt] paid for the tickets. We're going on a little vacation. I'll let you know when we get our return tickets."

For a few days, I didn't hear a word from him. But when he received the divorce papers, he exploded. I had left him. I was hurting the children. I had no right to do it. He was too perfect. I was too insane. No one would ever believe me. "You're filing for divorce because of violence?" he texted. "I'm a cop! No one's going to believe you!" In another message he said, "Come back or I'll ask for custody."

He also told me he knew social services had paid for the trip. I could no longer trust anyone, anywhere. He tried to interrogate the girls to find out what I was doing with my time, but my family put him on speaker phone when he called and gave him vague answers, instead of letting him speak to the girls. They refused to let the girls be dragged into it.

But I knew we eventually had to return to the city where we lived. I had to see my lawyer and the victim support group and to prepare for the divorce. My oldest daughter also had to go back for the start of school. Tom knew our return date. During the last week and a half, I got 15 to 30 texts a day, and he called every night. The closer the date got, the more threatening his messages became. "I won't let you leave," he said in a voicemail. "I won't let you hurt me. You want a divorce? Go jump off a bridge."

Naturally, I contemplated suicide. I told my doctor, "I can't get away from him, so I have to die." I started thinking about how I could do it. Since I felt worthless and totally alone, it seemed perfectly logical to me.

My doctor did everything he could to help me and didn't give in to Tom's intimidation. My husband showed up one day in uniform at my doctor's office asking where I was, how long I would be there and for what reason. First, he talked to the intern, who refused to answer. Tom went back later that day to see my doctor in person, but didn't manage to. My doctor and the intern didn't tell me all this at the time. Later, when I was better able to deal with it, I was told about this by the intern and the cop who was on patrol with my husband that day.

My doctor arranged for me to stay in a hospital until space was available in a women's shelter. The official reason for my hospitalization was exhaustion and depression. My doctor left clear instructions with the hospital staff that I was being threatened by an abusive police officer. "I am sending you Amy Morrison who is going through a very difficult divorce," he said in a note. "She is being subjected to domestic violence. She is now receiving assistance from a victim support group."

When I first arrived at the hospital, I told the staff I did not want to have any contact with my husband and that he might try to exploit his position as a police officer to get to me. The nurse who admitted me wrote this in my file. But the staff who were supposed to keep me safe ignored what my doctor and I had said.

When Tom showed up, the staff told him in my presence why I had been hospitalized and that I was waiting for a place in a women's shelter. Tom said he wouldn't let me take the kids to the shelter and that he'd put them in a nanny's care instead. A doctor told Tom he had the right to refuse to let my kids go with me to the shelter. (I later found out this wasn't true.) The doctor even asked Tom for his opinion about me. Everything Tom said was noted in my medical record as fact, despite many lies I pointed out.

The hospital's doctors and nurses even told me to go back to my "perfect husband" because I was making him suffer too much. A nurse told me it was inconceivable that a police officer could be violent and that I had to be lying. One psychiatrist tried to convince me there was no such thing as marital rape. Another psychiatrist forced me to write Tom a letter apologizing for making him suffer and for not being able to care for the kids. I also apologized for telling people he had insulted and raped me. The same psychiatrist tried to give me antipsychotic medication because she said I had made up the rapes. Other hospital staff finally dissuaded her.

I was very shaky when I was finally admitted to the women's shelter. The psychologist at the victim support group continued to see me regularly, and my doctor did a lot to help. And yet, I was on the verge of going back to Tom. His harassment and emotional blackmail continued. This perfect and kind police officer had been abandoned by a second wife, and under the same circumstances.

The day before we were to appear before the judge for the divorce, Tom sent me a text. "You know the judge is going to ask you tomorrow if you still want a divorce?"

"Yes," I replied.

"What are you going to say? You're going to say you love me too much. You're going to say that you don't want a divorce anymore."

But I didn't cave this time. Because if I had, I would have died.

I wrote back, "See you tomorrow."

A police officer makes a good impression in front of a judge. His uniform and work of serving and protecting are emphasized repeatedly. Tom's lawyer underlined his police status by frequently speaking of his exemplary and difficult work. She never spoke of him as a father or husband.

Compare this to a shattered mother with no job or money, needing all sorts of assistance and living in a shelter. Not only does she look bad, but the judge doesn't believe for an instant that a police officer could be capable of any form of violence at home.

The judge wouldn't let me talk about what I had gone through. The judge first met Tom and me separately and then together with our lawyers. When he saw us individually, he asked if I still wanted a divorce. "Would you like an amicable divorce?" he asked. "Why do you want a divorce?" For this last question, I wanted to explain that Tom was violent, but the judge cut me off after my first sentence. "He hurt me," I said, but the judge interjected: "It happens to all couples having problems. I'll see your husband now." I tried a second time by saying, "He harasses me." The judge cut me off again, saying: "Not my problem."

The judge did listen carefully, however, to what Tom had to say. Tom did a great job of playing the victim. He ended up getting the girls (even though he openly said he didn't want custody of them) and my car (which I had paid for and was in my name) for the entire time I was living at the shelter. As Tom had promised, he sent the girls to live with a nanny almost full time. I only got the girls and my car back when I finally had my own place, three months later.

The judge also forced me to go to my husband's apartment if I wanted to see the girls. He completely ignored Tom's threats about his gun in the closet and the death threat from the neighbor. I told the judge that my husband had suggested I commit suicide and that I had kept the voice message, but the judge wouldn't let me play it. The judge only listened to the upstanding police officer standing before him.

Before the court hearing, Tom's boss told his superiors why I had left Tom. The boss was worried about reprisals because his wife had invited me into their home. There was no response from the hierarchy even though a crime had been reported.

After I got custody of my children, the police administration section emailed to ask if my change of address was final and why I had moved. I responded saying I had left due to violence and was therefore not going back, and I sent a copy to the human resources division. Again, I never heard back. I followed up but still got no response. No one called to investigate the report of a crime. I didn't even get an acknowledgement that my email had been received.

I was 28 when I finally got the keys to my own apartment. I got my furniture back from Tom since I had paid for all of it. I got custody of our daughters, which was a relief to him because he was tired of taking care of them when the nanny wasn't around. Now he could tell the next girlfriend that I had taken his daughters away from him. He had to pay alimony because it was his responsibility and I had no money. It was an exact replica of what had happened with his first wife. I also couldn't move to another city because he said if I did, he would seek custody of the kids and win. "Your lawyer knows very well that I can win custody if I ask for it," he texted me. I was in no condition to see if he was lying or to fight him.

Just like with his first wife, he could now follow me to his heart's content or have me followed—which he certainly did and still does today, more than a year after I got my own apartment. Tom routinely interrogates the girls about our daily lives, but mostly, he uses his police contacts and resources to find out what he wants to know. He has access to my social services and medical files. He knows everything about my life. I have to be careful about what I tell authorities so he doesn't get his hands on it.

Tom and his police friends continue to follow me. Whenever I drive by a police car in the city, the vehicle always slows right down. A patrol cop sometimes follows me if I'm near my doctor's office and of course in my own neighborhood. When I go out with the girls, we are often followed for a while. If they follow us for too long, the girls eventually notice and say hi to the cops. My oldest daughter told me that when she is with her father, he shows her how he watches "mom's house."

Social services workers continue to give him confidential information about me. I know because my husband regularly tells me what he knows. It's his way of letting me know he's still in power, at least in part. The same people who are supposed to be protecting me and my children are quick to back down when confronted by a police officer. It's frustrating to see that my husband can do whatever he wants with the girls, but I'm completely ignored whenever I raise concerns about what my daughters have told me.

Tom likes to tell the girls that I abandoned them when I went into the women's shelter and that I'll do it again soon because I don't love them. He often talks to them about my death, which he presents as imminent. Obviously, this upsets them deeply. My younger daughter is always physically sick and vomits whenever she has to go to her father's house. Without fail, she gets sick at his place and suddenly feels better when she comes home.

I've told social services, but they don't believe me. I've told my doctor, but he can't do anything. I've told the victim support group, which talks with my daughter. My oldest daughter is being seen by a psychologist because she told my aunt, "Daddy hurt mommy at night, and she screamed at him to stop," and "Daddy hurt the cat."

Among our mutual acquaintances in the city, I'm seen as a crazy liar who made up stories in order to damage Tom's reputation. People ask me, "Do you realize what you're doing to him by saying he was violent?" I tell them, "Do you realize what he did to me with his violence?"

Just as Tom predicted, and because he carefully laid the groundwork while I was hospitalized and in the shelter, nobody believes me. This perfect policeman, who is always calm, can't be the man I'm describing. During my time in the hospital and shelter, he told his police colleagues, the nanny and people in our neighborhood that I was a violent and tyrannical woman who was completely insane. When people wanted to visit me in the hospital, he told them I was locked in isolation because I had tried to kill the kids.

They don't understand what happens when a police officer comes home from work, when he knows he will be protected by his co-workers, when he knows his uniform puts him above the law.

Leaving Tom was very difficult because he is not the stereotypical abuser, just like I'm not the stereotypical victim. His work is stable and respected in our society. I have a college degree and a middle class upbringing. Many people can't believe that domestic violence can happen with people like Tom and me. These stereotypes have prevented and still prevent many people from believing or helping me. They don't realize abuse happens in all kinds of families.

I was afraid that leaving Tom would hurt my children, even though I freed them just as I freed myself. While leaving Tom put my life in danger, what frightened me the most wasn't being killed, but being killed in front of the girls. Yet, they also needed to be saved. They had been living in an atmosphere of violence. They were born into it, and for the first years of their lives, it was all they knew.

Now that the three of us are living in a safe environment, their growth curves have shot up and the health care workers who treat them have noticed they are now more emotionally mature and open to the world. One of my daughters used to have eating problems, while the other one had problems with her joints. These problems have disappeared.

I idealized my husband while I put myself down. Tom was able to see I lacked self-confidence and realized that he could use my past trauma—particularly my mother's death when I was a young teenager—to dominate me. By the time I left Tom, I no longer existed as a person. I no longer lived. I was only his "thing." With the help of the victim support group, I was able to understand what had happened to me and start living again.

The most striking moment for me was when the city invited me to an event for new residents after I moved into my own apartment. I had actually been living in the city for a few years, but the apartment hadn't been in my name before. The city now considered me to be a "new" resident. It was at that moment that I felt like my own person again. I felt free to live.

I still get help from the victim support group. During sessions with my psychologist, I can see the progress I've made. I've managed to pick up my life where I had left off—and now, I have the love of my daughters. I'm working as a journalist again and am writing about the subjects that used to interest me. Therapy has taught me to no longer care about my husband's opinion. I've reconnected with friends I lost because of my relationship. I'm doing my favorite activities again—dancing, reading, writing and going to shows, especially jazz. I was never allowed to do these things when I was with Tom.

Most importantly, I no longer want to die. I'm no longer afraid of going home, and I sleep with my bedroom door open. I'm even wearing skirts and dresses, heels and make-up again. Tom never allowed me to do that unless it was for him. Now I'm doing it for me. I'm "me" again.

I meet with a domestic violence support group, where I have gone from being the one who listens to others, to the one who talks freely about how to leave the violence and deal with separation, even without any family or money. Even though our lives aren't financially stable, my children and I now have emotional stability, which is worth far more.

I sometimes talk to wives of violent police officers and try to offer advice on how to avoid falling into the same traps I faced. When our partners are cops, we have to be much more careful than most other women fleeing a violent spouse. We have to be very guarded about what information we give out, even to social services. I tell them to find someone they can trust who isn't linked to the authorities in any way. For me, it was my doctor and the psychologist from the victim support group. They were my strongest allies.

You don't need to file a complaint to get help for leaving a violent hus-band. Cops protect each other, so if you're having a hard time getting some-one to listen to you, you have to be willing to leave without any recognition of wrongdoing, as hard as that may be to accept. It took me a long time to really understand what the staff at the victim support group kept telling me: I'm a victim because of my husband's behavior, not because a court decided I was one.

If society has no idea what it's like for us to live in the shadow of these men, that's because it's easier that way. Police officers represent an institu-tion that's sometimes disparaged and sometimes revered. Society only sees their uniforms, not the men wearing them. People assume that cops, as society's guardians and protectors, must necessarily be exemplary in their private lives as well.

We easily forget that cops know how to circumvent or work the system that's in place to deter illegal behavior. The police have far-reaching networks—not just out of professional necessity, but because it's also in their and society's mutual self-interest, even though we turn a blind eye to it. We've put them in a position of power not only in public life, but in private life as well.

We want to believe in their integrity. The opposite would be disturbing. When these men demonstrate extreme behavior on the job, society is quick to denounce it. But we don't question what they do in their private lives. We should.

PART II

Licence to Abuse

By Alex Roslin

CHAPTER 2

"Unfounded"

Does a life matter? Can you imagine your child's or parent's life abruptly ending? It would matter to you. If they were murdered, you would probably be devastated, mindless with grief. If they were murdered by a person in public authority—their doctor, say, or teacher—it would be still more crushing and incomprehensible.

What if in your shock and grief you learned that a large portion of doctors or teachers—perhaps a quarter or more—secretly abused and in some cases killed vulnerable patients or students in a murderous rage, while their work colleagues mostly covered for them?

You would probably be deeply disturbed and furious. You might join other families to demand action. Public outrage would surely ensue. Prison would await the perpetrators and those who covered for them. Authorities would likely turn the entire profession upside down and inside out—replacing its leadership, forcing it to reform, holding inquiries. Society would be morally and legally compelled to make reparations to survivors and question how something so hideous could happen.

Exactly such abuse and killings are happening to the family members of police officers. Their predators are their own husbands, boyfriends and fathers, the men we often call heroes. They are far more violent at home than members of the public, whose laws they are hired to uphold. Their work colleagues often look away or derail inquiries. Incidents of horrendous violence—including murders—regularly come to light, with taxpayers on the hook to settle the lawsuits of victims' estates and families. Yet, governments and police have taken little or no action in response. Precious few academics and journalists have investigated the phenomenon. And it's gone largely ignored by domestic violence advocates and others who work with abused women.

In Amy Morrison's case, she writes of how her police officer neighbours ignored her cries, while one threatened to kill her. Other neighbours berated her. The police hierarchy was fully aware of the abuse, but no one ever called Amy to investigate or assure her family's safety. Even hospital staff dismissed her safety concerns and her doctor's note, insisted rape couldn't happen in a marriage and forced her to recant and apologize to her husband. The judge in her divorce case was equally disinterested.

But Amy did get help. She found people she trusted who lent an ear and helped her and her daughters get free—her doctor, social services workers, a victim support group, a few close friends, a police supervisor's wife. They were crucial lifelines assisting her to find the will, courage and tools to get through her darkest moments. She is now rediscovering peace and joy in life, while supporting other women on their path to survival.

Amy writes about how her husband often threatened her with the police gun he kept in the closet. Yet, she managed to avoid the fate of Lucie Gélinas, the mother of three gunned down by her RCMP ex-boyfriend on Montreal's busiest highway in 2001 (see introduction). But what if Amy's husband had followed through? We can imagine the headlines. "Police officer a suspect in wife's death," they may have said. And then, what? Would there finally have been action?

We may hope so. But Lucie Gélinas's story and many others suggest otherwise.

Lucie Gélinas and Jocelyn Hotte broke up three weeks before she died. It was common knowledge among her friends and co-workers that she lived those three weeks in fear of her ex-boyfriend, the Mountie crack shot. He frequently drove past Gélinas's apartment in the Montreal suburb of Laval, wrote down licence plate numbers of vehicles stopped near her home and parked his vehicle outside the seniors' home where she worked, witnesses testified at Hotte's murder trial. He once pushed his way into her apartment and checked her pager to see who had called.[17]

Gélinas grew increasingly frightened and told co-workers she was afraid for her three children's safety. One night while at work, she called her home 10 times to make sure her kids were okay. Hotte was apparently desperate to

---

[17] This account is based in part on testimony and evidence presented at Hotte's murder trial.

get back together. He offered Gélinas $10,000 and a dishwasher to have sex with him, one witness said.

Gélinas refused. She was happy and seeing a new man. But Gélinas was so worried about Hotte's behaviour that she asked her new boyfriend not to come to her apartment, scared that the Mountie would spot him. Despite her precautions, one of Hotte's relatives did see Gélinas walking down the street with another man and told Hotte.

Shortly afterward, on the evening of June 17, 2001, the enraged RCMP constable went to confront Gélinas at her home. The encounter left her in a panic. When Hotte was gone, she called her new boyfriend in tears.

"She said she was afraid she would suffer the same fate as her father," the boyfriend later testified in court. (Gélinas's father had been murdered by a deranged neighbour when she was 12.)

"Call the police," the boyfriend told Gélinas.

She did just that. "My ex-boyfriend, he's in the RCMP, I got death threats," she told the 911 dispatcher, sobbing. "He said, 'I'm giving you your last chance. Your father got shot.' He's crazy. I'm really scared." (Hotte, in his trial testimony, denied stalking or threatening Gélinas.)

Laval police constables Joël Sirois and Nathalie Rufer were sent to Gélinas's home that night in response to the 911 call. Gélinas asked them if they would take her complaint seriously given that Hotte was a cop. Constable Rufer insisted they would.[18]

Gélinas told the two officers Hotte was stalking her and that he seemed depressed and was acting strangely. She said the RCMP had previously disciplined him for stalking a female Mountie, with whom he had had a brief fling. Hotte had knocked on this woman's door several times a day, tailed her on the highway and accosted her in parking lots. He had shouted obscenities at her and attacked another cop in a courthouse for greeting the woman with the usual kiss on both cheeks that is common in Quebec.

The six months of harassment had been so upsetting that the woman quit the RCMP and moved to New Brunswick. But even that didn't stop Hotte, who tracked her down and slowly drove past her home several times—with Gélinas, of all people, in the car beside him.[19]

The two Laval officers listened to Gélinas for 30 minutes. They advised her to replace her locks and change her phone number, and then left. They

[18] Christiane Desjardins, "Procès du policier Jocelyn Hotte; Un appel de détresse de la victime jugé 'non fondé,'" *La Presse*, Nov. 20, 2002.

[19] George Kalogerakis, "Hotte jury not told how he stalked other woman; Testimony by Mountie's ex-colleague excluded for fear it could have tainted deliberations," *The Montreal Gazette*, December 11, 2002.

didn't write a police report. They didn't take action on Gélinas's complaint about being threatened and stalked, nor did they contact Hotte to check on his emotional state or get his side of the story. They didn't contact the RCMP to verify Hotte's background or tell the Mounties about the incident. Their only other action was to write a cryptic note in their log for the night: "Unfounded.... No threat, manipulation."[20]

Gélinas later told work colleagues the two officers "didn't want to take the complaint and wouldn't do anything."[21]

Six days after her fruitless 911 call, Hotte put five bullets into Gélinas and gravely wounded her three car passengers in a Mafia-style bloodbath. Tailed by a convoy of police cruisers, he then drove to a gas station a few minutes away where he was arrested after buying a bottle of pop.

Hotte was incarcerated in Montreal's Pinel Institute, a mental institution for the criminally insane, where he tried to kill himself. He later rejected a Crown proposal for a 16-year prison sentence, insisting instead on serving only 14 years.

The Crown put Hotte on trial for first-degree murder, which comes with an automatic life sentence and no chance of parole for 25 years, and three counts of attempted murder. The defence admitted Hotte killed Gélinas but sought a manslaughter conviction, which has no minimum sentence. Hotte's lawyers claimed he snapped because he was depressed and overworked and Gélinas provoked him.

Taking the stand in his own defence, Hotte expressed no regret for killing Gélinas and shooting her three friends, but said he had been depressed and overworked. He testified he had worked 70 to 80 hours a week in the months before the tragedy, including long shifts guarding dignitaries at that spring's protest-marred Summit of the Americas meeting of heads of state in Quebec City. "I had my feet on cement all day long. I was gassed twice. The hours were long. It was quite traumatizing," he said.

During the trial, Hotte's mother told reporters her son was taking more than 300 pills a month to control severe depression after his rampage. That didn't earn him much sympathy in court. "I read in the newspaper that Jocelyn Hotte takes a lot of pills," Pierre Mainville, who was paralyzed when Hotte shot him in the back, said during a sentencing hearing. "I wanted to say that I take more pills than him because of what he did. I found that funny."

---

[20] Desjardins, "Procès du policier Jocelyn Hotte.'"
[21] Christiane Desjardins, "Ce que le jury ne sait pas dans le procès Hotte," *La Presse*, December 11, 2002.

In December 2002, a jury found Hotte guilty on all counts. Judge John Gomery, in his remarks before sentencing Hotte, was flabbergasted that the accused hadn't expressed any remorse. "Is that too much to ask?" Gomery demanded. "Some sort of apology seeking forgiveness for the terrible hurt he's caused?... That's a little bit the problem with Mr. Hotte. He thinks only of himself."

Gomery sentenced Hotte to life in prison with no parole for 25 years, plus concurrent sentences of 20 years for the attempted murder of Pierre Mainville and 15 years each for passengers Hugues Ducharme and David Savard.

The survivors were pleased with the verdict, but they didn't think Hotte was the only guilty party. In 2004, the three men and Pierre Mainville's parents sued the city of Laval, its police department and the 911 call centre, saying the tragedy could have been prevented. The plaintiffs sought $1.7 million, saying Laval police should have taken Gélinas's 911 call more seriously. (They later increased the amount sought to $3.2 million.) The suit said the two Laval cops ignored a department directive on conjugal violence, which called for weapons to be taken from an individual if there were "reasonable and probable" security concerns.

I met Mainville in his lawyer's office in St-Jérôme, a town in the foothills of the Laurentian mountains where Mainville had lived most of his life, a 30-minute drive north of Montreal. In his early thirties with dark curly hair, he rolled into the office in a wheelchair. He had been sitting in the back of Lucie Gélinas's car and was paralyzed from the chest down when Hotte's bullet struck his T3 vertebra. He would never return to his job as a car test driver.

After the shooting, Mainville's mother moved in to help him care for himself. Three years later, he was still taking eight pills a day—down from 14 initially—in an attempt to control violent spasms that continually wracked his lower torso, but they didn't help much. "I have erectile difficulty. I need a catheter to go to the toilet. I have uncontrolled incontinence," he told me. He was seeing a psychologist once a week. "With an accident like this, you close in on yourself. I go out less among people. People look at me more than before. You don't necessarily want to be seen."

Mainville said he remained conscious that night as an ambulance crew took him from the bullet-riddled car to the Montreal General Hospital. "I asked the surgeon if I would live. He said, 'I don't know.'" Mainville spent seven hours in surgery while doctors removed the bullet from his back and implanted metal plates along the sides of his spine. He remained in the hospital more than two weeks, then spent a month in a rehabilitation centre learning to adapt to life as a paraplegic.

Mainville's two companions from that night were also still in therapy and hadn't returned to work three years after the attack. His childhood friend David Savard testified at Hotte's trial that he had a hard time concentrating and couldn't go anywhere near a highway. "I stay in a lot," Savard said. "I can't stand noise. If someone comes over, I feel like a target or in a state of danger."

Mainville's cousin Hugues Ducharme had been sitting in the passenger seat and was shot five times. He had 10 operations on his jaw and shoulder. He testified that his left arm was virtually nonfunctional and spoke of terrible psychological scars. "My curtains are always closed so no one knows I'm home," he said. "I'm afraid someone will come in. Often I don't answer the intercom or door. It's very hard for me to go outside."

Jean Bernier, the lawyer for Savard and Ducharme, said the attack was all the more tragic because it was preventable. "These people can't work. They can't restart normal lives," he told me. "If the RCMP had been informed before, they might have taken away [Hotte's] gun."

Jacques St-Pierre, the Sûreté du Québec provincial police officer who led the Hotte murder investigation, agreed that the RCMP should have been informed after Gélinas's 911 call. "It's possible [Gélinas's death] could have been prevented," he told me after the trial. "When you are in the presence of a police officer in a case like this, you should take action because this individual is armed. You shouldn't take chances.

"What they [the Laval police officers] should have done is make a police report, and they should have informed the RCMP," St-Pierre said. "If [Hotte] needed help, they would have been able to help him."[22]

Louis Bouthillier, the Crown prosecutor in Hotte's trial, agreed. In an interview after the trial, he said he had encouraged the three survivors of the attack to explore a civil lawsuit. "He was a time bomb, this guy," he said. "Someone should have set off the alarm, but nobody did. The only one who tried to do it was Lucie Gélinas, but she was met with indifference, at best, from the Laval police."

Judge Gomery also had harsh words for the Laval police officers. During the trial, he accused them of downplaying how worried Gélinas was in their testimony, which he called "clearly unbelievable" and "pretty strange."[23]

---

[22] St-Pierre retired from the SQ in 2002 and became deputy commander of a suburban police force east of Montreal.

[23] George Kalogerakis, "Laval police get a roasting for not aiding victim earlier," *The Montreal Gazette*, December 11, 2002, A10. During the trial, Gomery and prosecutor

"It's difficult for me to swallow their version of the events, but I understand they are probably a little uneasy about what happened after they effectively refused all help to this woman," Gomery said.

"It's not exactly what we want from our police corps. She reports a death threat, and the police act without even taking a report. I find this incomprehensible."[24]

During a break in the trial, even one of Hotte's defence lawyers agreed that Laval police should have done more. "If the RCMP had been advised by the Laval police of the incident, they might have taken action and this might not have happened," defence lawyer Johanne St-Gelais told reporters. "Lucie Gélinas would be alive, and Pierre Mainville wouldn't be in a wheelchair. Mr. Hotte should have been given treatment; he should have gotten medication. Obviously, whenever police arrive at a conjugal violence call, they should be prudent and make sure they take all necessary steps. If they had done more, we probably wouldn't be here."

Laval police weren't the only ones to face blame. The RCMP was also slammed for dismissing the warning signs about Hotte. When he harassed the female Mountie for six months, the force merely reprimanded him, docked him 10 days' pay and referred him to counselling.

"Any one of these abuses would have cost him [Hotte] his job if he'd worked in a bank, a hotel or even a newspaper office, but after six months of this kind of harassment, the worst the Mounties doled out was a suspension and some mandatory treatment for depression," *The Montreal Gazette* said in an editorial. "What were Hotte's superiors looking for? Foam flecks on his lips? Surely you don't need a degree in forensic psychology to read such blatant danger signals."[25]

Yet, far from taking stricter action, the RCMP later welcomed Hotte into its elite executive and diplomatic protection section, where he was a bodyguard for Canada's then-Prime Minister Jean Chrétien and other politicians. In the unit, Hotte was taught how to be even more dangerous. As part of the intensive training, he qualified as a crack shot and learned surveillance techniques and advanced driving skills—manoeuvering at high speeds,

---

Louis Bouthillier took the unusual step of cautioning the jury about the credibility of the testimony of the two Laval police officers, *The Gazette* noted. The move was especially surprising because the officers were the prosecutor's own witnesses. Bouthillier went so far as to declare one of the officers, Joël Sirois, a hostile witness because he wouldn't answer directly whether Lucie Gélinas was nervous the night of her 911 call.

24 Gomery later rose to prominence as head of a 2004-06 Canadian government public inquiry that probed irregularities in federal advertising contracts in Quebec.

25 Editorial, "Questions about Hotte," *The Montreal Gazette*, December 14, 2002.

backwards and in convoys, making sudden turns and stopping his vehicle on a button. Some of these skills were the very ones Hotte used to chase down his ex-girlfriend on the highway while peppering her car with bullets.

Every side in the trial agreed: Police should have done more to prevent the tragedy. Even Hotte said so. Years later in his cell, after the Supreme Court of Canada tossed out his final appeal of his conviction, Hotte wrote to the three survivors suggesting they sue the Sûreté du Québec provincial police, who he said should have protected his victims' car instead of pursuing him.[26] Hotte also said the RCMP was at fault because its work conditions were too onerous. He said the tragedy could have been avoided if the Mounties had given him time off work.

Hotte also authorized the RCMP to give his disciplinary and medical reports to the three men he shot to help them win their suit against the Laval police.[27] (Hotte died of pancreatic cancer while incarcerated in 2014. Under Canada's so-called faint-hope clause, he could have applied for parole in 2017.)

In March 2010, nearly a decade after Jocelyn Hotte's shooting spree, the survivors were finally vindicated when Quebec Superior Court Judge Steve Reimnitz ruled in favour of their lawsuit and decried the inaction of police. "The evidence has amply shown everything that could have been done by the Laval police and RCMP, if they had been duly informed of the facts reported by Gélinas to police on June 18.[28] From all the evidence, what would have been done could have prevented the murder and the damages caused to the plaintiffs," Reimnitz said in his judgment.

"An analysis of the facts reported by Gélinas does not justify the decision to write the note 'unfounded' in the [police] report."[29]

---

[26] "Coupable de meurtre; Jocelyn Hotte veut aider ses victimes!" TVANouvelles.ca, June 6, 2008, accessed April 26, 2015, http://tvanouvelles.ca/lcn/infos/faitsdivers/archives/2008/06/20080606-074348.html.

[27] "Poursuite de 3 millions contre la police de Laval," RadioCanada.ca, September 16, 2009, accessed May 14, 2015, http://www.radio-canada.ca/regions/Montreal/2009/09/15/006-Hotte-poursuite-police.shtml.

[28] There is a date discrepancy because Hotte confronted Gélinas the evening of June 17, while the two Laval police officers arrived at her home shortly after midnight on June 18.

[29] Charles Côté, "Laval tenue responsable dans l'affaire Jocelyn Hotte," LaPresse.ca, March 30, 2010, accessed March 18, 2015, http://www.lapresse.ca/actualites/justice-et-affaires-criminelles/201003/30/01-4265724-laval-tenue-responsable-dans-laffaire-jocelyn-hot-

If the officers had taken Gélinas more seriously, the RCMP could have taken away the weapon Hotte used days later to kill Gélinas, Reimnitz said. "The interpretation that the police officers made of what Gélinas perceived as a threat was not reasonable and constitutes one of the main elements for the conclusion of responsibility. This call was anything but a 'banal' call."

The city of Laval appealed the ruling, but it lost in 2012. It finally agreed to pay the plaintiffs $1.5 million to settle the case. Pierre Mainville worked hard to rebuild his life and went through extensive rehabilitation. He joined a mentor program that helps high-school dropouts and became Canada's top wheelchair fencer—the first Canadian to place in the sport's World Cup with a bronze in 2010. He competed in the Paralympic Games in Beijing (2008), London (2012) and Rio (2016) and is ranked 10th in the world. He has had two kids since the shooting.

"I believe a lot in the strength of the human spirit," he was quoted saying in 2009. "You can never prepare yourself for not walking again. But you can adapt. After it happened I gave myself a kick in the butt and said, 'This is my new life. I've got to look forward.'" He said he pursued the lawsuit "because I don't want something like this to happen again."[30]

How did Laval police and the RCMP react to the universal condemnation from all sides in the case, to the lost lawsuit and the embarrassing headlines about one of the bloodiest episodes in recent memory of police domestic violence anywhere worldwide?

Laval police were tightlipped. Lieutenant Gilles Moreau, head of its internal affairs section, told me his unit investigated the conduct of the two Laval cops who visited Gélinas, but refused to disclose the results. (*The Montreal Gazette* reported the two officers were cleared.[31]) Moreau also wouldn't say if his department changed any policies on dealing with officers accused of domestic violence. "We're going to reserve any comment," he said in an interview after the trial.

The RCMP, for its part, told me after the trial it didn't change anything in how it operates. "This is an isolated incident," Mountie spokesperson Ser-

te.php?utm_categorieinterne=trafficdrivers&utm_contenuinterne=cyberpresse_lire_aussi_4266376_article_POS4.

30 Ingrid Peritz and Les Perreaux, "Survivors of Mountie's rampage relive ordeal in courtroom," *The Globe and Mail*, September 17, 2009, A12, accessed March 18, 2015, http://www.theglobeandmail.com/news/national/survivors-of-mounties-rampage-relive-ordeal-in-courtroom/article4285979/.

31 George Kalogerakis, "Police work ripped; Laval cops criticized. But an internal probe cleared both officers," *The Montreal Gazette*, December 14, 2002, A4.

geant Jocelyn Mimeault said. "The important thing is we have internal mechanisms in place to recognize early signs of stress among members."

It wasn't just the Laval police and RCMP that didn't act. The governments to which they answer were also silent and did nothing to compel police officials to change. And no other police department or government in Canada heeded the lessons of the tragedy either, as far as I could tell.

The inaction also isn't peculiar to this incident or country. The Hotte killing is actually an instructive, if extreme example of an epidemic of police domestic violence that continues to be generally condoned today in the U.S., Canada and worldwide, except in the most egregious cases.

No inquiry or study has ever investigated how widespread the abuse is in any country outside the U.S.—though some Canadian police officers say it is as prevalent in Canada as south of the border. No Canadian police force, so far as I could find, automatically fires an officer convicted of domestic violence. Very few have a specific policy on procedures to follow when an officer is accused of domestic violence, so as to avoid conflict of interest. And none have adopted the model policy on the issue recommended over 15 years ago by the International Association of Chiefs of Police to all its 21,000 member chiefs, including those in Canada.

Many Canadian police departments don't even compile data on how many of their officers commit abuse. And despite new gun-control legislation in 2015, Canada still lags about 20 years behind the U.S. in keeping firearms out of the hands of abusers. [32]

Canada seems to be in a different galaxy. But Canada is far from unique. It is representative of the international inaction on the problem. Just how far have Canadian and other police forces fallen behind? How bad is the problem around the world—and what are the impacts? Are there any solutions? The questions are relevant in any country where little awareness exists about the abuse epidemic, including the U.S.

In our search for answers, we will meet the two people most responsible for our present understanding of police domestic violence: an Arizona sociologist who served on an FBI advisory panel and whose grandfather started the first African American-owned detective agency; and a highly decorated police detective with a PhD and a side interest in hypnosis.

---

[32] See more on the Canadian and U.S. gun legislation in Chapters 7 and 8.

CHAPTER 3

Stumbling Onto a Secret

Leanor Johnson was excited as she drove past the high-tech office complexes of the I-270 corridor just outside Washington, D.C.'s Capital Beltway. Nearly a year of effort had paid off. She had finally broken into the secretive world of the police.

Johnson, a sociologist, had won a major government grant to research how women deal with conflict and stress in male-dominated jobs. She decided to focus on policewomen. But getting the okay from police to study their highly secretive world had nearly ended in failure.

After months of shut doors and unreturned messages, Johnson finally lucked out by getting introduced to a police chief who gave her a thumbs-up to study his officers. Johnson wanted to interview both female and male cops to see how their work affected their home lives differently. The police chief agreed. Even better, the officers' spouses were excited about the study and wanted to participate, too. It was the first time an outsider had asked them what it was like to be married to a cop. They would have a lot to say about it.

To Johnson, the study seemed like a no-brainer. Few professions are more in the public eye than policing. She imagined cops would have a lot of interest in knowing how the stress of their jobs and the power of the uniform impact their family life. But as important as the subject was, Johnson quickly learned it was acutely sensitive for the police. She didn't know it yet, but good reasons existed for the lack of transparency. She was about to stumble onto a secret the police didn't want outsiders to discover.

Johnson's destination was the sprawling campus of Westat, a large research institute in Rockville, Maryland, where she was a senior researcher.

(In the midst of her study, she changed jobs to become a professor of family studies at Arizona State University.)

Helping Johnson with the study was Veronica Nieva, a psychologist. Nieva was already in the interview room. She flashed Johnson a big smile. "So are you ready?" she asked.

"I've been ready a *looong* time," Johnson said.

Before long, there was a knock on the door.

"Come in," Johnson said.

A woman opened the door. Subject no. 1—we'll call her Claire—was early. Her eyes surveyed the room, then she took the seat at the table across from the researchers.

"I saw this flyer," she said. "I decided to come because it's anonymous and confidential and you're way out here. If you were doing this at the police station, I wouldn't have come.

"I have something I want to talk to you about, and I really don't care what you want to talk to me about. I'm going to tell *you* what I want you to know about *my* stress."

The two researchers glanced at each other.

"*Okaaay,*" Johnson thought to herself. "Now what do we do?"

They set aside their questionnaire and listened. Claire proceeded to talk virtually nonstop for two hours, unburdening herself of a remarkable story. She started by describing how wonderful her husband was.

"He's a great police officer who is very effective on the street and cares about prostitutes. He takes the time to talk to them about getting off the street and changing their lives," she said.

Claire continued, "Sometimes, he cares so much that he has sex with them."

She then talked about how her husband beat her up.

"Why don't you go to a shelter?" Johnson asked at one point.

Claire gave her a hard look. "I can't," she said. "I'm afraid of the police department finding out and firing my husband. We have children. Who will support them?"

As a researcher, Johnson knew she wasn't supposed to show any expression. It had been a tough two hours. When Claire was gone, she and Nieva looked at each other in astonishment. A police officer beating up his wife? This was unexpected.

"I can't imagine this being a real problem in the police community," Johnson said to Nieva. "It's probably just an odd case."

Nieva agreed. Surely Claire's story was an aberration. When they met the second wife, however, she also said she was being assaulted at home. So did the next wife, and the one after that. Johnson and Nieva were surprised but still skeptical.

It must be some kind of freak coincidence, they reasoned. Or maybe the first woman had some friends who were also being abused, and she had told them about the study. The friends may have figured that since Claire had had a good therapeutic experience, they would go meet the researchers, too.

After all, police officers are sworn to uphold the law and protect the public. How could they be assaulting their own wives and girlfriends? It didn't make sense.

Leanor Johnson's accidental discovery of police domestic violence in the mid-1980s led to the first detailed picture of the abuse epidemic raging in many law enforcement homes. Johnson went on to dedicate a significant part of her career to the issue, spending the next six years researching it, writing several important papers and serving on a Federal Bureau of Investigation advisory board on police stress and family violence.

The chance manner of her breakthrough also revealed how extremely hidden the problem was and why no one had explored it before—and very few others have even now, more than 25 years later.

Johnson succeeded through ingenuity, luck and perseverance that had its roots in her own upbringing. When she was growing up in the upscale southern California enclave of Pasadena, her Jamaican-born father often took the family on trips to visit his land of birth. He would use the opportunity to tell his three children the story of his former schoolmate in Jamaica, who had overcome desperate poverty to become the police chief of Kingston, the capital.

"You see him?" their father asked. "He used to be so poor when we were in Port Antonio that his mother would take a yam sack and cut three holes, one for his head and two for his arms. That would be his uniform for school. Then when he came home, he would take his uniform off. He went naked so they kept it looking nice. And now he's chief of police of Kingston."

Her father told this story as a lesson in grit and achievement, but it also embedded in Johnson's young mind a special emotional connection with cops. That childhood bond was reinforced by family legends about her renowned grandfather. He had passed away when she was young, but her father loved to talk about how his dad came to New York City during the Depression and started what he believed was the first African American-owned private detective agency in the country.

"He put away a lot of criminals because no one suspected him of being a detective," her father said.

These early positive impressions of lawmen and detectives were a sharp contrast with Johnson's experiences with cops while growing up in the Los Angeles area in the 1960s and early 1970s. Her family's encounters with the police were typical of those of many African Americans.

One of the most jarring episodes took place at the Rose Parade, the colourful New Year's Day pageant that Pasadena holds each year before the Rose Bowl college football championship. It was a family tradition to attend the parade.

Sophie, a relative of Johnson, was dropping everyone off in the car and then planned to drive home because she was having a migraine headache.[33] A police officer ordered Sophie to move the car, but she hesitated as everyone piled out. Johnson recalls how the officer, growing impatient, reached across Sophie's chest, grabbed the keys and dragged her from the vehicle. Three other officers joined in, and together the four of them threw her to the ground where she was handcuffed.

The family was stunned. Sophie was a genteel piano composer and classically trained soprano with postgraduate degrees. Despite attempts to explain the situation, Sophie was forced to lay flat on the cold ground. She was soon shivering because she didn't have her coat on. When Johnson approached with Sophie's coat, a police officer warned her to stay back.

"If you put the coat on her we're going to arrest you," he said.

The police eventually agreed not to charge Sophie if she didn't bring charges against the officer, Johnson said. "This was a person who never had premarital sex, who's never drank, never smoked. It was very horrible."

The episode was traumatic for the family, but it wasn't the only brush with belligerent cops. Police officers seemed to make a habit of harassing Johnson's father, a successful real-estate broker and exporter-importer, as he walked down the street with his briefcase, she said.

"Hey, boy, come over here," the cops would call out to him. "Just get over here."

Johnson said, "My father was always fighting that kind of discrimination." But she refused to become bitter. If anything, the incidents fostered in her an even greater curiosity about cops and a longing to know what was in their minds. She wanted to find out why they acted the way they did and to

---

[33] Johnson asked that Sophie's full name be omitted because Sophie still experiences post-traumatic stress from the incident and fears possible police retaliation if she speaks out.

see if she could help them change for the better. She would soon have her chance.

She got a PhD in sociology specializing in family studies and, after joining Arizona State University, co-authored a pioneering text, *Black Families at the Crossroads*, one of the first books on the evolution of African American families in the U.S.[34] She also founded the university's African and African American Studies Department, which she headed for seven years.

In 1983, she got a grant from the U.S. government's National Institute of Mental Health to study women in nontraditional jobs. She chose female police officers. Her plan was to investigate how they handled the conflict of working in the male-dominated police world.

But when she approached police departments to get access to officers for the study, she met resistance right away. Some said they were interested, but months would tick by without a commitment. Many officials made it clear they didn't like the study.

"Our women are doing just fine," one police commander told her. "They're just doing a great job, and there's no conflict."

After months without a police department onboard, Johnson and her research partner Veronica Nieva realized what the problem was. The police weren't comfortable with women being in the title of the study. So they changed the title. The study would now be about work-family stress among cops. In fact, they had always intended to study stress among both male and female officers.

Police were immediately more receptive. "You're talking about the stress we have? Oh yeah, we have stress," they would tell the researchers. But the departments still wouldn't grant access to officers. The distrust of outsiders was too strong. One day, Johnson mentioned her frustration to her dean at the university. He offered to write a letter of introduction to a friend who worked in a large U.S. police department.

Within days the department's commissioner agreed to let his officers participate in the study and referred Johnson and Nieva to four other police departments on the east coast that also agreed to participate. They had finally broken into the closed policing community. The study could proceed. Johnson was getting a good sense of the kind of world she was entering. Only a trusted few got access.

The five departments turned out to be a good sample. The commissioner who was their main contact ran a large 3,000-member urban police force.

---

[34] Robert Staples and Leanor Boulin Johnson, *Black Families at the Crossroads: Challenges and Prospects* (San Francisco: Jossey-Bass, 1993).

They also had two midsized suburban departments with 1,000 members each and two small rural forces.

They started with a round of pre-interviews with officers and spouses to shape the study and narrow down their questions. The first ones were done with officers and spouses from one of the suburban departments. That is where Claire and the other abused wives came forward.

The researchers decided to disregard these initial accounts. They had a major study to do and no time to get sidetracked. They went back to the commissioner who was their contact and asked to do pre-interviews at his large urban police force. He was a giant of a man who enjoyed reminding them the study's fate was in his hands.

"Docs, I'll just tell you right here," he said, "I could have dragged you on for a whole year, and you would never have gotten to first base."

He now had a surprise for them. He said he wanted to choose the officers they interviewed. Johnson's heart sank. "Oh Lord, it's going to be the stars of the department," she thought. "That is not scientifically cool. He's going to bias the sample."

But they were stuck. This man was their ticket in, and there was no study without his blessing. They decided to go with his star officers. Johnson, Nieva and two other researchers each took a list of officers and spouses. At the end of the first day, they came together to compare notes. They were stunned. Everyone had more stories about domestic violence.

Now there was no getting around the fact that they were onto something significant. Abuse in the homes of cops appeared to be widespread. After all, even the commissioner's handpicked cops were involved. Claire and her friends hadn't been aberrations at all.

But just how prevalent was it? What was going on in police homes? Johnson and Nieva decided they had to find out. It was not what they had set out to research, but how could they ignore this astounding problem? They refocused their study to include questions about domestic violence.

Given the police mistrust of outsiders, the researchers figured they should explore the situation as gingerly as possible. They figured the abuse was going to be a touchy subject, and they didn't want to scare anybody off. They would hint at it and leave it to the subjects to talk, if they chose. As it turned out, they did not have trouble getting officers and spouses to open up. Many were as eager to unburden themselves as Claire.

When Johnson presented her landmark findings at the U.S. House of Representatives Select Committee on Children, Youth and Families in May 1991, the room was floored.

A remarkable 40 percent of 728 officers admitted they had "gotten out of control and behaved violently" toward their spouse or children in the previous six months, Johnson told the committee in a hearing called "On the Front Lines: Police Stress and Family Well-Being."[35]

The number was mind-boggling. It means 360,000 of the 900,000 sworn law enforcement officers in the U.S. today could be violent at home. And if the problem is similar in other countries, 28,000 of Canada's 70,000 cops could be abusive, along with 52,000 of the 130,000 police officers in England and Wales.[36]

The rate was several times the level reported in the general population. For comparison, 1.5 to 4 percent of U.S. and Canadian women report domestic violence by an intimate partner in the previous year, while 6 to 14 percent of children are estimated to be physically abused each year.[37] (We don't know exactly how many times Johnson's numbers are above the public average because no data exists on the combined abuse rate for spouses and children for the previous six months in the wider population.)

- **U.S.**—Of 8,000 U.S. women surveyed in 1995 and 1996 by the Centers for Disease Control and Prevention (CDC), 1.5 percent said an intimate partner had physically assaulted or raped them at least once in the previous year.[38] In 2010, 4 percent of 9,086 American women told the CDC they had experienced physical violence by an

---

[35] Leanor Boulin Johnson, Prepared statement before the U.S. House of Representatives Select Committee on Children, Youth and Families (Washington, D.C.: May 20, 1991), 32-48, accessed March 18, 2015, http://files.eric.ed.gov/fulltext/ED338997.pdf.

[36] As we see in Chapters 5 and 8, the police domestic abuse rate in the U.S. today probably hasn't changed materially since 1991, while cops in other countries such as Canada likely have similar abuse rates.

[37] Ruth Gilbert et al., "Burden and consequences of child maltreatment in high-income countries," *The Lancet* 373, no. 9657 (January 3, 2009): 68-81, accessed May 3, 2015, http://www.thelancet.com/journals/lancet/article/PIIS0140-6736%2808%2961706-7/abstract.

[38] Patricia Tjaden and Nancy Thoennes, *Prevalence, Incidence, and Consequences of Violence Against Women: Findings From the National Violence Against Women Survey* (Washington, D.C.: U.S. Department of Justice, November 1998), 2, accessed March 18, 2015, https://www.ncjrs.gov/pdffiles/172837.pdf.

intimate partner in the past year.[39] (It's important to note abuse is usually underreported and that the actual numbers are probably higher.)

- **Canada**—Domestic violence rates in Canada are generally in line with those in the U.S. In a 2009 Statistics Canada survey of 9,233 women, 1.9 percent said they experienced spousal violence (including sexual assault) by a current or former partner in the previous year.[40] In Statistics Canada surveys in 1999 and 2004, 2 to 3 percent of women said they experienced spousal violence in the previous 12 months.[41]

While no clean comparison could be made between Johnson's cops and the wider population, abuse was clearly much more rampant in police families. Johnson also heard from 479 police spouses. Ten percent reported being physically abused at home in the prior six months. This rate was also much higher than the U.S. average—but curiously, well below the 40-percent rate admitted by police officers. Johnson suspected that the spouse number was lower because the questionnaires were usually mailed to the homes of the families. Many couples filled them out together, which could have caused spouses to be fearful to report abuse.

An additional 10 percent of spouses said their partner physically abused their children. And 20 to 30 percent of spouses said their mate "frequently became verbally abusive" to them or their children. They said officers often treated family members like "citizens," were overly critical and expected the last word.

The domestic reign of terror was coupled with other serious troubles. Spouses often told Johnson their husbands were emotionally distant and kept their work troubles bottled up inside. The cops felt that "rugged indi-

---

[39] Black et al., *The National Intimate Partner and Sexual Violence Survey*, 38. This survey also said 0.6 percent of women reported an intimate partner had raped them in the previous year. In total, 5.9 percent of women reported physical violence, rape and/or stalking in the previous year.

[40] Statistics Canada, *Family Violence in Canada: A Statistical Profile* (Ottawa: 2011), 17, accessed March 18, 2015, http://www.statcan.gc.ca/pub/85-224-x/85-224-x2010000-eng.pdf. The available statistics don't offer perfect comparisons between the U.S. and Canada because the U.S. data is based on married and unmarried intimate partners, while the Canadian data is for only married and common-law partners.

[41] Statistics Canada, *Family Violence in Canada: A Statistical Profile 2005* (Ottawa: 2005), 17, 18, accessed March 18, 2015, http://data.library.utoronto.ca/datapub/codebooks/cstdli/gss/gss18/85-224-xie2005000.pdf.

vidualism"—"going it alone and being extra tough"—was an essential part of the job. "The most frequent complaint reported by both spouses and officers was the officers' inability to leave the job at work," Johnson said.

The tough guy act had a price: alcoholism, emotional exhaustion and an uncaring attitude toward civilians. Under the surface many were confused and angry. Some told their wives everything was under control, but in their sleep they grinded their teeth so much they needed major dental care. Thirty-six percent of the officers felt worried or guilty about excessive alcohol use. Thirty percent reported suicidal thoughts.

Especially challenging was the plight of many women married to officers of colour, who faced extra obstacles to reporting the abuse. "They may experience a triple guilt trip from turning on both an officer and intimate partner as well as exposing yet one more person of color to what they may perceive to be an unjust prosecuting system," Johnson wrote in a subsequent paper. [42]

As a stark sign of the trouble in police homes, nearly 90 percent of spouses wanted police departments to offer psychological counselling and marriage-enrichment programs to cops and their families. Over three-quarters wanted alcoholism treatment and stress reduction programs.

"To me these statistics are neither cold nor distant," Johnson told the Congressional representatives. "During the course of our study, an officer dedicated to our efforts committed suicide, two women officers shot their husbands, a male officer killed his estranged wife, and dozens of spouses in stable marriages shared with us heart rendering testimonies about their work-family tensions and hardships."

Doing the study deeply touched Johnson. "The wives felt their spouses were doing a public service, but yet felt so cheated because no one was paying any attention to their families and how the job interferes with their functioning," she said in an interview. "They felt trapped. If they complain, they put their spouses' job into jeopardy. If they don't complain, they're miserable and don't have a way of correcting that."

Johnson still keeps in touch with many of the families. "I got to know the families really well, and I felt their pain," she said. "I kind of rejoice in their joys when they have them, and I really got close to them. My heart just went out to them in a way that I'm surprised because I know first-hand what police

---

[42] Leanor Boulin Johnson, "Police Officers and Spousal Violence: Work-Family Linkages," in *Continuing the War Against Domestic Violence*, 2nd ed., ed. Lee E. Ross (Boca Raton, Florida: CRC Press, 2014), 189-210.

brutality can do, and I certainly don't condone that. But on the other hand, I think as a scholar it is my duty and my mission to tease out all sides to a story."

Johnson's study provoked strong reactions. Penny Harrington, a former chief of police in Portland, Oregon, and the first woman to head a major U.S. police department, remembers scoffing when she first heard the horrendous data and similar numbers in a second study that came out not long after (see Chapter 4).

But Harrington changed her mind when she took a closer look at the research and saw it was methodologically sound. The numbers helped turn Harrington, a police officer for over 20 years, into a leading critic of how police forces handle family violence by officers.

"As a police officer I was aware of a few cases, but I was never aware of the depth of the problem. I had no idea," said Harrington, who after leaving the police founded the National Center for Women & Policing. She is now chair of the center's board. "It's a horrible, horrible problem. Close to half of all 911 calls are for family violence. If the statistics are true, you've got a two-in-five chance of getting a batterer coming to answer your call."

Leanor Johnson's study helped convince Congress to amend the Omnibus Crime Control Act of 1991 to include funds for police departments to provide therapy and other support services for officers and their families. The plan was to create a network of family support centres modeled on those at U.S. military bases.

The amendment got bipartisan support in the House of Representatives and Senate. But the crime bill was flawed in the eyes of President George Bush Sr., who had lobbied Congress to expand use of the death penalty. When his measures were cut, Bush threatened to veto the legislation. Enthusiasm for the bill collapsed, and it died in Congress.

It wasn't long, however, before tragedy showed the consequences of inaction and thrust abusive cops squarely back into the public eye. The scene was a Los Angeles neighbourhood just a short drive from where Johnson grew up.

CHAPTER 4

"I Just Couldn't Walk Away"

The Los Angeles Police Department had known for months that Victor Felix Ramos was a troubled cop. Ramos, 29 years old, lived with his wife Melba, 26, and their three young kids in the LA suburb of Glendale, which borders Pasadena. A clear sign of trouble came in May 1992 when Ramos showed up at his wife's work. He dragged her by her hair, threw her to the ground, pointed a gun at her, trashed her office and hung her by a hook in the bathroom.[43]

Melba, covered in bruises and suffering back pain, reported the incident to police. Her husband wasn't charged. Instead, Victor's guns were confiscated for 16 days and he agreed to get counselling. Internal affairs conducted an investigation, but its report failed to note that Victor had pointed a gun at his wife. He was back on patrol after a month.

At home, the violence reportedly continued. In one argument, Victor put his gun to his head and threatened to shoot himself, authorities said. In July, Melba, tired of years of abuse, filed for separation.

In August 1992, Victor kicked down the door of Melba's apartment and burst in. He fired eight shots from his 9 mm Beretta service pistol into Melba and 13 into her new boyfriend, Gregory Thomas, stopping only to reload,

---

[43] Kathy Braidhill, "A deadly force—domestic violence in the Los Angeles Police Department," *Los Angeles Magazine*, October 1997.

then killed himself with a bullet in the heart. The couple's three sons, aged 3, 5 and 6, huddled in a bedroom all night until police discovered them and the three bodies the next morning.

The families of Melba Ramos and Gregory Thomas sued the city, saying the LAPD had let Victor Ramos have his guns back despite evidence that he was distraught and had made threats of violence. The department was also faulted for not taking firmer action against him after he assaulted Melba at her workplace.

During the court case, retired LAPD Assistant Chief David Dotson acknowledged in a sworn statement that the department had covered up abuse in the ranks. "It was the department's practice to treat police officers accused of domestic violence differently than civilians accused of domestic violence....

"Rather than arresting the accused police officers for domestic-violence misconduct and using the criminal justice system, the department would use internal disciplinary measures," Dotson said. [44]

The lawyer for the two families compelled the LAPD to disclose records of internal investigations of police officers accused of domestic violence. The lawyer hired a friend with extensive human resources management experience, Bob Mullally, to analyze the records. [45] Mullally was taken aback by what he read.

"I figured the police would be policing themselves," he later told the *LA Weekly*. Instead, he said, "kids were being beaten. Women were being beaten and raped. Their organs were ruptured. Bones were broken. It was hard cold-fisted brutality by police officers, and nothing was being done to protect their family members." [46]

More than 70 officers were investigated for domestic violence from 1990 to 1993, the documents showed. The allegations, which also included child molestation, led to administrative discipline against several officers and a few firings, but not one cop was prosecuted. [47]

After Mullally's analysis was shared with city officials, they quickly agreed to pay the plaintiffs $2.15 million to settle the lawsuit. One of the terms was that the damaging records be kept secret. A city official admitted the settlement was agreed to solely to keep the records from the public eye. [48]

---

[44] Braidhill, "A deadly force."

[45] Mullally had been the state of South Dakota's personnel commissioner and personnel director.

[46] Jim Crogan, "Life of a Whistleblower," *LA Weekly*, June 5, 2003, accessed March 18, 2015, http://www.laweekly.com/news/life-of-a-whistleblower-2136507.

[47] Tony Ortega, "Blind Justice," *New Times LA*, January 11, 2011, accessed March 18, 2015, http://truthinjustice.org/mullaly.htm.

[48] Ortega, "Blind Justice."

But Mullally was frustrated at the thought that the domestic violence and impunity would be covered up. "I just couldn't walk away and pretend I hadn't seen it," he later told the *Rapid City Journal* newspaper.[49] He had a special connection to the issue because his own late father had been abusive: "It's terrorizing, especially for a kid, especially by a trusted adult." In 1997, Mullally leaked the files to a local CBS TV affiliate, which aired an explosive two-part series. CBS journalist Mike Wallace later covered Mullally's whistleblowing in a segment on the program *60 Minutes*.

The disclosure forced the LAPD to act. The department's then-Inspector General Katherine Mader launched what appears to have been the first official investigation worldwide into how police handle domestic violence in the ranks.

Mader's 1997 report was scathing. Mullally had been right. The inspector general found a massive cover-up inside the LAPD going back years. Ramos was far from the only abuser who had gotten virtually no punishment. In fact, that was the norm. Known batterers on the force usually got only mild, in-house discipline and rarely faced criminal prosecution. Many internal investigations "lacked objectivity or were otherwise flawed or skewed," the report said.[50]

The inquiry reviewed 227 investigations of officers for domestic violence between 1990 and 1997. Abuse allegations were sustained (i.e. upheld) in 91 cases. But prosecutors usually declined to lay charges. Only 18 cases resulted in a criminal charge (or one in five of those sustained). Just four cases led to a conviction, and only one cop was fired. The three other convicted cops were merely suspended—for as few as five days.

The most common punishment was a brief suspension of one to four days or an admonishment. Over three-quarters of abusive officers had no mention of the incident in their performance records. When discipline was men-

49 Steve Miller, "New life but no regrets: Mullally out of jail," *Rapid City Journal*, July 16, 2003, accessed March 18, 2015, http://rapidcityjournal.com/news/local/new-life-but-no-regrets-mullally-out-of-jail/article_4c94d409-339a-5d56-bbf9-d98838783286.html.

50 Katherine Mader, *Domestic Violence in the Los Angeles Police Department: How well does the Los Angeles Police Department police its own? The Report of the Domestic Violence Task Force to the Board of Police Commissioners* (Office of the Inspector General, Los Angeles Police Department, July 22, 1997).

tioned, the description "tended to minimize the misconduct," Mader said. Twenty-nine percent of abusive cops went on to get a promotion.[51]

Tellingly, male cops were treated much more indulgently than female officers and civilian LAPD employees when facing abuse accusations. Just 38 percent of allegations against male officers were upheld—compared to 60 percent of those against female cops and 70 percent of those against civilians. Male cops appeared to be protecting their own.

Mader's report singled out some of the more remarkable stories. One LAPD member made terrorist threats following a conflict with his wife. He served several days in jail, but was then allowed back on the job as an instructor in an elite police program.

Another officer backhanded and slapped his wife, a fellow cop, in the face, threatened to kill them both, then committed himself for psychiatric treatment. Shortly afterward, he was appointed to teach at the LAPD academy. There was no mention of the episode in the officer's performance evaluation, and he was rated as "problem free."

One officer punched the complainant with his fist, grabbed her by the hair, threw her and caused her to fall. Not long after, his supervisor wrote that "[the officer] has consistently displayed a calm and professional demeanor even when dealing with the most highly agitated and stressful situations."

Mader's inquiry wasn't easy to complete. Even locating the records was a challenge; many were misfiled or missing. Was the LAPD worse than other departments in dealing with abuse? Mader's staff contacted large police forces across the U.S. to find out, but almost none tracked domestic violence by officers.

"Traditionally, as demonstrated through the statistics in this report, law enforcement agencies have 'gone easy' when addressing domestic violence committed by law enforcement personnel," Mader's study said.

The impacts went beyond police families. Many cops, unsurprisingly, were similarly lax in investigating domestic violence in other people's homes. "Some of the reasons for laxity in pursuing Department personnel have applied equally to lay investigations," Mader wrote. (We return to this problem in Chapter 6.)

Mader's report made headlines and prompted the creation of a domestic violence unit in the LAPD's internal affairs division. But Bob Mullally, the whistleblower who finally induced the LAPD to investigate the problems,

---

[51] California law and LAPD policy required police to write a crime report for all domestic violence cases, whether or not an arrest was made. That was not done in 93 of the 227 investigations (or 41 percent).

fared worse than any of the cops he exposed. In a cruel twist, a judge convicted him in 2001 of violating a court order for disclosing the LAPD records to a journalist. Mullally served 45 days in a federal prison. It was an extraordinary contrast to the easy lot of the many officers who got away with abuse or covering it up.

Undaunted, Mullally has since campaigned to promote awareness of domestic violence. "I'd feel worse," he told reporters after his conviction, "if I stood by and said nothing."[52]

It turned out the LAPD's lackadaisical approach to disciplining abusive cops was indeed the norm across the U.S. and in other countries. Prior to Mader's report, another study had come out in 1995 from the Arlington Police Department and the Southwestern Law Enforcement Institute, both in Texas. Led by Arlington police Lieutenant Larry Boyd, the study surveyed 123 U.S. police departments about discipline for domestic violence and made some interesting discoveries.

Less than 6 percent normally terminated an officer for a first sustained domestic violence incident. Fifty-two percent said counselling would be the usual discipline. Even after a second sustained incident, just 19 percent said termination was typical, while 48 percent said suspension and days off without pay was the norm.

And only 9 percent of the departments said they had different or higher standards for police officers involved in domestic violence. "Internal affairs units and the disciplinary actions meted out tend to regard domestic assault as more a private than a criminal matter," the study said.[53]

And it isn't just police in the U.S. who ignore abuse in their ranks. In fact, the problem appears to be a worldwide phenomenon, though it has gotten even less attention in other countries than in the U.S. (See Chapter 8 for a detailed look at the situation in Canada.)

- **Britain**—In the UK, a government inquiry in 2014 stumbled across abuse in police homes during a broader investigation that found police grossly mishandle domestic violence in the general population. Police domestic violence "is an uncomfortable fact that cannot be ig-

---

[52] Ortega, "Blind Justice."

[53] Larry Boyd et al., "Domestic Assault Among Police: A Survey of Internal Affairs Policies" (Southwestern Law Enforcement Institute and Arlington Police Department, 1995), accessed March 18, 2015, http://www.cailaw.org/media/files/ILEA/Publications/domestic_99.pdf.

nored," the inquiry said. "Some of the victims we spoke to in our focus groups had been in abusive relationships with police officers. They described their utter lack of confidence in the police response and fear that the service would 'look after its own.' It is vital for public confidence that those police officers who are perpetrators of domestic abuse are brought to justice. Forces should also have consis-consistent and robust disciplinary policies to deal with this issue."[54]

- **Australia**—Similar concerns have been expressed in Australia. "Domestic abuse is still perceived to be essentially a private family matter," Alan Corbett, a former state legislator and teacher in Australia, said in a submission to a government inquiry on family violence. "Unless the abuse impacts on the capacity of an officer to do their job or adversely impacts on the public perception of the service, the [Queensland Police Service] will not get involved."[55]

In the Australian state of Queensland, for example, police don't publicly disclose abuse incidents involving officers or keep track of such cases, Corbett said. In the state of Victoria, 190 police officers were subject to court-issued protection orders related to family violence between 2011 and 2014, according to police documents Corbett obtained through a freedom-of-information request. Officers breached protection orders 41 times over the same period.[56]

Corbett's research was highlighted in a government inquiry into domestic violence in the state of Victoria in March 2016. Citing "cultural attitudes held among members of Victoria Police that are consistent with family violence risk factors, victims of family violence perpetrated by police members can face additional barriers to reporting," the inquiry said. "Transparency and rigour in relation to

---

[54] Her Majesty's Inspectorate of Constabulary, *Everybody's business: Improving the police response to domestic abuse* (London: March 27, 2014), 35, accessed April 20, 2015, https://www.justiceinspectorates.gov.uk/hmic/wp-content/uploads/2014/04/improving-the-police-response-to-domestic-abuse.pdf.

[55] Alan Corbett, "Domestic Abuse by Police Officers" (submission to the Queensland Premier's Special Taskforce on Domestic and Family Violence, edited version, April 10, 2014), accessed April 20, 2015, https://www.facebook.com/AustralianChildrensRightsParty/posts/589716234464317 (Part A) and https://www.facebook.com/AustralianChildrensRightsParty/posts/589715997797674 (Part B).

[56] Alan Corbett, "The Thin Blue Line Of Violence in Australian Police Families," NewMatilda.com, August 31, 2015, accessed July 26, 2016, https://newmatilda.com/2015/08/30/thin-blue-line-violence-australian-police-families/.

how Victoria Police deals with family violence within its own ranks are critical to ensuring that the public has confidence in the ability of police to respond effectively to family violence in the broader community." The inquiry called on Victoria state police to review how they handle abuse in their ranks within 12 months.[57]

- **South Africa**—Police in South Africa have an especially poor record. They in some cases "discourage women [abused by officers] from laying charges against colleagues" or refused outright to lay charges, one study found. Some abused police spouses said when they called police, responding officers greeted the abuser as a friend and shook his hand.[58]

One woman's story was especially disturbing. She filed several police complaints about abuse but was ignored. Her officer husband once beat her in front of his police friends "who did nothing but stand around and laugh," the study said, citing the wife's family. When she tried to flee in a car, he pulled her out by her hair and went on beating and kicking her. He later shot her six times in the back. Instead of being jailed, the officer waited in the police station with his colleagues and friends until his bail was paid by a supervisor, who took him to his own home to spend the night. The officer was convicted for the murder but sentenced to only four years in prison. He didn't lose his job and instead was only suspended pending his appeal of the sentence.

Another horrendous incident took place in June 2015 when South African police Constable Ronnie Masie stormed a Johannesburg police station and shot and murdered his girlfriend Sowela Anna Nkuna, a police commander and two others. Masie was later killed by a police tactical team. He had remained a cop even after Nkuna filed numerous complaints of domestic abuse, her family members said. A month before the killing, he reportedly held Nkuna hostage at gunpoint, fired shots into the street and threatened to kill responding officers.[59]

---

[57] State of Victoria, *Royal Commission into Family Violence; Summary and recommendations* (Victorian Government Printer, 2016), accessed August 3, 2016, http://files.rcfv.com.au/Reports/RCFV_Full_Report_Interactive.pdf.

[58] Jennifer Nix, "To Protect and Abuse: An exploratory study discussing intimate partners of police as victims of domestic abuse" (paper presented to the Centre for the Study of Violence and Reconciliation, Johannesburg, South Africa, June 4, 1998), accessed November 28, 2016, http://www.csvr.org.za/wits/papers/papnix.htm.

[59] Kutlwano Olifant and Karishma Dipa, "Killer cop had history of violence," IOL.co.za, June 5, 2015, accessed August 28, 2015,

The LAPD was far from unique in covering up for its officer-batterers.

Back in the U.S., the Victor Ramos murder-suicide put the abuse epidemic back on the public agenda. What helped keep it there and convince Congress to take action again was the work of a couple of Arizona cops who decided they had to do something about the abusers they worked alongside.

Detective Albert "Bud" Seng of the Tucson Police Department lived two hours south of sociologist Leanor Johnson's university office, down Inter-state Highway 10. In the late 1980s, he didn't yet know of Johnson's work, but he had concerns of his own about cops who abused at home.

Seng would often see telltale signs of domestic violence at police social events—arguments with threatening body language, heightened tension between spouses. Lots of cops came right out and told him they were getting physical at home.

Seng was an unusual police officer with eclectic interests. Highly deco-rated and a leading armed robbery investigator, he had a master's degree in counselling and studied hypnosis. On the side, he had a private therapy practice for fellow cops and their spouses. He was often surprised at how frequently he heard about domestic violence from clients. He began to sus-pect that what he saw was a mere teardrop in an ocean of sorrow.

Seng wanted to find out more but could not find any research on cops and conjugal violence. No one had done a study. He was at a loss to understand how widespread the violence was, why it happened and how to stop it.

Abuse at home seemed like a major occupational hazard for cops, but Seng found himself staring into a black hole of information. He decided he had to do something and without intending to—much like Leanor Johnson—went on to cause an upheaval in law enforcement.

Born in Louisville, Kentucky, to a German dad who was a manager at Canada Dry, Seng had two big dreams as a young man in the Sixties, both related to helping others. The first was to join the Peace Corps. He signed on in 1965 for two years in India. The other was to become a cop.

In 1969, Seng joined a small police department in a Detroit suburb. After three years, he left in search of better weather and fresh air and wound up in Arizona. He settled in the sun-drenched oasis of Tucson, nestled in a valley under five spectacular mountain ranges.

Seng joined the Tucson Police Department and soon made detective, working in the larceny, burglary and robbery details. He coached little league

http://www.iol.co.za/capetimes/police-top-brass-to-face-tough-parliamentary-questions-1.1900683#.VeECU_lVhBd.

soccer, became a union delegate and was decorated multiple times, winning medals of service, merit and valour. He was named Officer of the Year in 1987. Ever humble, he shies away from questions about what he did to earn the honours.

When he wasn't earning medals, Seng studied clinical hypnosis and used the insights to help fellow officers having trouble with things like stress, quitting smoking or weight loss. He became president of the Arizona Hypnosis Investigators Association.

While taking a course on forensic hypnosis—used by police to help witnesses remember traumatic events—Seng got to know the department's colourful staff psychologist. Harold Russell was a retired U.S. Army colonel who had served in France in World War II and did postdoctoral work at Harvard. Russell had moved to Tucson when he left the army and joined the city police in 1972 as Arizona's first police psychologist. He quickly became renowned in law enforcement, co-writing a widely used police textbook and helping to found the field of police psychology. He taught at the FBI Academy and many universities and trained officers in hostage negotiation, defusing confrontations and dealing with disturbed people without lethal force.

The two men were soon close pals. Seng liked Russell's Irish sense of humour, and "Doc Russell," as everyone called him, became Seng's mentor. It was Russell who encouraged his protégé to go back to university to get his master's degree in counselling. On graduating, Seng kept doing detective work but also opened his private counselling practice, which he expanded into a full-time job when he retired in 1992. (Seng went on to earn a PhD in biblical studies in 2015.)

"People think, 'How does a Peace Corps volunteer become a police officer, and then how does a police officer become a counsellor?' But I saw them as all related—as helping people," Seng said in an interview. "Working with people had always fascinated me. Of course, as a police officer you're constantly helping people in crisis situations, so I thought it was just kind of a natural progression into full-time counselling."[60]

Russell, like Seng, was taken aback by how many cops confided that they abused their spouses and by the lack of research. But what to do? They got their answer when they met Peter Neidig.

Neidig was a consultant to the U.S. military who had pioneered studies into conjugal violence among soldiers. One study he co-authored found

---

[60] Seng still works part-time as a therapist.

soldiers engaged in "severe aggression" at home three times more often than a comparable U.S. civilian population.[61]

Seng and Russell shared their concerns with Neidig about the abuse in cops' homes. Neidig was intrigued. The trio agreed to replicate Neidig's military surveys in the police community. The research became a labour of love. It took 18 months, and the men got no grants from police or government, paying out of their own pockets to travel across the country to survey officers.

They developed a questionnaire to hand out at law enforcement conferences and in-house training sessions in the U.S. Southwest. A broad gamut of cops completed the survey from a variety of large and small police departments.

The researchers also traveled to Pittsburgh to hand out their questionnaire at the 1991 national convention of the Fraternal Order of Police, the largest U.S. law enforcement association with about 250,000 members at the time.[62] They got a tremendous response there, with over 1,000 officers and spouses answering the questions.

As fate would have it, sociologist Leanor Johnson was also there. She had been invited to the convention to present her findings as a keynote speaker and saw Seng and his partners passing out their questionnaire. After Johnson's presentation, the next speaker was President George Bush Sr.

He used the opportunity to make a rousing tough-on-crime speech that some reporters described as the kickoff for his (ultimately unsuccessful) 1992 reelection campaign. "Values is [sic] what we're talking about. It's what drives you in your careers," Bush told the audience. "Our administration will help you take criminals off the streets.... Now, you keep up the good work. Thanks for what you've done." To Johnson's ears, Bush's remarks were highly ironic. If the president had been in the room to hear her presentation, he would have learned that a sizeable portion of the audience was likely committing criminal violence at home.

But as Seng learned, many cops weren't happy about the abuse being exposed. Despite plenty of responses at the convention, he and Russell faced a lot of police suspicion and sometimes anger about their project, including in their own department. "Many officers became defensive and didn't like the

---

[61] R. E. Heyman and P. H. Neidig, "A comparison of spousal aggression prevalence rates in U.S. Army and civilian representative samples," *Journal of Consulting and Clinical Psychology* (April 1999): 239-242, accessed March 19, 2015, http://www.ncbi.nlm.nih.gov/pubmed/10224734.

[62] The group has about 325,000 members today.

study, didn't agree with it, and occasionally we'd be challenged: 'This is b.s. I don't believe this kind of thing,'" Seng said.

"Law enforcement people are not particularly fond of mental health people, and law enforcement is a very closed society. They don't like the dirty laundry being exposed to the public. But I don't like it either. I mean, I was a cop for 25 years."

The only reason the three researchers got any cooperation was that Seng and Russell were cops themselves, Seng said. "We had a difficult time getting them to cooperate as is. So with an outside researcher or clinician it would be very difficult to get that kind of information."

They published their findings in 1992. It turned out Leanor Johnson's results weren't a fluke. Even Seng was surprised by the high level of abuse. Forty-one percent of 385 male officers said there had been violence in their relationship in the previous year (regardless of who committed the violence), Seng and his team reported in the journal *Police Studies*. They also found:

- The male cops' domestic violence rate was corroborated by the two other groups in the survey—female spouses (37 percent of whom reported relationship violence) and female officers (40 percent of whom did so).
- Twenty-eight percent of male officers admitted they had been violent toward their spouse at least once in the previous year. This rate was up to 15 times higher than among the public. The 115 female spouses in the survey also corroborated this number—25 percent saying they had been abused in the prior year.
- The 40 female officers in the survey disclosed being abused at an even higher rate—37 percent saying their spouse had been violent toward them in the previous year. As well, 27 percent of female cops said they had assaulted their spouse. (One factor could be that many female officers—just over half, according to one study—are married to male cops.)[63]

---

[63] Peter H. Neidig, Harold E. Russell and Albert F. Seng, "Interspousal Aggression in Law Enforcement Families: A Preliminary Investigation," *Police Studies: International Review of Police Development* 15 (Spring 1992): 30-38. See Chapter 3 for reported domestic violence rates in the wider U.S. and Canadian population. Sociologist Leanor Johnson's research identified another possible factor in abuse involving female officers: They may retaliate violently if their spouse is abusive. For the female police marriage data, see Carol A. Archbold and Kimberly D. Hassell, "Paying a marriage tax: An examination of the barriers to the promotion of female police

And the actual abuse rates were likely higher because of "the tendency to underreport socially undesirable events," the study said. "We felt that number was a conservative number," Seng told me, referring to the 41-percent figure for male cops. "It could easily have made the 50-percent mark."

Cops were involved not only in far more abuse than civilians, but also more brutal, extreme violence. The researchers asked the respondents to categorize the violence as "minor" or "severe." Minor violence included throwing something at the spouse, pushing, grabbing, shoving, slapping, kicking, biting and hitting with a fist. Severe violence included choking, strangulation, beating up the spouse and using a gun or knife.

Eight percent of male officers reported "severe violence" in their relationship in the previous year. And an amazing 20 percent of the female officers surveyed said their spouse had engaged in "severe violence" against them.

There were other surprises, too:

- Half of cops on the midnight and swing shifts reported violence at home.
- Narcotics officers reported severe violence at a rate seven times higher than uniformed cops.
- Nearly half of officers who worked over 50 hours a week reported domestic violence.

Age also played a role. A remarkable 64 percent of cops in their 20s reported violence at home. The abuse fell off as cops got older. "The significant relationships found between work related variables such as current assignment, shift and hours worked per week, and marital aggression, suggest that marital violence in law enforcement officer families can be understood, at least in part, as a function of the unique demands of the profession and of specific working conditions experienced in discharging those responsibilities," the study said.

Verbal abuse was a big problem too, as Leanor Johnson had found. "The thing that struck me the most was that we were measuring physical violence, but a greater part—and a really troublesome part—was the verbal abuse that goes on below that line and is totally devastating to the relationship and to the woman," Seng told me.

---

officers," *Policing: An International Journal of Police Strategies & Management* 32, no. 1 (2009): 60-61, accessed May 3, 2015,
http://www.researchgate.net/publication/230814737 Paying a marriage tax An examination of the barriers to the promotion of female police officers.

"There was a tremendous amount of verbal abuse reported, and we could see huge numbers of spouses out there and other family members—kids and so on—who were subject to daily verbal abuse."

Seng and his team later published a separate study based on their survey at the Fraternal Order of Police convention. In that survey, 24 percent of male officers reported violence in their relationships.[64] These officers were older and higher ranked than those in the first study, and their lower abuse rate is consistent with Seng's finding that the problem seemed to fall off as cops get older.

The biggest danger of an explosion came during separations. An incredible 66 percent of officers who were divorced or separated reported domestic violence in the prior year, and 17 percent reported severe violence, Seng's first study in *Police Studies* said. The rate of severe violence was about three times that of cops with intact marriages. "Officers who are experiencing marital separations should be considered at high risk for violence," the study said.

Just months after these fateful words were published, the point was underlined in dramatic fashion when LAPD officer Victor Ramos killed his estranged wife Melba and her new boyfriend, then himself. Had police heeded the study's warning, these lives may not have been lost and their children orphaned.

---

[64] P. H. Neidig, A. F. Seng and H. E. Russell, "Interspousal Aggression in Law Enforcement Personnel Attending the FOP Biennial Conference," *National FOP Journal* (Fall/Winter 1992): 25-28.

CHAPTER 5

Why Are So Many Cops Abusive?

L eanor Johnson and Albert Seng had made an astonishing discovery, but it raised a new question: Why are so many cops abusive at home? The answer is crucial. Without it, how can the violence be stopped? As it turns out, the answer also helps tell us a couple of other things—first, how widespread the abuse is today and, second, how the problem hurts everybody in one way or another.

The epidemic of police domestic abuse appears to have three main causes:

- power and control
- derogatory attitudes toward women
- impunity—a de facto licence to abuse

POWER AND CONTROL

The police have enormous power over our lives. "Even the lowest man on the totem pole [in the police] has more power—the power of life and death—than any CEO," said Anthony Bouza, the former Minneapolis Police Chief who also commanded the Bronx forces in the New York Police Department, in his memoir.[65] That kind of power can be alluring to batterers. For them, domestic violence is usually a way to control a partner or child.

"Batterers are typically attracted to professions where they can have power and control over people. It stands to reason that you would see that among police officers," Dottie Davis, a retired deputy chief of the Fort Wayne Police Department in Indiana, told me in an interview.

Davis served as a police officer for 32 years and has first-hand knowledge of police domestic violence. She has spoken widely about her former marriage to an abusive tactical-squad officer.

"The first time we fought... he leg-swept me to the floor with a forearm across my chest and laughed in my face," she told the *Post-Tribune* newspaper of Northwest Indiana. "I thought, 'He's right. If I don't get better, I'll never make it as an officer.' I never thought that I was just assaulted by a man who loved me."[66]

Davis had five miscarriages due to the violence and stress of the six-year relationship. Her husband once threw her across a room and on another occasion sent their two-year-old daughter flying with a kick in the back because she spilled her cereal, she told me. The assault on her daughter prompted her to file for divorce. Her husband moved out, but Davis said that when he got the divorce papers he returned to the home and began to strangle Davis. She escaped by hitting him with a phone and rushing outside, where she yelled for a neighbour to call police.

"It was never daily constant battering. That was part of the confusion. It could go months before another physical assault. Other forms of abuse would be present, but he could also be quite doting and loving, which was very crazy-making. He had very few coping skills for any time of stress. Batterers have really weak egos," she said.

Davis went on to chair the Indiana Governor's Council for the Prevention and Treatment of Family Violence and authored her department's protocols on officer-involved domestic violence and crisis intervention. She has since also testified as an expert witness in over a dozen criminal and civil trials related to domestic violence, helping victims' estates and families win several million dollars in jury awards due to inadequate police protection. "Batterers are attracted to this job. We should do a better job of screening," she said.

No one suggests that all police officers have a need for power and control. Many enter policing with the best intentions—to help others and serve their

---

[65] Anthony V. Bouza, *The Police Mystique: An Insider's Look at Cops, Crime, and the Criminal Justice System* (New York: Plenum Press, 1990), jacket.

[66] Christin Nance Lazerus, "Cop tells her story of childhood abuse," *Post-Tribune* of Northwest Indiana, April 5, 2014.

community—and act with honour and courage. But some people seem to be attracted to the job for other reasons—because they like the power of a gun, badge and uniform, because of insecurity or a hunger to be in control. Some cops also develop controlling behaviours on the job.

In fact, an officer's survival often depends on quickly imposing control. It's a key part of the job. "If *ask* and *tell* do not work, you *make* the person do what you want," wrote Tim Barfield, a police chief near Cleveland, Ohio, in an article on officer survival. It's important for officers to impose their will without hesitation to manage critical situations before they get to "bang," a police term for spinning out of control, said Barfield, a 34-year veteran cop.

"Failure to take control puts control into the realm of the violator. The longer that a suspect is allowed to refuse to comply with a lawful command, the closer to bang you get," Barfield wrote. "If voluntary compliance does not work, be prepared to use force. The sooner you control the situation, the more likely you'll have a good day."[67]

But that same impulse can morph into abuse when the officer is at home. This problem was highlighted in the Federal Bureau of Investigation's milestone *Domestic Violence by Police Officers* report. The 426-page document is a fascinating collection of papers presented at a landmark conference on police domestic violence organized by the FBI at its behavioral science unit in Quantico, Virginia, in 1998.

Over 50 police officers, psychologists, academics and other experts made presentations, including sociologist Leanor Johnson. She also served on an FBI advisory board on police stress and family violence that counselled the bureau on the planning of the conference and writing of the report.

Police domestic violence is a "serious problem... well known to all who work in or with the police profession," said the report's introduction, co-written by FBI Supervisory Special Agent Donald Sheehan and Vincent Van Hasselt, a Florida police officer and police psychology professor at Florida's Nova Southeastern University, who has also taught at the FBI Academy.[68]

"Does police culture encourage and foster domestic violence? Many attributes apply to police officers. Most of them have positive connotations. Let us take control as an example. It stands as an attribute absolutely required in a successful police officer. What citizen wants a police officer who cannot

---

[67] Tim Barfield, "How cops can stay 'left of bang' in a critical incident," PoliceOne.com, January 14, 2016, accessed August 3, 2016, http://www.policeone.com/officer-survival/articles/64071006-How-cops-can-stay-left-of-bang-in-a-critical-incident/.
[68] Vincent Van Hasselt and Donald C. Sheehan, introduction to *Domestic Violence by Police Officers*, ed. Donald C. Sheehan (Quantico, Virginia: Behavioral Science Unit, FBI Academy, 2000), 1-9.

control an unruly individual or volatile situation? Police routinely exert control in the course of daily events. A virtue on the job, however, can degenerate into a vice in the home, if misapplied," Sheehan and Van Hasselt said. "Job positives become home negatives."

Officers tend to display "overprotectiveness and restrictiveness for [their] spouse and children.... They may also appear guarded, moralistic, rigid and authoritarian," the two officers wrote. Police are taught that "any response other than compliance threatens an officer's safety or survival.... Noncompliance from a spouse or child may inappropriately appear as a challenge or threat requiring a forceful response to control the situation. Unfortunately, physical force becomes a solution or coping strategy at home."

Sergeant Robert Sgambelluri of the Illinois State Police concurred with this in a paper in the FBI report. "Police officers are trained to take control and are controlling individuals," he wrote. "When a situation has deteriorated beyond their verbal control, or they lose control because of some intervening element, they are trained to take physical control....

"Policing attracts and encourages characteristics associated with authoritarianism. The ability to establish power and control, while an underlying motive of domestic abuse, is an essential job skill for police. Officers who display this ability achieve higher status as leaders among their peers. The police culture itself encourages isolation, a need for control and a sense of entitlement, all traits present in a domestic abuser."[69]

Jean-Michel Blais is chief of the Halifax Regional Police, in Canada. He disagrees that power and control are to blame for elevated abuse in police homes. "My ex would raise that: 'You're used to having control all the time.'... I think it's an easy answer," he told me in an interview.

Blais does believe domestic violence is more common in Canadian police homes than in the general population, though he's skeptical it is in the 40-percent range. "That just doesn't jive with what my experience has been. But then on the other side, you never know what goes on in the hearts of men. There is a lack of proper studies that have been done in Canada," he said.

But instead of power and control, Blais blamed the abuse on the stress of police work, coupled with substance abuse. "I think the rate of mental health challenges [among police officers] is higher than in the general population, and eventually some of those mental health conditions, exacerbated by

---

[69] Robert Sgambelluri, "Police Culture, Police Training, and Police Administration: Their Impact on Violence in Police Families," in *Domestic Violence by Police Officers*, 309-322.

alcohol and drugs, end up leading to domestic violence," he said. "We're dealing with human beings, and human beings have problems."

Blais has a law degree and joined the Halifax police as chief in 2012 after 25 years at the RCMP, where he was a chief superintendent. As a Mountie, he was director of the internal disciplinary system and adjudicated over 75 disciplinary cases involving RCMP officers. He is also co-chair of the labour relations committee of the 1,000-member Canadian Association of Chiefs of Police.

Blais was stationed in Manitoba when RCMP Constable Jocelyn Hotte murdered his ex-girlfriend and shot her three companions in 2001. "It woke everybody up to the realities of what goes on in people's lives," he said of the tragedy. "It added to the sense of what constitutes harassment." But when asked what changes the RCMP made in response, he said, "I don't know if I recognize any particular changes."

On the subject of domestic abuse, Blais said repeated exposure to traumatic situations takes a toll on the mental health of cops. Imagine, he said, a scale of 0 to 100, with 0 representing extreme mental illness and 100 being perfect mental health. "When someone joins the police, he may be at 70. Then he comes across his first dead body or car accident or beaten child, and his resiliency goes down to 65. Eventually it goes back up, but not all the way to 70. Then the next incident takes it down even more. He may be at 30 after a number of years," he said.

"Policing changes who you are as an individual. When you have to deal with the entire problems of society for your entire career, it takes a very special individual to be able to deal with this all the time.... When they're done their shift, they may try to compensate by getting themselves tanked up. They go off into a corner, drink it or create a fantasy world....

"Perhaps police officers drink and some have consumed other licit and illicit drugs, and the inhibition mechanisms they have to normally keep them in check are gone. And that's what may lead to domestic violence."

Indeed, it's clear that stress and burnout from police work can significantly affect officers' health and quality of life. Cops in the U.S. have dramatically shortened lifespans, a 2013 study found, with white male officers living 21.9 fewer years than white male Americans overall.[70] By the average police retirement age of 57, a white male officer can expect to live just six more years, while U.S. white males live 31 extra years on average. Stress, heart disease and obesity are thought to be among the main culprits.

---

[70] John M. Violanti et al., "Life Expectancy in Police Officers: A Comparison with the U.S. General Population," *International Journal of Emergency Mental Health and Human Resilience* 15, no. 4 (2013): 217-228.

Police families face a "high-risk lifestyle" marked by burnout, "domestic strains" and "exceptionally high divorce rates (nearly 75 percent in large metropolitan areas)," according to the FBI's *Domestic Violence by Police Officers* report.[71]

But abuse counsellors I interviewed disagreed that such pressures are at the root of domestic violence. While stress, alcohol and drugs may aggravate abuse in some cases, they say, violence at home is usually about getting power and control over a spouse or child.

"Many people experience extreme stress without becoming violent," said Dale Trimble, a long-time registered clinical counsellor in British Columbia who set up a pioneering program to counsel abusive men. "To put it on stress is saying, 'It doesn't have to do with me.' It's a way of diffusing responsibility."

Lundy Bancroft is a veteran counsellor of abusive men and battered women in Massachusetts. He made a similar point in his best-selling book *Why Does He Do That?: Inside the Minds of Angry and Controlling Men*: "When a man starts my program, he often says, 'I am here because I lose control of myself sometimes. I need to get a better grip.' I always correct him: 'Your problem is not that you *lose* control of yourself, it's that you *take* control of your partner. In order to change, you don't need to *gain* control over yourself, you need to *let go* of control of her.'... This is one of the single most important concepts to grasp about an abusive man."[72]

Indeed, cops aren't the only professionals whose job involves lots of stress. Firefighters and airline pilots often rank higher than police on lists of

---

[71] Van Hasselt and Sheehan, introduction to *Domestic Violence by Police Officers*, 2. The stresses on police families can also be seen in the results of a recent informal poll on a U.S. police wife's blog. The blog asked readers if they were seeing a therapist. Of 173 respondents, 24 percent said they were, while another 6 percent said they did so "occasionally" (as of the poll results in August 2015). An additional 45 percent answered, "No, but I probably should." The reported therapy rate, albeit not scientific, is many times the U.S. average. For comparison, 3 percent of Americans report being in therapy. See "Poll Results: Do you see a therapist?" APoliceWife.Blogspot.com, accessed August 29, 2015, http://poll.pollcode.com/yw2k_result?v (webpage inactive as of November 28, 2016). For the U.S. therapy rate, see M. Olfson and S. C. Marcus, "National trends in outpatient psychotherapy," *American Journal of Psychiatry* 167, no. 12 (December 2010): 1456-63, accessed March 24, 2015, http://www.ncbi.nlm.nih.gov/pubmed/20686187.

[72] Lundy Bancroft, *Why Does He Do That?: Inside the Minds of Angry and Controlling Men* (New York: The Penguin Group, 2002), 54.

the most stressful jobs[73]—but they haven't been linked to extreme levels of abuse at home.

"Stress is a nice easy way to excuse the issue. That's usually the first thing an abuser says: 'I'm under a lot of stress,'" said George Rigakos, a professor in the law department at Ottawa's Carleton University who has studied police attitudes toward domestic violence.

Leanor Johnson, the sociologist in Arizona, found evidence for the notion that police domestic violence is related to control. Cops in her study who were violent at home tended to rate high on a psychological test for controlling traits. The test, called Authoritarian Spillover, asks respondents if they agree with statements such as, "My job conditioned me to expect to have the final say on how things are done in my household," and, "I catch myself treating my family the way I treat civilians." Meanwhile, Johnson found very little relationship between domestic violence and alcohol use.[74]

What's more, if job stress were really the cause of abuse, the problem should presumably get worse as cops get older—not better. But as Arizona cop Albert Seng and his team found, abuse actually declined as cops got older, while cops in their 20s were among the worst abusers.

"I think it [policing] attracts the kind of personality that likes to be in control," Seng told me. "We often joke in counselling that cops are control freaks. They always have to be in control. You've got to be a take-charge kind of person to be a cop. If you're not, geez, you're going to get run over. So when you have a control type personality and then you work at a job that requires you always to be in control, when you go home from work you kind of have an expectation of control in your family.

"You can't run a home like you do a crime scene or an auto accident, but a lot of cops try to do that. Domestic violence is in fact a control issue. If I can't control my wife through persuasion or manipulation or sweet talk, then I have to resort to the threat of violence or intimidation."

---

[73] "The Most Stressful Jobs of 2015," CareerCast.com, accessed March 19, 2015, http://www.careercast.com/jobs-rated/most-stressful-jobs-2015. See also Susan Adams, "The Most Stressful Jobs of 2015," Forbes, January 7, 2015, accessed April 23, 2015, http://www.forbes.com/sites/susanadams/2015/01/07/the-most-stressful-jobs-of-2015/.

[74] Leanor Boulin-Johnson, "Burnout and Work and Family Violence Among Police: Gender Comparisons," in Domestic Violence by Police Officers, 107-121. Johnson did find a relationship between authoritarian attitudes and "external burnout" (e.g. treating civilians like objects or feeling callous or hardened emotionally). She believes that while domestic violence is a control issue, burnout from street patrol can make officers more authoritarian, thus indirectly contributing to abuse at home.

DEROGATORY ATTITUDES TOWARD WOMEN

Negative views of women are likely a second cause of elevated rates of police domestic violence.

"Most batterers hold traditional values and the belief that the man is entitled to be the 'head of the household.' Many male police officers are conservative people who share these traditional family values," said an article co-written by Diane Wetendorf, a retired Chicago-area abuse counsellor, and Dottie Davis, the retired Fort Wayne, Indiana, deputy police chief.

"This group of men accepts a man's violence against a woman as a necessary reminder of her place. Male dominance that is reinforced by police culture breeds strong resistance to considering domestic violence a criminal offense."[75]

George Rigakos, of Carleton University's law department, saw this attitude when he studied how police in British Columbia responded to domestic violence calls. Rigakos's specialty is the political science of policing, a field that studies how politics and economics influence the role of police.

Officers in his study made an arrest in only 35 percent of cases of an abusive spouse breaching a peace bond (a criminal court-issued protective order) and in just 21 percent of cases involving the breach of a civil court-issued restraining order. "There is a strong basis for calling the current system a hoax on the victims, a promise to protect them that will not be kept," Rigakos quoted U.S. criminologist Lawrence Sherman saying.[76]

When Rigakos asked officers to explain the low arrest rates, he said he came across "a conservative attitude toward women." The officers typically judged battered women in unflattering terms and tended to be unsympathetic and unhelpful unless the abused woman was "a Betty Crocker type [who] kept the house clean and had an apron on when she came to the door," Rigakos said. He recalled one male officer telling him, "Most of these things are started by the women anyways. It's just that they're smaller and end up losing the fight."

Carol-Ann Halliday experienced derogatory police attitudes toward women firsthand. She was a member of the Vancouver Police Department for 30 years, retiring as a detective in 1999. She was the department's first

---

[75] Diane Wetendorf and Dottie L. Davis, "The Misuse of Police Powers in Officer-Involved Domestic Violence" (2015), accessed May 3, 2015, http://www.abuseofpower.info/Wetendorf_Misuse2015.pdf.

[76] George S. Rigakos, "Situational Determinants of Police Responses to Civil and Criminal Injunctions for Battered Women," *Violence Against Women* 3, no. 2 (April 1997): 204-216.

female street supervisor and the first female detective in its major crimes unit.

During her time in major crimes in the 1980s, the unit was full of "chauvinist pigs," Halliday told me. "Nobody would work with me. They made the new guy do it." Things went from bad to worse when she got involved with the 3,000-member International Association of Women Police, eventually becoming its president. "They were badmouthing me because I was on this women's group. They all started picking on me."

A lot of male officers were in love with the power of being a cop, and this attitude caused strife in their homes, Halliday said. "The job brings it out. It gives this licence, and all of a sudden they realize all the power they have," she said. "I can see how that spills over a lot. They just think, 'I am the man. I am the boss. I am the power. I can do whatever I like.' I am sure that's what breaks up a lot of [police] marriages."

Such attitudes aren't unique to Canadian police. In a 2006 survey of 873 U.S. police officers (most of them men), only 7.2 percent said they'd be equally comfortable with a female or male boss. Just 7.1 percent agreed that "women are just as capable of thinking logically as men."[77]

"Machismo is central to police culture," said University of Maryland law professor Leigh Goodmark in a 2016 paper on police domestic violence. "Violence and the denigration of women are endemic in such hegemonic or hypermasculine settings." Spousal abuse, Goodmark suggested, is "a predictable consequence of an ideology prevalent in law enforcement." And despite the entry of women into policing, the "hypermasculine" police culture is actually getting more entrenched as U.S. police become more militarized, increasingly using military-style equipment, training and tactics, she said.[78]

IMPUNITY—LACK OF DETERRENCE

A third reason so many cops abuse at home seems to be simply that they can get away with it. They effectively have a licence to assault their spouses and

[77] Amy Dellinger Page, "Judging Women and Defining Crime: Police Officers' Attitudes Toward Women and Rape," *Sociological Spectrum* (July 2008): 389-411, accessed April 23, 2015,
http://libres.uncg.edu/ir/asu/f/page_2008_judging_women.pdf.
[78] Leigh Goodmark, "Hands Up at Home: Militarized Masculinity and Police Officers Who Commit Intimate Partner Abuse," BYU Law Review 1183 (May 2016), accessed December 14, 2016,
http://digitalcommons.law.byu.edu/cgi/viewcontent.cgi?article=3002&context=lawreview.

kids. "A major influence in the use of domestic violence is a lack of deterrence. If there is no sanction, then it's obvious the offence goes on," Carleton University professor George Rigakos told me.

That is particularly true for police officers because of the so-called "blue wall of silence"—an unwritten Mafia-like code of protecting fellow officers from investigation. Cops learn early on to cover for each other—or as police call it, extend "professional courtesy." Failing to do so exposes a cop to ostracism, harassment and the frightening prospect of not getting timely back-up on a call.

Anthony Bouza, the former Minneapolis police chief and New York Police Department commander, explained how the code of silence works in his memoir *Police Unbound*. "'Stand-up guys,' who protect the brethren, keep quiet and back you up, are proudly pointed out; and pariahs among the force come in all shapes, sizes and levels of opprobrium, sharing only the visceral contempt of their associates," he wrote.

"'Rats' are scorned, shunned, excluded, condemned, harassed and, almost invariably, cast out. No back-up for them. They literally find cheese in their lockers. Unwanted items are delivered to their homes. The phone rings at all hours—followed by menacing silences, anonymous imprecations or surprisingly inventive epithets. The police radio crackles with invective. The message is eloquent and pervasive. Remarkably, the brass joins in."[79]

Domestic violence is already difficult enough to report in other families. Abused women experience about four violent incidents on average before calling police. Shelters are chronically underfunded, making it harder to disclose abuse and get help. One survey found Canadian shelters turned away 539 abused women and accompanying children on a random day in 2014—more than half the time because they were full. Hundreds of U.S. communities have adopted "nuisance property" laws that pressure landlords to evict tenants if police are repeatedly called to their home, including for domestic abuse. Such laws further dissuade survivors from seeking help because they fear losing their home.[80]

---

[79] Bouza, *Police Unbound*, 17-18.

[80] Twenty-two percent of abused Canadian women reported the incident to police, according to Statistics Canada, *Family Violence in Canada: A Statistical Profile* (2011), 8. In the U.S., 27 percent of abused women reported the assault to police. See U.S. Department of Justice, *Practical Implications of Current Domestic Violence Research*, 5. For shelter survey data, see Sara Beattie and Hope Hutchins, "Shelters for abused women in Canada, 2014" (Statistics Canada, last modified July 6, 2015), accessed July 8, 2015, http://www.statcan.gc.ca/pub/85-002-x/2015001/article/14207-eng.htm. Regarding the nuisance laws, see Erik Eckholm, "Victims' Dilemma: 911 Calls Can Bring Eviction," *The New York Times*, August 16,

The spouses and children of violent officers face even greater obstacles. They rarely call 911 because they know a co-worker of their partner may come to their door or derail any investigation. Experts point out that abusive cops are trained to use physical force and have guns, which they often bring home. And if a cop's wife runs, where will she hide? Staff at many women's shelters say they are often powerless to protect abused police family members.

"Police officers generally know exactly where the shelters are in the community," Laurie Parsons, then coordinator of the Mission Transition House in Mission, British Columbia, told me in 2003 when I was researching my first stories on the issue. She said she regularly got calls from abused partners of cops seeking advice. "What stands out is the intensity of their fear. The women don't feel safe to stay in the local shelter. There really is no shelter she [the abused police spouse] can be entirely safe at.... Mostly, we don't see the wives of these officers. Those women are not free to leave [their spouse]."

Incredibly, some shelters even reportedly turn police spouses away. In one account, a survivor said she was turned away from over a dozen shelters in her county when she told staff that her perpetrator was a police officer. "We then tried three other counties—again we were turned away because [he] is a police officer," she said. [81]

Police wives and girlfriends are often reluctant to complain about abuse because they are scared, embarrassed or afraid their partner may lose his job, which could make him angrier and jeopardize the family's financial stability, said Jean-Michel Blais, chief of the Halifax Regional Police. "It [abuse] isn't something you advertise openly unless you know there's going to be safety," he told me. "If you go forward, you also recognize very quickly that this person could lose his job."

In his previous job at the RCMP, Blais headed the internal disciplinary process, where he said he often saw abused spouses drop complaints out of fear that their husband would get fired. "It's very difficult to deal with. That is going to put more pressure on the family and increase the violence," he said. "I saw this all the time."

But a cop's risk of getting fired over a domestic violence allegation is actually quite small. In fact, exaggerating that risk is a trick cops often use to manipu-

2013, accessed August 31, 2015, http://www.nytimes.com/2013/08/17/us/victims-dilemma-911-calls-can-bring-eviction.html?_r=0.
[81] Wetendorf, *When the Batterer Is a Law Enforcement Officer*, 28.

late abused spouses into dropping their complaint, said former Chicago police officer Gina Gallo in an eye-opening article in the monthly *Police: The Law Enforcement Magazine*.

Gallo, who is also author of the book *Armed and Dangerous: Memoirs of a Chicago Policewoman*, wrote that spousal abuse "may be one of the best-kept secrets in law enforcement."[82] Gallo extensively quoted Dennis Banahan, a retired Chicago Police Department homicide lieutenant, who talked about the tactics responding officers used to shield abusive cops and pressure spouses to stay quiet.

"She'd be told that an arrest would serve no one's best interests, and would absolutely jeopardize the officer's job, thereby threatening the family's security. That was a rationale I always found particularly offensive. In effect, that's telling a bleeding victim, 'Hey, sorry about the broken arm and that your nose will never be the same again, but drop a dime on this guy and you'll all be in the welfare line tomorrow,'" Banahan said.

As a rookie cop, Banahan said other officers taught him how to sabotage a police domestic violence case. "The first officers arriving at the scene of any cop-involved domestic violence call were expected to be the primary spin doctors.... I know it sounds horrible. But one of the first lessons police learn is to protect each other, and it's that sense of loyalty that dictated our actions.... It was also about protecting a brother cop's career," he said.

If the spouse wouldn't drop the complaint, cops could deliberately botch the case in other ways. They'd neglect to file an official report, withhold information from the abused person, not offer her the option to sign the complaint or not give her the standard victim's information rights sheets that other abuse survivors got.

If a police spouse asked for a peace bond, she could be told those don't exist in Illinois. The officer wouldn't bother to mention that such orders simply had a different name in the state—an order of protection.

The inaction—and consequent murders of several police spouses—haunted Banahan. "When I became a homicide detective, that's when I saw the results," he said. "Too many bricks in that Blue Wall of Silence triggered more domestic homicides and suicides than I care to think about."

A female police officer in New York shared similar experiences with Gallo. "I've gone in on domestic violence calls knowing in advance that since a

---

[82] Gina Gallo, "A Family Affair," *Police: The Law Enforcement* Magazine, February 2005, accessed April 17, 2015,
http://www.policemag.com/channel/patrol/articles/2005/02/a-family-affair.aspx.
Gina Gallo, *Armed and Dangerous: Memoirs of a Chicago Policewoman* (New York: Tom Doherty Associates, 2001).

police officer was involved in the dispute, no action would be taken other than medical treatment," she said.

"Our standard procedure was to separate all parties and convince the victim that a cooling-off period would be enough to restore the peace, which was a bogus bill of goods that nobody believed."

Little wonder then that abused spouses of cops are reluctant to call 911. "A victim calls 911—well, guess what? Their statement is right on the screen for every fellow officer and every friend of that officer to read and to make a call and let him know what she just told the dispatcher," Dottie Davis, the retired deputy police chief in Fort Wayne, Indiana, was quoted saying in a *The New York Times*-PBS investigation into police domestic violence in 2013.[83]

Davis said officers often don't take complaints seriously. She said she herself called police after she was assaulted by her officer husband, but the cops who responded took his side, even though Davis too wore a badge. "They worked with him, and he stood up and shook both their hands and began to apologize immediately, and so I knew right then that not much was going to be done," Davis told *The New York Times*. The responding officers agreed not to report the incident and said they would "swear the dispatchers to secrecy."

As if that wasn't bad enough, Davis said, after reporting the assault "I was ostracized by my co-workers because you don't rat on another cop.... Even though his behavior was criminal and we were arresting other people for it, because he was a police officer, he was exempted."

When Davis spoke about officer-involved domestic violence at a conference of the International Association of Women Police in Toronto in 2000, she said 19 percent of over 50 female officers in the session came forward to tell her they had also been abused by an intimate partner who was a fellow cop. "They were extremely upset because their abusers were primarily promoted while they were reassigned and ostracized," she said.

Another problem: Complaints to police tend to be funneled into the internal disciplinary process—which unfolds behind closed doors—instead of a criminal trial that takes place in public and leads to embarrassment for the

---

[83] Sarah Cohen, Rebecca R. Ruiz and Sarah Childress, "Departments Are Slow To Police Their Own Abusers," *The New York Times*, November 23, 2013, accessed March 19, 2015, http://www.nytimes.com/projects/2013/police-domestic-abuse/. See also "A Death in St. Augustine," PBS *Frontline*, November 26, 2013, accessed March 19, 2015, http://www.pbs.org/wgbh/pages/frontline/criminal-justice/death-in-st-augustine/transcript-53/.

police department, said Amy Ramsay, a police sergeant in Ontario and former president of the International Association of Women Police. [84]

Except in extreme cases, the internal disciplinary process typically results in a reprimand or a few days' lost pay, not firing. "Generally, very little is done. If anything happens at all—and I say that with some reservation, because usually nothing does happen—generally it's dealt with internally. I've heard enough things from my own experience to know it's not very well handled," Ramsay said.

Even in the unusual case of a police officer facing a criminal investigation or charges, he has an advantage because he knows how to work the justice system. The accused may have friendly working ties with prosecutors and may be defended by a high-powered lawyer paid for by the police union. Police officers also know how to make sure they don't leave evidence of their abuse that will stand up in court, retired Deputy Chief Dottie Davis told me. "These types of batterers know where to hit you where other people can't see."

"The police officer is going to be a much more credible witness in the eyes of the judge," said Pamela Cross, a lawyer in Kingston, Ontario, and one of the province's leading domestic violence legal experts. "He's going to be better at testifying. The judge might know him. He might have worked with the Crown attorney two weeks ago."

And even in the extremely rare cases where there is a criminal conviction, police officers often get a slap on the wrist and keep their job anyway. Judges seem reluctant to sentence cops to jail time for domestic violence convictions, often preferring probation, community service or a discharge.

The average citizen has about a two times greater chance than a cop of being convicted or incarcerated when charged with a criminal offence, according to a study of the U.S. National Police Misconduct Reporting Project. [85] The average sentence is also 40 percent longer for the public than for cops.

Canada's justice system is similarly lenient toward cops. Canadian civilians have a 28 percent higher chance of being convicted than police officers when charged with a comparable domestic violence offence—and a whopping

---

[84] Ramsay asked that her police agency not be named because of concerns about possible repercussions at work.

[85] David Packman, *2010 NPMSRP Police Misconduct Statistical Report –Draft* (National Police Misconduct Reporting Project, Cato Institute, April 5, 2011), accessed December 7, 2016, http://www.policemisconduct.net/2010-npmsrp-police-misconduct-statistical-report/.

seven times greater chance of being sentenced to prison time. That's according to a 2015 study by Danielle Sutton, a PhD sociology student at the University of Guelph in Ontario.[86]

Sutton analyzed the results of 264 Canadian domestic violence cases from 2000 to 2014, half of them involving police officers, the other half involving civilians. Her study appears to be the first ever study of officer-involved domestic violence in any country outside the U.S.

The justice system's lenient treatment of cops stands out all the more, Sutton found, because police officers are two times more likely than civilians to use a weapon in the incident.

In the very rare cases when cops are convicted of domestic violence, they often still stay on the job. As strange as it may sound, breaking the law doesn't seem to disqualify anyone from employment as a law enforcer, at least not if the crime is domestic violence.

Philip Stinson is a criminologist at Ohio's Bowling Green State University and himself an ex-cop. In a U.S. justice department-funded study, he reviewed news reports on 324 cases of U.S. police officers arrested for domestic violence from 2005 to 2007. Only 49 percent of convicted officers lost their job through termination or resignation, according to the study Stinson co-authored, titled "Fox in the Henhouse." And just 32 percent of cops convicted of misdemeanour domestic assault lost their job.[87]

The findings are all the more remarkable, Stinson noted, because a U.S. law bars anyone convicted of misdemeanour domestic violence from carrying a firearm, which means they effectively can't be a cop. But even this seemingly straightforward rule is regularly flouted, as he found.

Virtually no police departments in the U.S. or Canada automatically fire officers convicted of domestic violence. Most decide on the discipline on a case-by-case basis. "It's not automatic, even if an officer is found guilty of a criminal charge," Sergeant Gilles Fortin, of the RCMP's internal-

---

[86] Danielle Sutton, "News Coverage of Officer-Invoved Domestic Violence (OIDV): A Comparative Content Analysis," a thesis presented to the University of Guelph in partial fulfillment of requirements for the degree of Master of Arts in Criminology and Criminal Justice Policy (Guelph, Ontario: August 2015), accessed November 28, 2016, https://atrium.lib.uoguelph.ca/xmlui/bitstream/handle/10214/9099/Sutton_Danielle_201508_MA.pdf?sequence=1.

[87] Philip M. Stinson and John Liederbach, "Fox in the Henhouse: A Study of Police Officers Arrested for Crimes Associated with Domestic and/or Family Violence," *Criminal Justice Policy Review* 24 (2013), accessed March 20, 2015, http://scholarworks.bgsu.edu/cgi/viewcontent.cgi?article=1005&context=crim_just_pub.

investigations section in Montreal, told me in 2000. "There are no strict rules [at the RCMP] on when he would be fired."

"It's very difficult to fire an officer," Staff Sergeant Karen Moffatt, then commander of the Ontario Provincial Police detachment in London, Ontario, said in an interview in 2000. The sanctions for spouse abuse, Moffatt said, usually ranged from temporary suspension to a temporary demotion or being assigned for a while to desk duties. After that, the officer typically went back to regular duties, which could include responding to domestics.

Seventeen years after these interviews, the situation remains largely the same. Only about one in five police forces worldwide typically fires an officer even after a second domestic violence conviction or sustained complaint, according to results of a survey I sent to 178 police departments in the U.S., Canada and eight other countries in 2015. In Canada, the portion is even lower—with one in seven departments saying they typically fire the officer. As a sign of how little research exists on the issue, my survey is the first ever done of how police in various countries handle domestic violence among officers. (Read more results in Chapter 8 and Appendix E.)

In Quebec, the province where RCMP Constable Jocelyn Hotte murdered his ex-girlfriend Lucie Gélinas in 2001, the situation is only mildly better. The province's Police Act says cops convicted of an indictable offence (the equivalent of a felony in the U.S.) must be automatically fired. But this law contains a gaping loophole. If the offence could also have been prosecuted as a summary offence (i.e. a minor or petty crime, equivalent to a misdemeanour in the U.S.), convicted officers can keep their job if they can show that "specific circumstances justify another sanction," the law says. Since assault and uttering threats can be prosecuted in Quebec (as in the rest of Canada) as either an indictable or a summary offence, the loophole means cops convicted of domestic violence can still keep their job.

It all adds up to a de facto licence for cops to commit violent crime at home. "Most families will not 'air dirty laundry,' so what happens behind closed doors remains within the family unit," wrote Texas State University criminal justice professor Wayman Mullins and Michael McMains, then a psychologist with the San Antonio Police Department, in a paper in the FBI's *Domestic Violence by Police Officers* report. "Officers can engage in virtually consequence-free abuse with little or no negative ramifications, a truly win-win situation for the abuser."[88]

Deborah Harrison, a sociologist at the University of New Brunswick, came to a similar conclusion when she studied what she calls the "serious

---

[88] Wayman C. Mullins and Michael J. McMains, "Impact of Traumatic Stress on Domestic Violence in Policing," in *Domestic Violence by Police Officers*, 257-268.

and significant problem" of domestic violence in the military. Her four-year study, which was endorsed by the Canadian military, gives a disturbing inside look at how a hierarchical, male-dominated organization covers up domestic violence.

The study included interviews with 126 abused military spouses and Canadian Forces members. Harrison published the results in her book *The First Casualty: Violence Against Women in Canadian Military Communities.*

Just like cops, many soldiers engaged in highly controlling behaviour to keep abuse secret. "Early in their marriages, many military members instruct their spouses not to discuss difficulties with other members of the military community. Abusive members instruct their spouses especially vigorously. The result is a strong taboo amongst spouses against disclosing problems," Harrison said in a report on her results submitted to Canada's defence minister.[89]

The taboo was reinforced by the military's inaction on complaints. When abused spouses worked up the courage to complain to military supervisors, they often got little help. Responses included: "Big deal—it happens all the time. Go home," and, "Goodbye—I don't want to know." "Or they [spouses] are told that they have 'asked for' the abuse by being unsupportive of their husbands' careers," wrote Harrison, who was a member of the Canadian Forces Advisory Council to the federal Department of Veterans Affairs.

Some supervisors also reacted by telling the husbands, "Get your wife under control so she will shut up." Supervisors even actively helped the perpetrator—lying about his whereabouts so he couldn't be served with a summons, discouraging spouses from testifying in court or threatening to arrest an abused spouse for "trespassing" on a base.

"An army supervisor told us that woman abusers are considered to be assets to some units because their abuse has proven these members [are] 'mean' enough to engage in frontline combat," Harrison wrote.

---

[89] Deborah Harrison, *The First Casualty: Violence Against Women in Canadian Military Communities* (Toronto: Lorimer, 2002). See also Deborah Harrison et al., *Report on the Canadian Forces' Response to Woman Abuse in Military Families* (submitted to the Minister of National Defence, Canada, May 2000), accessed March 19, 2015, http://www.unb.ca/fredericton/arts/centres/mmfc/_resources/pdfs/familyviolmilitaryreport.pdf. Harrison is a former director of the University of New Brunswick's Muriel McQueen Fergusson Centre for Family Violence Research. Arizona cop Albert Seng and his team found that spousal violence was at similarly high levels in the police and military—with 28 percent of male cops admitting they assaulted their spouse in the prior year, compared to 27 percent of soldiers. See Neidig, Russell and Seng, "Interspousal Aggression in Law Enforcement Families," 34.

"I think it goes by the situation and the wife," one supervisor told Harrison's team. "Like if she's a real... bitch or... has not supported him... or we figure that she's doing that to get money out of it, we'll do everything for him."

Harrison's conclusion: "Any occupation that exercises power and violence is going to have a problem with family violence."

Understanding why police domestic violence is so widespread also helps us answer another question: how prevalent it may be today in the U.S., Canada and elsewhere. After all, Leanor Johnson and Albert Seng released their studies in the 1990s—and only surveyed U.S. cops. More recent studies haven't been done in the U.S., and no prevalence studies have been done at all in any other country. How do we know the abuse epidemic is still going on? And how do we know cops in Canada, the UK and elsewhere are similarly violent?

Like using a pinhole projector to indirectly see a solar eclipse, we can get an indirect picture of the abuse by looking at whether the reasons behind it are still present today in the U.S., Canada and elsewhere. If they are, it's reasonable to expect the situation everywhere is materially the same today. And the news isn't good. Despite some changes in police departments in the past 25 years, the root causes of the abuse persist at the heart of policing—power and control, derogatory attitudes toward women and impunity.

First, power and control. Despite improved codes of conduct and pre-hire screening, police in the U.S., Canada and most other countries continue to play the same social role as 25 years ago—maintaining order. That means a critical part of a cop's job is still exercising power and control. Nothing different there.

If anything, that role has probably sharpened in the wake of 9/11 and other terrorist attacks and as income inequality and economic dislocation have deepened in the past two decades, fuelling social unrest (see Chapter 9).

As for derogatory attitudes toward women, police departments in the U.S. and elsewhere are still overwhelmingly male dominated, even if some have hired more women. In Canada, only 21 percent of cops are women, while in senior ranks the figure is just 11 percent, according to Statistics Canada. The rates are even lower in the U.S., where only 12 percent of all police officers are women and a mere 1.6 percent of police chiefs are female.[90]

---

[90] Hope Hutchins, *Police resources in Canada, 2014* (Ottawa: Statistics Canada, 2015), 14, accessed June 28, 2015, http://www.statcan.gc.ca/pub/85-002-x/2015001/article/14146-eng.pdf. For the U.S. data, see U.S. Department of Justice,

It's no surprise then that conservative attitudes toward women still seem to prevail in the police. (As we'll see in the next chapter, such attitudes have been on full display in Canada in a massive sexual harassment scandal rocking the RCMP and in the bungled police investigation of one of the country's most notorious serial killers.)

Would hiring more women make a difference? The evidence is unclear. A U.S. study found that a male cop costs police departments up to 5.5 times more on average than a female cop in civil lawsuit payouts for use of excessive force. This suggests hiring more women could help change the culture of policing.[91]

And yet, a different picture emerged in Carleton University professor George Rigakos's study of how cops responded to domestic violence calls. He found that female officers didn't arrest protection order violators any more than male cops. "This suggests that male and female officers are either equally socialized into the police occupational culture or, as institutions often do, [police] tend to hire in their own image," Rigakos wrote.[92] Given the treatment of officers who buck the strict norms of the police world, the female cops may also have feared ostracism and career repercussions if they acted differently than the men.

Office of Community Oriented Policing Services, "Women in Law Enforcement," *Community Policing Dispatch* 6, no. 7 (July 2013), accessed March 21, 2013, http://cops.usdoj.gov/html/dispatch/07-2013/women_in_law_enforcement.asp. See also Kevin Johnson, "Women move into law enforcement's highest ranks," *USA Today*, August 14, 2013, accessed March 21, 2013, http://www.usatoday.com/story/news/nation/2013/08/13/women-law-enforcement-police-dea-secret-service/2635407/.

[91] Kim Lonsway et al., "Men, Women, and Police Excessive Force: A Tale of Two Genders" (National Center for Women & Policing, April 2002), accessed July 13, 2015, http://womenandpolicing.com/PDF/2002_Excessive_Force.pdf. Another study found male cops were responsible for 99.1 percent of police sexual misconduct cases. See Philip M. Stinson et al., "Police sexual misconduct: A national scale study of arrested officers," *Criminal Justice Policy Review*, Paper 30 (2014), accessed July 14, 2015, http://scholarworks.bgsu.edu/cgi/viewcontent.cgi?article=1029&context=crim_just_pub. Women officers also tend to be more empathetic toward others, more respectful toward citizens, less cynical, less likely to be the target of citizens' insults or attacks, more supportive of community policing and more concerned, patient and understanding in domestic violence calls, according to research cited in Kim Lonsway et al. "Hiring & Retaining More Women: The Advantages to Law Enforcement Agencies" (National Center for Women & Policing, Spring 2003), accessed September 7, 2015, http://womenandpolicing.com/pdf/newadvantagesreport.pdf.

[92] Rigakos, "Situational Determinants of Police Responses to Civil and Criminal Injunctions for Battered Women," 211.

Hiring more women is thus probably not enough. Deeper change is needed in the culture of police and its function of power and control.

Finally, despite better police accountability in some jurisdictions, the same impunity largely reigns for police in the U.S., Canada, the UK and elsewhere. Abusive cops still get treated with stunning leniency, as we'll see in the next chapters.

All this means domestic violence in police homes today most likely remains an epidemic in the U.S. and is likely at comparable levels in Canada and any other country where police have a similar structure.

Albert Seng, the police detective in Arizona, told me as much when I first spoke with him in 2003. He speculated that the abuse in police homes had possibly increased since his study. "Life has gotten even more difficult and more complex in the last decade," he said.

When I caught up with him again more recently, I asked if he thought police had made any progress in the years since he did his research. "I would have to say no," Seng said. "We have stricter laws on domestic violence and the use of weapons, but other than that I think much of the same behaviours are continuing now."

CHAPTER 6

How the Abuse Epidemic Hurts Us All

U nderstanding why police domestic violence is so widespread also helps us see how it hurts everyone, not just police families.

The most obvious impact is on abuse calls at other people's homes. How police handle 911 domestic calls is a critical issue for police, governments and society. As we saw in the introduction, domestic violence is the single most common reason the public contacts the police in the U.S., accounting for up to 50 percent of calls in some communities. The situation is similar elsewhere. In Australia, for example, police describe domestic violence as "the majority of your shift" and "by far the biggest call for service.... It's the core business."[93]

Violence against intimate partners costs an estimated CAD$7.4 billion per year in Canada (USD$5.5 billion). In the U.S., the most recent estimate in 2003 put the cost at $8.3 billion annually (a conservative and dated figure that didn't include the burden on the criminal justice system or quality of

---

[93] U.S. Department of Justice, *Practical Implications of Current Domestic Violence Research*, 1. See also Friday et al., "Evaluating the Impact of a Specialized Domestic Violence Police Unit," 9, 12; and Vieser, "Police hire 2 to investigate domestic violence in Statesville." For the Australian information, see Clare Blumer, "How police navigate the complex terrain of domestic violence," ABC.net.au, June 1, 2015, accessed August 28, 2015, http://www.abc.net.au/news/2015-06-02/police-domestic-violence/6488828.

life), while the cost in the UK is more realistically estimated at £15.7 billion (USD$19.3 billion) each year and in Australia at USD$15.7 billion.[94]

Worldwide, the cost of spousal abuse is estimated at USD$4.4 trillion annually, or over 5 percent of the planet's economy, with child abuse costing another $3.6 trillion. Spousal abuse alone costs over 25 times as much as all wars (both civil and external) and terrorism put together each year, according to a study by Oxford University economist Anke Hoeffler and Stanford University political scientist James Fearon.[95]

Family violence is also closely connected to mass shootings. In nearly two-thirds of such tragedies in the U.S., the shooter killed an intimate partner or family member, according to a study of 110 mass shootings (defined as the killing of four or more people with a gun) from 2009 to 2014. The killer had a prior domestic violence charge in a fifth of the incidents.[96]

And yet, as we saw in the last chapter, police often downplay domestic abuse or investigate it poorly, treating it as a private matter rather than a crime. It was exactly this problem that led the FBI to organize its landmark 1998 conference on abusive cops and issue its report *Domestic Violence by Police Officers*. "Only a small proportion of perpetrators [of domestic violence] experience conviction and punishment for their offense," wrote police officers Vincent Van Hasselt and Donald Sheehan in the report's introduc-

---

[94] Public Health Agency of Canada, "The economic burden of family violence," last modified August 4, 2014, accessed November 28, 2016, http://www.phac-aspc.gc.ca/sfv-avf/info/fv-econo-eng.php. For the U.S. data, see Centers for Disease Control and Prevention, "Intimate Partner Violence: Consequences," last modified March 3, 2015, accessed August 10, 2015, http://www.cdc.gov/violenceprevention/intimatepartnerviolence/consequences.html. For the UK data, see Sylvia Walby, "The Cost of Domestic Violence: Up-date 2009," Project of the UNESCO Chair in Gender Research, Lancaster University, November 25, 2009, accessed August 28, 2015, http://www.edvitaly-project.unimib.it/wp-content/uploads/2013/12/Cost_of_domestic_violence_update-1.doc. For the Australian data, see "The cost of domestic violence: Australian economy 'robbed' of billions," News.com.au, November 22, 2015, accessed December 28, 2016, http://www.news.com.au/national/the-cost-of-domestic-violence-australian-economy-robbed-of-billions/news-story/655a55c524aabdb4640e3bfdeac2865e. For more on the impacts of domestic violence, see the resources in Appendix F.
[95] Anke Hoeffler and James Fearon, "Conflict and Violence; Assessment Paper: Benefits and Costs of the Conflict and Violence Targets for the Post-2015 Development Agenda" (Copenhagen Consensus Center, 2014), accessed December 28, 2016, http://www.copenhagenconsensus.com/sites/default/files/conflict_assessment_-_hoeffler_and_fearon_0.pdf.
[96] "Analysis of Recent Mass Shootings" (Everytown For Gun Safety, July 2014), accessed July 18, 2015, http://everytown.org/article/analysis-of-mass-shootings/.

tion. An arrest occurred in just one in five cases in which there was *prima facie* (i.e. clear) evidence for an arrest, according to data they cited. [97]

Why so few? Some responding officers may be batterers themselves, Van Hasselt and Sheehan said. "If a police officer batters himself, his ability to conduct an objective investigation of the problem in other cases decreases. Indeed, data show [that] where a police officer approves of domestic violence and resorts to physical abuse in his own marriage, he grows less likely to arrest others for the offense," they said. "Police officers in relationships characterized by severe conflict may view domestic violence as more normal and tend to identify with the male offender."

Two official investigations in the U.S. have also made the connection between a permissive attitude toward abusive cops and poor investigations of violence against other women.

- **Puerto Rico**—The U.S. justice department raised the concern in a 2011 investigation of what it called a "staggering level of crime and corruption" in the Puerto Rico Police Department—including rampant domestic abuse among officers. The investigation found amazingly lax discipline for abusive cops. Of 98 officers with two or more domestic violence arrests from 2007 to 2010, 84 were still on active police duty (or 86 percent). Even among the 17 cops with three or more domestic violence arrests, 11 (or two-thirds) were still on duty.

  Unsurprisingly, Puerto Rican police also had a miserable record of handling violence against women in general, the investigation said, blasting the department for its "longstanding failure to effectively address domestic violence and rape in Puerto Rico" in the wider population. The failures were so grave that when taken with the impunity for abusive officers, they "may qualify as evidence of discriminatory intent" and a violation of the Fourteenth Amendment of the U.S. Constitution, which guarantees equal protection to all under the law, the justice department said. [98]
- **Los Angeles**—Katherine Mader, the inspector general of the Los Angeles Police Department, raised a similar concern in her 1997 investigation of domestic violence by LAPD cops, as we saw in Chapter 4. "Some of the reasons for laxity in pursuing Department personnel

---

[97] Van Hasselt and Sheehan, introduction to *Domestic Violence by Police Officers*, 1, 4.
[98] U.S. Department of Justice, Civil Rights Division, *Investigation of the Puerto Rico Police Department* (September 5, 2011), 7, 16-18, 54, 57-8, accessed May 21, 2015, http://www.justice.gov/crt/about/spl/documents/prpd_letter.pdf.

[for domestic violence] have applied equally to lay investigations," she said. [99]

Diane Wetendorf, the retired Chicago-area domestic violence counsellor, agrees that the two issues are closely tied. "Through the experiences of hundreds of victims of police officer batterers, I have learned that domestic violence within police ranks is a litmus test of law enforcement's commitment to public safety," she said in a guidebook for abuse counsellors. [100]

"If it looks the other way when violence against a woman is perpetrated by one of their own, no woman in that community, or our wider society, can count on police protection," said Wetendorf, who created the AbuseOfPower.info website, which offers advice to survivors of police domestic violence.

How police handle violence against women in the general population has long frustrated abuse survivors and counsellors. While many cops do a good job, others fail to take the problem seriously or to properly investigate, while departments often leave domestic violence units understaffed. The issue has been national news in Canada for several years due to mishandled police investigations of reports of missing women and the related case of serial killer Robert Pickton, as we'll see later in this chapter.

In the Toronto Police Service, an internal audit in the late 1990s found officers exhibited "a high degree of non-compliance" with the department's domestic violence policy when responding to citizen calls. A report wasn't written as required by policy in 55 percent of domestic incidents. [101]

Leighann Burns is executive director of Harmony House, a women's shelter in Ottawa. "I've been working in this field for 25 years, and throughout that entire time, women have reported to me time and time again that they have called police for help and didn't get it—[that] they didn't get the help that they needed, that police discounted what they said, or minimized it, or dismissed it, and left without laying charges," Burns said in a CBC story. [102]

---

[99] Mader, *Domestic Violence in the Los Angeles Police Department*, 45.

[100] Wetendorf, *When the Batterer Is a Law Enforcement Officer: A Guide for Advocates*, 5.

[101] Sergeant Nadia Horodynsky, "A Report to the Domestic Violence Review Advisory Committee" (Toronto Police Service, November 28, 2001).

[102] "Mandatory domestic violence charges too infrequent, women say," CBC.ca, November 25, 2014, accessed April 23, 2015, http://www.cbc.ca/m/news/canada/ottawa/mandatory-domestic-violence-charges-too-infrequent-women-say-1.2847529. The problems echo Carleton University professor George Rigakos's study that found police in British Columbia often failed to arrest abusers for breaching protection orders (see Chapter 5).

Burns was concerned that police in Ottawa had started laying far fewer domestic assault charges than before. They laid 670 charges in 2013, down from nearly 950 in 2009—a drop of 30 percent—even though the number of calls remained the same.

Ottawa police Staff Sergeant Isobel Granger, head of the partner assault unit, told CBC her unit was stretched. "Just to put it in context for you, we have 19 investigators and we have 4,500 files that come through the office a year," she said. "So we are really busy.... There is no downtime."

It wasn't the first time concerns had been raised about this unit's severe understaffing. More than a decade earlier, a memo written by the unit's investigators said they needed at least 50 percent more personnel. The 2003 document was made public at a disciplinary hearing in 2010 of a detective in the unit, Constable Jeffrey Gulick, who was convicted of assaulting four police officers. Ironically, they had been answering a domestic dispute at Gulick's own home. (See Chapter 8 for more on this episode.)

Gulick's disciplinary hearing provided a rare look at the horrendous work conditions in an understaffed domestic violence unit. Life in the unit was highly stressful due to the inadequate resources, testified Ottawa police Constable Anne Menard, who said that at one point she had 84 active files. "It was waking up in the middle of the night, being cold, shaking, being afraid that one of my victims would be murdered or hurt badly because I couldn't get to the file," Menard said.[103]

Similar problems exist in other countries:

- **Britain**—In the UK, a scathing government inquiry in 2014 slammed police for "alarming and unacceptable weaknesses" in domestic violence investigations in the general population. Most abuse survivors "experienced very poor attitudes at some point from responding officers. Victims told us that they were frequently not taken seriously, that they felt judged and that some officers demonstrated a considerable lack of empathy and understanding."

  Police took photos of injuries in only 46 percent of cases, while interviews with neighbours were done less than a quarter of the time, the inquiry found—even though these were recommended practices for domestic abuse investigations in the UK.[104]

  The inquiry's report came out a month after an outcry over two British cops who were recorded calling an alleged teen survivor of

103 Meghan Hurley, "Partner-assault unit rife with stress," *The Ottawa Citizen*, January 13, 2010, B1.
104 Her Majesty's Inspectorate of Constabulary, *Everybody's business*, 11-12, 55-57.

domestic abuse a "fucking slag" and a "fucking bitch" in a message the officers inadvertently left on her phone.[105]

In May 2016, British Home Secretary Theresa May (who went on to become prime minister) ordered another inquiry into police handling of domestic violence after evidence of improper investigations and some officers exploiting their authority to develop inappropriate relationships with domestic abuse survivors.

- **Australia**—A 2015 government inquiry in Australia's state of Queensland reported "many stories about the shortcomings of police responses" on domestic violence, which it attributed partly to "a culture in some areas that does not give sufficient weight to what is seen as 'just a domestic.'"[106]

At a national Australian inquiry on the same issue, the first survivor to testify said that when she called police after her husband raped and repeatedly hit her, she heard officers laughing with her attacker. The mother of four said her spouse was controlling and kept the phone in a locked room. He forced her and their kids to sleep in a car parked outside his work when he was on the night shift. A shelter told her she could only bring two of her kids to stay with her.[107]

- **South Africa**—Police response to domestic violence in South Africa seems especially atrocious. "The police are probably the biggest problem with domestic violence," a South African rape counsellor said in one study. "It's completely acceptable to believe that women are a bunch of whiny, nagging, horrible bitches and they should be kept in their place."

Another South African counsellor agreed: "[Many] police have really ingrained attitudes about their roles in society, especially

---

[105] Vikram Dodd, "Police officers alleged to have called woman 'slag' in voicemail message," *The Guardian*, February 19, 2014, accessed April 23, 2015, http://www.theguardian.com/uk-news/2014/feb/19/police-woman-slag-voicemail-alleged.

[106] Quentin Bryce, *Not Now, Not Ever – Putting an End to Domestic and Family Violence in Queensland* (Special Taskforce on Domestic and Family Violence in Queensland, February 28, 2015), accessed August 28, 2015, http://www.qld.gov.au/community/getting-support-health-social-issue/dfv-read-report-recommendation/index.html.

[107] Danny Morgan, "Family violence royal commission: Rape victim heard police laughing with abusive partner, inquiry hears," ABC.net.au, July 13, 2015, accessed August 28, 2015, http://www.abc.net.au/news/2015-07-13/rape-victim-heard-police-laughing-with-abuser-royal-commission/6616688.

about men's and women's roles in society…. There's a lot of traditional thinking that the husband is entitled to beat his wife."[108]

In 2015, South African police came under fire in the country's parliament from women's groups that said officers were failing to act against abusive men. Of 156 police stations, only one was fully compliant with the country's domestic violence legislation, an audit found. Over 300 complaints were filed against police for noncompliance with domestic violence legislation from October 2013 to March 2014. Officers were disciplined in 57 of the cases. Their punishment: a verbal or written warning.[109]

On top of the direct effects on abuse survivors, mishandled domestic violence calls impact all of society in other ways. Children who witness abuse and don't get timely help can perpetuate the abuse cycle with their own kids. Mishandled 911 calls are also a major potential source of legal liability for police and communities. As we saw in the cases of Jocelyn Hotte in Montreal, Victor Ramos in Los Angeles and David Brame in Tacoma, survivors or families can sue if police mess up. In other words, we all pay as citizens and taxpayers.

Police domestic violence also hurts us all in other major ways. Officers who assault their spouse or child are also more likely to flout other laws, including on the job.

"Not surprisingly, an association exists between severely conflicted police families and the officer's level of effectiveness and judgment in the work place, both of which increase the risk for use of excessive force," said police officers Vincent Van Hasselt and Donald Sheehan in their introduction to the FBI's *Domestic Violence by Police Officers* report.[110]

An extreme example was highlighted in the U.S. Department of Justice investigation of misconduct in the Puerto Rico Police Department in 2011. Officer Javier Pagán Cruz was found guilty of first-degree murder and weap-

---

[108] Nix, "To Protect and Abuse."

[109] Aarti J Narsee, "Domestic Violence Act given a black eye," *The Times* of South Africa, May 28, 2015, accessed August 28, 2015,
http://www.timeslive.co.za/thetimes/2015/05/28/Domestic-Violence-Act-given-a-black-eye. See also Siyanbonga Mkwanazi, "Police top brass to face tough parliamentary questions," *Cape Times*, August 17, 2015, accessed August 28, 2015,
http://www.iol.co.za/capetimes/police-top-brass-to-face-tough-parliamentary-questions-1.1900683#.VeECU_IVhBd.

[110] Van Hasselt and Sheehan, introduction to *Domestic Violence by Police Officers*, 4.

ons violations after being videotaped standing over a civilian who was lying on the sidewalk and shooting him multiple times in 2008.

At the time, Cruz was the subject of seven civilian and internal complaints, including a domestic violence complaint for allegedly beating and threatening an intimate partner with a firearm, a complaint for insubordination and one for immoral conduct. An internal affairs report said he had a "bad attitude" and a "tendency for being an aggressive person," yet he was allowed to remain in the department's tactical operations unit.[111]

Indeed, 21 percent of U.S. police officers arrested for domestic violence were previously named as defendants in at least one federal court civil-rights lawsuit, according to ex-police officer Philip Stinson's "Fox in the Henhouse" study.[112] "The finding suggests that misconduct associated with the perpetration of domestic and/or family violence may not be isolated; but rather, indicative of officers with performance problems in other areas," the study said.

Police misconduct is so closely linked to domestic violence that misconduct can actually be a warning sign for abuse, according to the International Association of Chiefs of Police. In its model policy on police spousal abuse, which the 21,000-member association recommends all its members adopt, the IACP advises police supervisors to watch officers for certain behaviours that are "potentially indicative of domestic violence." These warning signs include "excessive and/or increased use of force on the job," "unusually high incidences of physical altercations and verbal disputes," complaints from citizens and fellow officers about "unwarranted aggression and verbal abuse" and "inappropriate treatment of animals."[113]

The correlation is buttressed by the findings of sociologist Leanor Johnson. Her research found:

- Seventy-three percent of male cops who admitted being violent toward their spouse also admitted they had been violent toward citizens.

- Seventy-five percent of male cops who admitted being violent toward their children were also violent toward citizens.

[111] U.S. Department of Justice, Civil Rights Division, *Investigation of the Puerto Rico Police Department*, 20-1.

[112] Stinson and Liederbach, "Fox in the Henhouse," 18-19, 24.

[113] "Domestic Violence by Police Officers Model Policy," International Association of Chiefs of Police, accessed March 20, 2015,
http://www.theiacp.org/MPDomesticViolencebyPO.

- Abusive police officers also have more conflicts with other cops. Of male officers who reported being violent toward a fellow cop, 81 percent said they had also behaved violently toward their spouse.[114]

Most of this police violence, whether on the job or at home, has the same root causes—that is to say, one or more of the following: abuse of power, derogatory attitudes toward women and impunity. These same three problems that lie at the heart of policing also play a central role in some of the most important controversies embroiling police in our time.

TARGETING AFRICAN AMERICANS AND ABORIGINAL PEOPLE

In the U.S., abuse of police power and lack of accountability have sparked mass protests against police killings of African Americans and led to the rise of the Black Lives Matter movement.

In Baltimore, Lieutenant Brian Rice was the most senior of six city cops charged in the death of Freddie Gray, an African American man who suffered fatal spinal trauma after being arrested in 2015. Gray's death sparked days of protest in Baltimore, culminating in a city-wide curfew and deployment of the National Guard.

Rice faced six charges stemming from the incident, including involuntary manslaughter, second-degree assault and misconduct in office. He and the other officers pleaded not guilty. Rice and two other officers were acquitted, while a third officer's case ended in a mistrial and charges were dropped against the remaining two officers. Nonetheless, Baltimore city officials agreed to a $6.4-million wrongful death settlement with Gray's family.

And in an extraordinary development, prosecutors publicly slammed city police for undermining their case against the officers. The two lead prosecutors said the lead police detective in the investigation sabotaged the case and that police failed to execute search warrants for officers' cellphones.

Rice made headlines because he had previously been disciplined and had his guns taken away in 2012 after concerns were raised about his mental health by his ex-girlfriend, a fellow Baltimore police officer who also has a child with Rice, according to news reports.[115] In a separate incident, Rice had

---

[114] Boulin-Johnson, "Burnout and Work and Family Violence Among Police: Gender Comparisons," 112, 118.

[115] Jeff Horwitz, Juliet Linderman and Amanda Lee Myers, "Records show worries over Baltimore officer's mental health," Associated Press, May 1, 2015, accessed June 8, 2015, http://news.yahoo.com/records-show-worries-over-baltimore-officers-

reportedly been disciplined and had his guns removed again after being accused of engaging in a "pattern of intimidation and violence" against his ex-girlfriend's then-husband, a Baltimore firefighter, who said Rice's behaviour caused him "to have constant fear for my personal safety" and a "fear of imminent harm or death."

After Gray's death, the U.S. justice department investigated the Baltimore Police Department and found a long history of unconstitutional practices targeting African Americans for stops and arrests. African Americans made up 95 percent of the 410 people stopped 10 or more times from 2010 to 2015. Only 3.7 percent of pedestrian stops led to citations or arrests, the investigation found. One African American man was stopped 30 times in less than four years, but none of the stops led to a citation or criminal charge. Yet, despite targeting African Americans, police found contraband twice as often when searching white people as black people during vehicle stops.[116]

The justice department found similar patterns of racial discrimination when it investigated city police in Cleveland, San Francisco and Ferguson, Missouri, following the shooting deaths of other African Americans.

In New York City, police used a controversial tactic known as "stop-and-frisk" about 5 million times over 10 years before a federal judge ruled in 2013 that the stops violated constitutional rights because they intentionally discriminated by race. About 83 percent of the stops targeted black people and Latinos. The stops, while highly damaging to police-community relations, were also ineffective for crime prevention. Just 3 percent of arrests stemming from the stops led to a conviction, while only 0.1 percent led to an arrest for a violent crime, a New York attorney general report found.[117]

Similar police abuses occur in communities across the U.S. Unarmed black Americans are five times as likely to be shot and killed by police as

---

mental-health-071656472.html. See also Jon Swaine and Oliver Laughland, "Freddie Gray officer threatened to kill himself and ex-partner's husband, court document alleges," *The Guardian*, May 5, 2015, accessed August 11, 2015, http://www.theguardian.com/us-news/2015/may/05/freddie-gray-baltimore-police-brian-rice; and see Jon Swaine and Oliver Laughland, "Baltimore police warned of Freddie Gray officer's feud with man he got arrested," *The Guardian*, May 12, 2015, accessed August 11, 2015, http://www.theguardian.com/us-news/2015/may/12/freddie-gray-officer-feud.

[116] U.S. Department of Justice, Civil Rights Division, *Investigation of the Baltimore City Police Department* (August 10, 2016), 7, 28, accessed October 11, 2016, https://www.justice.gov/opa/file/883366/download.

[117] Julia Dahl, "Stop and Frisk: AG's report says only 3 percent of NYPD arrests using tactic end in conviction," CBSNews.com, November 14, 2013, accessed October 11, 2016, http://www.cbsnews.com/news/stop-and-frisk-ags-report-says-only-3-percent-of-nypd-arrests-using-tactic-end-in-conviction/.

unarmed white Americans, according to a *Washington Post* study of 1,502 police shootings in 2015 and 2016.[118] The newspaper also debunked a some-times-made claim that police target black people more because they commit more crime. Thirteen percent of black people shot and killed by police were not armed, compared to 7 percent of white people, the newspaper said. In other words, black people were less likely to be armed, yet far more likely to be shot and killed by police.

A 2016 study by the New York-based Center for Policing Equity supported this conclusion. It found police were nearly 30 percent more likely to use force—anything from Tasers to baton strikes and pepper spray—when arrest-ing black people than whites.[119]

The problems go beyond the U.S. In the UK, where police use a similar tactic called "stop and search," a black person is far more likely to be stopped than a white person, according to an investigation by UK newspaper *The Independent*. In London, black people were 3.2 times more likely to be stopped than whites, while in one county, a black person was 17.5 times more likely to get stopped.[120]

In Canada, it's called "carding." In Toronto, Canada's largest city, one in four people whom police carded were black, even as black people made up only 8.3 percent of Toronto's population, *The Toronto Star* newspaper reported in a 2012 investigation.[121] Black people were more likely to be

---

[118] Wesley Lowery, "Aren't more white people than black people killed by police? Yes, but no," *The Washington Post*, July 11, 2016, accessed October 11, 2016, https://www.washingtonpost.com/news/post-nation/wp/2016/07/11/arent-more-white-people-than-black-people-killed-by-police-yes-but-no/?hpid=hp_no-name_whiteshootings-pn-8am-1%3Ahomepage%2Fstory&utm_term=.4185456f4fa5.

[119] Timothy Williams, "Study Supports Suspicion That Police Are More Likely to Use Force on Blacks," *The New York Times*, July 7, 2016, accessed October 11, 2016, http://www.nytimes.com/2016/07/08/us/study-supports-suspicion-that-police-use-of-force-is-more-likely-for-blacks.html?&moduleDetail=section-news-5&action=click&contentCollection=U.S.&region=Footer&module=MoreInSection&version=WhatsNext&contentID=WhatsNext&pgtype=article&_r=0.

[120] Nigel Morris, "Black people still far more likely to be stopped and searched by police than other ethnic groups," *The Independent*, August 6, 2015, accessed October 12, 2016, http://www.independent.co.uk/news/uk/crime/black-people-still-far-more-likely-to-be-stopped-and-searched-by-police-than-other-ethnic-groups-10444436.html.

[121] Jim Rankin and Patty Winsa, "Known to police: Toronto police stop and document black and brown people far more than whites," *The Toronto Star*, March 9, 2012, accessed April 25, 2015, http://www.thestar.com/news/insight/2012/03/09/known_to_police_toronto_police_stop_and_document_black_and_brown_people_far_more_than_whites.html.

carded than white people in every one of the city's 70-plus patrol zones. Their chance of being stopped went up in mostly white neighbourhoods.

The police behaviour is "reminiscent of apartheid South Africa and the pass laws which were used there to control the movement of blacks in the country," said Akwasi Owusu-Bempah, then a member of a Toronto police liaison committee with the black community and now an assistant professor of sociology at the University of Toronto. Police in Toronto stopped black people at an even higher rate than in New York. [122]

Police also single out Aboriginal people. A Canadian study found that police in one large city were 1.4 times more likely to stop a First Nations person than a white person. [123] Meanwhile, the incarceration rate of Aboriginal adults in Canada is estimated to be 10 times higher than that of non-Aboriginals. Over 60 percent of detainees in some prisons are Aboriginal. [124]

After much public outcry about carding in Ontario, the provincial government in 2016 issued regulations that sought to end discriminatory police stops. But despite such reforms in some communities, police still use various versions of carding and stop-and-frisk in many cities in the U.S., the UK, Canada and elsewhere.

And the tactic could get new life after Donald Trump's election as U.S. president in 2016. He enthusiastically praised stop-and-frisk during his campaign, dismissing the judge's ruling that it is unconstitutional and the evidence that it is ineffective. "We need law and order in the inner cities," Trump said during one presidential debate. "Stop-and-frisk had a tremendous impact on the safety of New York City. Tremendous beyond belief."

POLICE SEXUAL MISCONDUCT—DRIVING WHILE FEMALE

Police sexual misconduct is another dark secret of law enforcement—one rooted in all three of the problems that also fuel domestic violence in police homes.

---

[122] Jim Rankin et al., "As criticism piles up, so do the police cards," *The Toronto Star*, September 27, 2013, accessed October 12, 2016, https://www.thestar.com/news/gta/knowntopolice2013/2013/09/27/as_criticism_p iles_up_so_do_the_police_cards.html.

[123] "Police stop more blacks, Ont. study finds," CBC.ca, May 26, 2005, accessed October 12, 2016, http://www.cbc.ca/news/canada/police-stop-more-blacks-ont-study-finds-1.565724.

[124] Government of Canada, Office of the Correctional Investigator, "Aboriginal Offenders – A Critical Situation," September 16, 2013, accessed October 12, 2016, http://www.oci-bec.gc.ca/cnt/rpt/oth-aut/oth-aut20121022info-eng.aspx.

Diana Guerrero was a 17-year-old high school police intern in New Mexico when she was sexually assaulted by sex-crimes detective Michael Garcia of the Las Cruces Police Department. "It had never occurred to me that a person who had earned a badge would do this to me or anybody else," Guerrero later said. "I lost my faith in everything, everyone, even in myself," she told the police officer's trial, as she detailed her resulting struggles with depression and post-traumatic stress.

Michael Garcia was sentenced to nine years in prison in 2014 and, in a separate case that year, an additional 11 years in prison after admitting he had molested a young female family member.

Diana Guerrero sued the city of Las Cruces, saying a culture of sexism and harassment had created the conditions for her assault. Officers referred to female secretaries as "whores," nicknamed a female officer whose call number was 704 "7-0-whore" and grabbed their penises in front of female employees, asking to be touched, the suit said. The city agreed to pay Guerrero $3 million to settle the case in 2016.

Guerrero's story was recounted in an Associated Press investigation of police sexual misconduct. It found that 550 U.S. cops lost their law enforcement licence from 2009 to 2014 due to sexual assault, sexual shakedowns or gratuitous pat-downs, while another 440 lost their licence for other sex offences or misconduct.[125]

"It's so underreported and people are scared that if they call and complain about a police officer, they think every other police officer is going to be then out to get them," Chief Bernadette DiPino of the Sarasota Police Department in Florida was quoted saying.

A little-known type of police sexual misconduct occurs during traffic stops. The problem has been dubbed "driving while female." That's when officers use trumped-up or minor traffic stops to sexually harass, sexually assault, stalk and occasionally even kidnap young women, often teenagers, according to a pair of University of Nebraska studies.

One of the studies reviewed 183 cases of U.S. police officers accused of sexual abuse in 2002 and 2003 that resulted in official action, such as discipline or criminal charges. Traffic stops were the scene of over a third of the cases, and 40 percent involved a teenager.

Police departments fail to properly investigate or curtail the misconduct with better policies and training, the researchers found. They noted that the problems are "symptomatic of a pervasive sexist culture" in policing, which

---

[125] Matt Sedensky and Nomaan Merchant, "Betrayed By the Badge," Associated Press, November 1, 2015, accessed August 3, 2016, http://interactives.ap.org/2015/betrayed-by-the-badge/?SITEID=apmobile.

they said also leads to discrimination and sexual harassment against female officers and "a systematic failure" to investigate police domestic violence.[126]

The disturbing findings were buttressed by another study in 2011 by the U.S. National Police Misconduct Reporting Project. Citing FBI crime data, the study found that U.S. police officers committed over two times more sexual assaults per capita than the general population. The rate was 68 sexual assaults for every 100,000 cops versus 29 per 100,000 for the public.[127]

The study also found that minors made up 52 percent of the alleged survivors of serious sexual misconduct by cops, such as sexual assault or battery, and that sexual misconduct was the second most common form of wrongdoing reported, after excessive force.

Still more disturbing revelations about sexual misconduct came in the U.S. justice department investigation of the Baltimore police in 2016. It found that some officers coerced prostitutes into providing sexual favours in exchange for avoiding arrest. The police department failed to adequately investigate.[128]

In Australia, cops have also come under fire for sexual misconduct. Some police officers sexually preyed on domestic violence survivors whom the officers had met while investigating abuse, *The Sydney Morning Herald* newspaper reported in 2015. The news came amid a human rights investigation of police for widespread sexual harassment and discrimination against female police colleagues.[129]

"The abuse of civilian victims of crime by police and the problem of sexual harassment and discrimination inside the force are viewed by senior police as over-lapping issues because they share a root cause—the abuse of power by some police to prey on, harass or discriminate against others," the newspaper

---

[126] Samuel Walker and Dawn Irlbeck, "Driving While Female: A National Problem in Police Misconduct" (Police Professionalism Initiative, University of Nebraska at Omaha, March 2002), accessed July 14, 2015, http://samuelwalker.net/wp-content/uploads/2010/06/dwf2002.pdf. See also Samuel Walker and Dawn Irlbeck, "Police Sexual Abuse of Teenage Girls: A 2003 Update on 'Driving While Female'" (Police Professionalism Initiative, University of Nebraska at Omaha, June 2003), accessed July 14, 2015, http://samuelwalker.net/wp-content/uploads/2010/06/dwf2003.pdf.

[127] Packman, *2010 NPMSRP Police Misconduct Statistical Report –Draft*.

[128] U.S. Department of Justice, *Investigation of the Baltimore City Police Department*, 149-150.

[129] Nick McKenzie and Richard Baker, "Police prey on victims of domestic violence," *The Sydney Morning Herald*, November 30, 2015, accessed December 8, 2016, http://www.smh.com.au/national/investigations/police-prey-on-victims-of-domestic-violence-20151129-glaqax.html.

said. (See below for a more detailed discussion of sexual harassment of female police officers.)

"The masculine police world is aggressively libidinous," said former New York Police Department commander Anthony Bouza in his memoir. "What this means is that contacts with women—at traffic stops, for example—have to be monitored and controlled. It also means a higher-than-normal level of sensitivity is essential to combat sexual harassment or exploitation within the ranks. Like the military, the world of cops is too often given to the excesses of sexual predators—at all levels and ranks."[130]

SEXUAL HARASSMENT AND ABUSE IN THE RANKS

In Canada, all three problems that fuel police domestic violence—abuse of power, derogatory attitudes toward women and impunity—are also at the heart of a major sexual harassment scandal rocking the RCMP.

The scandal erupted when RCMP Corporal Catherine Galliford went public in 2011 about enduring years of sexual harassment by fellow Mounties, which led to her suffering debilitating post-traumatic stress. Galliford was the force's prominent public face in British Columbia as the spokesperson in several high-profile cases.[131]

The harassment started while Galliford was still an applicant seeking to join the Mounties, she said in a lawsuit against the federal and provincial governments and individual officers.[132] She said an RCMP officer stalked and "aggressively pursued" her, "forcing himself upon her sexually [and] threatening her that if she did not gratify him sexually, he would make sure that she did not get accepted into the RCMP." Later, once in the RCMP, the same officer "threatened to shoot" Galliford if she broke off the relationship, she said. Galliford said she complained to a superior and that the officer was charged, but the case was botched and he was allowed to stay in the RCMP.

---

130 Bouza, *Police Unbound*, 21.
131 "B.C. Mountie alleges years of sexual harassment," CBC.ca, November 7, 2011, accessed March 20, 2015, http://www.cbc.ca/news/canada/british-columbia/b-c-mountie-alleges-years-of-sexual-harassment-1.1034369.
132 *Catherine Galliford v. Marvin Wawia et al.*, Notice of civil claim (Supreme Court of British Columbia, Vancouver Registry, May 9, 2012), accessed March 20, 2015, http://www.cbc.ca/bc/news/bc-120509-galliford-lawsuit.pdf. See also Nancy Macdonald and Charlie Gillis, "Inside the RCMP's biggest crisis," *Maclean's*, February 27, 2015, accessed May 5, 2015, http://www.macleans.ca/society/inside-the-rcmps-biggest-crisis/.

More harassment came, Galliford said, from a drunken RCMP inspector who groped her in his car during her time at the Mountie training academy. She also said an RCMP staff sergeant groped her in a hotel room and exposed his penis to her, while superiors and colleagues frequently propositioned her sexually and insisted she sit on their knee.

The harassment didn't come only from RCMP members, she said. A Vancouver city police officer who was her supervisor on a joint police task force often made suggestive comments and once exposed his penis to her in a car while on duty, she said. Another time, a Vancouver police detective told Galliford in front of two RCMP members that "he fantasized about [British Columbia serial killer Robert] Pickton escaping from jail, hunting her down, stripping her naked and hanging her from the meat hook and gutting her like a pig," the suit said, noting that the two RCMP members laughed.

After 18 years on the force, Galliford said she developed "extremely severe" post-traumatic stress, had panic attacks, threw up at work, lost hair and weight, began drinking to cope and started to stutter. She became a recluse in her mother's house—unable to go outside due to agoraphobia, let alone go to work.

In a statement of defence, the RCMP acknowledged that the officer who allegedly threatened to shoot Galliford was disciplined after her complaints. Yet, the RCMP denied "each and every allegation" in Galliford's suit, said she abused alcohol and insisted that any injuries or damages she may have suffered were due to her own "negligence."[133]

Pursuing the suit drained Galliford's life savings, and her lawyer believed the opposing lawyers were trying to bleed her dry, *Maclean's* reported.[134]

Galliford's revelations prompted a slew of other lawsuits from female RCMP officers alleging sexual harassment and abuse. In 2012, Janet Merlo, a retired Mountie, became the lead plaintiff in a proposed class action lawsuit against the RCMP. She said she suffered post-traumatic stress and depression from continual sexual harassment, derogatory comments and discrimination during her 19 years in the force. The toll included losing her marriage.

Merlo penned a book about her experiences titled *No One To Tell: Breaking My Silence on Life in the RCMP*.[135] She recalls a note that was passed

---

[133] *Catherine Galliford v. Marvin Wawia et al.*, Response to civil claim (Supreme Court of British Columbia, Vancouver Registry, July 16, 2012), accessed March 20, 2015, http://www.cbc.ca/bc/news/bc-120717-rcmp-galliford-response.pdf.
[134] Macdonald and Gillis, "Inside the RCMP's biggest crisis."

around to female officers in her detachment, titled "Training Courses Now Available for Women." It included options such as "Silence, the final frontier, where no woman has gone before," "PMS, your problem, not his" and "Communications Skills 1: Tears – the last resort not the first."

Merlo also recounts penning a scathing note when she filled out an RCMP exit questionnaire on leaving the force in 2010. "The RCMP is 100 years behind in its treatment of women," she wrote. "Sexual harassment is rampant. There is no accountability other than to quietly transfer the offending members and return results of investigations to those who speak out as 'unfounded.'"

Nearly 500 active and former female RCMP officers and civilian members eventually joined Merlo's suit. The plaintiffs' lawyers said the RCMP's "paramilitary culture" was behind a "systemic problem" of sexual harassment, rape and gender discrimination that led to severe stress, suicide attempts, broken relationships and shattered careers among the plaintiffs.[136]

"I don't think there's been a female in the outfit who hasn't been approached sexually," said Mike Webster, a Victoria, British Columbia, police psychologist who has treated Mounties and other officers for over 30 years, in a CBC story about Galliford's allegations. "Senior [RCMP] executives for decades have been accountable to no one and they've created a toxic work environment, high levels of employee stress and a culture of fear."[137]

An internal RCMP survey in 2012 found female officers didn't trust the force's system for handling harassment complaints and believed that harassers generally didn't suffer consequences while supervisors could target complainants and hurt their careers, *The Globe and Mail* newspaper said.[138]

The avalanche of allegations prompted the RCMP to overhaul how it responds to harassment complaints in 2013. Additional changes were later enshrined in amendments to the RCMP Act. But despite the changes, little seems to have improved on the ground.

In 2014, then-opposition Liberal Member of Parliament Judy Sgro called for an inquiry into sexual harassment in the RCMP after hearing "horrible

---

135 Janet Merlo, *No One To Tell: Breaking My Silence on Life in the RCMP* (St. John's, Newfoundland: Breakwater Books, 2013).

136 "RCMP face sexual harassment class-action suit," CBC.ca, March 27, 2012, accessed August 11, 2015, http://www.cbc.ca/news/canada/british-columbia/rcmp-face-sexual-harassment-class-action-suit-1.1153130.

137 "B.C. Mountie alleges years of sexual harassment," CBC.ca.

138 Daniel Leblanc, "Female Mounties fear backlash over reporting harassment, report shows," *The Globe and Mail*, September 17, 2012, accessed March 21, 2015, http://www.theglobeandmail.com/news/national/female-mounties-fear-backlash-over-reporting-harassment-report-shows/article4550565/.

and graphic" accounts from dozens of active-duty and former Mounties. "Our offices continue to receive emails from RCMP staff. The emails provide a grim look into the past and offer little hope for the future," Sgro and Liberal Senator Grant Mitchell wrote in *The Huffington Post*.

"These are individuals who have either experienced harassment, with no repercussions for the harassers, or are currently being harassed but are having difficulties navigating the cumbersome review and complaints process. They are asking us: 'What's actually changed?' and more importantly, 'What's next?'... It's clear that there is a disturbing culture of sexual harassment and bullying within the organization," they wrote.[139]

In fact, some of the changes reportedly made things worse. A new provision in the amended RCMP Act gave the commissioner of the Mounties the power to medically discharge officers if doing so contributed to the "promotion of economy and efficiency." "It's the equivalent of giving the schoolyard bully the power to get rid of his victims," said Greg Passey, a psychiatrist who treats Mounties and soldiers at an operational stress injury clinic funded by the federal Ministry of Veterans Affairs.

Passey knew several RCMP officers who were being discharged under the new rule, he told *Maclean's* magazine in 2015. Most were on medical leave due to harassment. "It boggles the mind. If you come forward, they label you a troublemaker. They do everything they can to make you go away, and the supervising officers doing the harassing get promoted," said Passey, who spent 22 years in the military and whose uncle and father-in-law were both Mounties. "I used to be very proud of our force," he said, but now "there is no way I would ever allow my daughters to serve in the RCMP."[140]

As an aside, the sexual harassment scandal raises another interesting question. If a female RCMP officer has such a difficult time getting a fair hearing from fellow officers, what chance does a non-cop have—such as an abused police spouse?

After the 2015 election of Liberal leader Justin Trudeau, the RCMP finally entered settlement talks on the harassment lawsuits. In May 2016, the RCMP settled Galliford's suit (details weren't disclosed), then in October 2016, it settled two class action cases led by Merlo and former Mountie Linda Davidson. The RCMP apologized to the women and set aside $100 million to cover claims of about 1,000 women expected to come forward.

---

[139] Grant Mitchell and Judy A. Sgro, "Give Harassed RCMP Officers Real Change, Not Lip Service," *The Huffington Post*, September 4, 2013, accessed March 21, 2015, http://www.huffingtonpost.ca/grant-mitchell-/rcmp-harassment-_b_3869232.html.
[140] Macdonald and Gillis, "Inside the RCMP's biggest crisis."

But even after her settlement, Galliford was not convinced the RCMP had changed. She said the RCMP had offered "beautiful words on paper," but independent investigators were still needed to look into complaints. "Why would you go to a senior officer in the RCMP to complain about harassment in the RCMP?" she said, adding that she would advise young women against joining the force. "I would tell them to look in other directions."[141]

Sexual harassment of female officers isn't just a Canadian problem. In Australia, a human rights investigation—one of the largest inquiries worldwide into sexual harassment in the workplace—found that 40 percent of female officers in the state of Victoria said they had been sexually harassed by male colleagues. Only one in 10 filed a complaint about the harassment or reported it. The main reasons for not reporting were fear of repercussions for career or reputation and the belief that reporting wouldn't make any difference. Nearly 2 percent of female cops said they had been raped or experienced attempted rape by a male cop in the previous five years.[142]

"It's the same mentality as domestic violence but being perpetrated by the organisation," one female officer told investigators. "The nightmares I have are horrendous. I am really fearful.... The guys were drinking and screwing around. They just regarded us as part of their property."

Another said: "From day dot, you are exposed to comments about boobs, you... see them perving on women, you have to hear about who sleeps with who. That was the day my bubble burst. I thought it would pick up but it was a slow decline." One female officer said she was stalked by a male colleague, but a supervisor dismissed her concerns. The police hierarchy still wouldn't act even after the officer raped her and went on harassing her, she said. "Management didn't do anything despite my repeated pleas for assistance. People would joke about the perpetrator's behaviour all the time, saying things like 'he will just get them drunk, it's not rape then,'" she said.

---

[141] Ian Bailey, "B.C. Mountie says she was blindsided by sexual-harassment suit settlement," *The Globe and Mail*, May 3, 2016, accessed May 3, 2016, http://www.theglobeandmail.com/news/british-columbia/bc-mountie-says-she-was-blindsided-by-sexual-harassment-suit-settlement/article29836349/.
[142] Victorian Equal Opportunity and Human Rights Commission, *Independent review into sex discrimination and sexual harassment, including predatory behaviour in Victoria Police* (Victoria, 2015), 13-16, 77, 87, 105, accessed December 8, 2016, http://www.humanrightscommission.vic.gov.au/our-resources-and-publications/reports/item/1336-independent-review-into-sex-discrimination-and-sexual-harassment-including-predatory-behaviour-in-victoria-police-phase-one-report-2015.

BOTCHED INVESTIGATIONS OF MISSING WOMEN AND SEXUAL ASSAULT

Meanwhile, as if chronic sexual harassment weren't enough, RCMP Corporal Catherine Galliford made still more explosive revelations of wrongdoing—again, rooted in police power, anti-women attitudes and impunity.

Galliford said sexist attitudes among police led them to bungle investigations into reports of dozens of women who had gone missing in British Columbia and the related case of Robert Pickton, one of Canada's most notorious serial killers.

Pickton was charged in 2002 with killing 26 women, many of them of First Nations descent. He was convicted of six second-degree murder charges and sentenced to life in prison with no chance of parole for 25 years. (Prosecutors stayed 20 other charges of first-degree murder because Pickton had already gotten the maximum possible sentence.[143])

Galliford was a member of a joint RCMP-Vancouver Police Department task force that investigated the missing women reports and Pickton's possible involvement. Galliford said police had enough evidence by the late 1990s to execute a search warrant at Pickton's farm, but they didn't proceed until 2002 while Pickton continued his killing spree, murdering 14 more women by some estimates.

Instead of doing a proper investigation, police officers watched porn, engaged in sexual liaisons and harassment, and left work early "to go drinking and partying," Galliford told *The Vancouver Province*.[144] When police finally searched Pickton's farm, Galliford said she confronted a top RCMP officer, saying, "You've known this since 1999." She said the officer ignored her. "He is a misogynist, which is probably why he blew off the missing women investigation," she said.

---

[143] Police found remains or DNA evidence from 33 missing women at Pickton's pig farm, but he reportedly told an undercover cop he killed 49 women. See Camille Bains, "For the 98 children who lost their mothers to Robert Pickton, $50,000 each," The Canadian Press, March 18, 2014, accessed August 11, 2015, http://www.theglobeandmail.com/news/british-columbia/for-the-98-children-who-lost-their-mothers-to-robert-pickton-50000-each/article17554682/.

[144] Suzanne Fournier, "Cops watched porn, skipped work instead of investigating missing women: Officer," *The Vancouver Province*, November 23, 2011, accessed March 21, 2015, http://www.theprovince.com/news/Cops+watched+porn+skipped+work+instead+investigating+missing+women+Officer/5757752/story.html. See also Ken MacQueen, "The RCMP: A Royal Canadian disgrace," *Maclean's*, November 18, 2011, accessed June 11, 2015, http://www.macleans.ca/news/canada/a-royal-canadian-disgrace/.

"There was a police indifference and that, I believe, is why it went on for so long [before Pickton was arrested], and why so many women lost their lives," she told CBC News.[145] A public inquiry in 2012 confirmed many of Galliford's criticisms, lambasting police for "blatant failures" and "systemic bias."[146] The RCMP and Vancouver police apologized for their inaction.

Families of the murdered women sued the federal, British Columbia and Vancouver governments, slamming the mishandled police investigation. Those governments agreed in 2014 to pay $4.9 million to settle the suit.

Yet, despite the lessons of the affair, the then-Conservative government of Stephen Harper doggedly refused to heed calls for an inquiry into reports that as many as 4,000 indigenous women across Canada had gone missing or been murdered since the 1980s, with many of the cases unsolved. In 2016, Justin Trudeau, the newly elected Liberal prime minister, finally ordered an inquiry.

The Baltimore police are a remarkable example of how power, impunity and anti-women attitudes can combine to create a tsunami of police misconduct and botched investigations of violence against women.

The same U.S. justice department investigation that found racial discrimination and sexual misconduct in the Baltimore police in 2016 also uncovered a disturbingly poor record of investigating sexual assault in the general population.

The department "makes minimal to no effort to locate, identify, interrogate or investigate [sexual assault] suspects," the justice department found. "We found this to be true even in cases where the suspects had been identified or were easily identifiable on the basis of the victim's testimony."

Officers routinely blamed sexual assault survivors for getting raped and discouraged them from filing a complaint—for example, asking questions such as "Why are you messing that guy's life up?" One detective in the department's sex offense unit reportedly complained: "In homicide, there are real victims; all our cases are bullshit."

---

[145] "Pickton investigators were indifferent, Mountie says," CBC.ca, November 23, 2011, accessed March 21, 2015, http://www.cbc.ca/news/canada/british-columbia/pickton-investigators-were-indifferent-mountie-says-1.1112656.

[146] Wally T. Oppal, *Forsaken: The Report of the Missing Women Commission of Inquiry* (Victoria, British Columbia: Missing Women Commission of Inquiry, November 19, 2012), accessed March 21, 2015, http://www.missingwomeninquiry.ca/obtain-report/.

And not surprisingly, Baltimore police also enjoyed remarkable impunity. Of 1,382 allegations of excessive force against city cops from 2010 to 2015, only 2.2 percent were sustained (i.e. deemed credible), an exceptionally low rate. One officer had been the subject of about 125 complaints—many due to allegations of unwarranted strip and cavity searches in public—but the department had sustained only a single minor misconduct complaint against him.

The impunity was enforced by vicious retaliation against officers who dared to report misconduct or resisted orders to conduct discriminatory stop-and-frisks. One detective who reported two fellow cops for using alleged excessive force was repeatedly called a "rat," had pictures of cheese left on his desk, found a dead rat on his car with its head severed and failed to get a response to his calls for police backup. After he reported the dead rat to internal affairs, investigators took a year and a half to contact him and then did so only after the incident got substantial media coverage.[147]

The spousal abuse epidemic in police families clearly has broad impacts that go far beyond the world of law enforcement and is closely connected to a host of other social ills that are major preoccupations in our communities. All of these problems share one or more of the same root causes—police power, anti-woman attitudes and impunity.

All of these root causes were again at centre stage in a horrific murder-suicide in the U.S. Pacific Northwest, which for the first time focused a national spotlight on the violence raging in police homes and finally convinced some officers that change could wait no longer.

---

[147] U.S. Department of Justice, *Investigation of the Baltimore City Police Department*, 122, 146, 151-153.

CHAPTER 7

"Daddy Shot Mommy!"

B ack in Washington, D.C., Arizona cop Albert Seng's 1992 study helped get police family violence back on the agenda in Congress. Domestic violence activists scored a breakthrough in 1996 when the so-called Lautenberg Amendment, also known as the Domestic Violence Offender Gun Ban, was enacted into law.

Senator Frank Lautenberg, a feisty World War II veteran and Democrat from New Jersey, introduced the provision as part of a reform of the Gun Control Act. "If you beat your wife... you should not have a gun," Lautenberg said on the Senate floor. His amendment prohibited anyone with a misde-meanour conviction for domestic violence from buying, possessing, selling or transporting firearms and ammunition. The ban applied even to those who needed a gun for their job, such as the 740,000 sworn law enforcement officers and 3 million active-duty soldiers and reservists then employed in the U.S.[148]

---

[148] The Gun Control Act of 1968 already barred anyone with a felony conviction from possessing a firearm, but an exception was made for guns issued to police officers and other government personnel for duty. A 1994 amendment extended the prohibition to anyone subject to certain kinds of domestic violence protection orders (though again service weapons issued to police and other government employees were exempted). To qualify, the protection order must be issued by a court after a hearing in which the defendant had an opportunity to participate; it must bar the defendant from harass-ing, stalking or threatening an intimate partner or the partner's child; and it must include a finding that the defendant is a credible threat to the victim or prohibit the use of force against the victim or attempts or threats to use force.

Most abuse experts welcomed the measure. They noted that domestic violence involving a firearm was 23 times more likely to result in death than assault with other weapons or physical force. The gun lobby and police unions were not so happy. This was, after all, the land of gun rights enshrined in the Second Amendment. The National Rifle Association called Senator Lautenberg "an unprecedented danger to civil liberties." Some gun-rights activists said the measure was inspired by "feminazis."

Gun lobbyists launched a withering campaign to kill it. Their allies in Congress introduced a slew of amendments to repeal the measure or modify it to exclude cops and soldiers. A barrage of lawsuits challenged its constitutionality in court. Police groups argued that the law discriminated against cops and unfairly deprived them of their livelihood.

One of the groups that filed a court challenge was the Fraternal Order of Police. In a congressional hearing in March 1997, Bernard Teodorski, the group's vice president, warned that the measure could lead to the firing of "hundreds—perhaps thousands—of... good veteran law enforcement officers who made a mistake—a terrible, but forgivable mistake." Teodorski seemed untroubled by his implicit acknowledgement that "hundreds" or "perhaps thousands" of cops were convicted domestic violence offenders.[149]

Teodorski complained that police departments were rifling through officers' records in search of misdemeanour convictions. "This is not an indication that chiefs and police administrators support this new law," he said. "Indeed, most do not. Nor is there any evidence that suggests domestic violence or abuse is prevalent or common among police officers as opposed to any other group in society."

Teodorski's remarks were quite odd considering that his own group's journal had not long before published the study of Albert Seng and his team, showing that domestic violence was indeed far more prevalent among cops than other people. Teodorski's organization had also heard sociologist Leanor Johnson speak about her research at its 1991 convention. In a final irony, Teodorski made his remarks just days after the city of Los Angeles

---

[149] Bernard H. Teodorski, Statement before the U.S. House of Representatives Subcommittee on Crime, Committee on the Judiciary (Washington, D.C.: March 5, 1997), 30-50, accessed June 14, http://commdocs.house.gov/committees/judiciary/hju58106.000/hju58106_of.htm. Teodorski's statement also gave some troubling examples of how officers with misdemeanour domestic violence convictions were able to skirt the firearms prohibition. One officer, who had pleaded guilty to a misdemeanour domestic assault on his wife, had his guilty plea set aside by a judge who ruled that the conviction created a "manifest injustice." The officer got to keep his gun and job.

agreed to pay $2.15 million to settle lawsuits over police officer Victor Ramos's murder-suicide.

Not all cops were against the Lautenberg Amendment. Ronald Hampton, executive director of the 35,000-member National Black Police Association, supported the measure in his testimony to Congress. Police must "not be above or beyond the laws of this country," he said.

Hampton criticized other police groups for opposing the ban. "At a time when the relationship between the community and the police is constantly deteriorating, we believe this effort by police unions and other associations is misguided and will result in the continued widening gulf between the community and the police," he said.[150]

The measure's merits were plain enough that it survived the various challenges and remains in force today. The debate focused renewed attention on the trouble in police families. It also finally prompted some police and public officials to recognize the problems and take tentative steps toward reform. Some realized they had a huge potential liability time bomb in the ranks. They wondered how many other Victor Ramoses lurked out there, about to saddle them with costly, embarrassing lawsuits. If for no other reason, many departments acted out of pure self-interest—to minimize liability.

In 1999, another important breakthrough came when the International Association of Chiefs of Police, based in Alexandria, Virginia, developed a model policy on abusive cops that it recommended for adoption to its 21,000 members in over 100 countries. The policy calls for a "zero tolerance" approach and "a definitive statement that domestic violence will not be tolerated." Other recommendations:[151]

- **Terminate abusers**—Automatically fire officers convicted of a misdemeanour domestic violence criminal offence and those found through an internal administrative investigation to have committed domestic violence.
- **Review records**—Check records of all employees for misdemeanour domestic violence convictions (which preclude the officer from possessing a firearm under Lautenberg) and protection orders.

---

[150] Ronald E. Hampton, Statement before the U.S. House of Representatives Subcommittee on Crime, Committee on the Judiciary (Washington, D.C.: March 5, 1997), 80-83, accessed June 11, 2015, http://commdocs.house.gov/committees/judiciary/hju58106.000/hju58106_of.htm.
[151] "Domestic Violence by Police Officers Model Policy," International Association of Chiefs of Police.

- **Screen hires**—Thoroughly investigate potential new employees to screen out abusers or those with abusive tendencies, including applicants with a history of violence, sexual assault or stalking. Checks should include driver's records, protection orders, misconduct in previous police jobs and psychological screening for abusive tendencies.

- **Monitor**—Watch officers for potential warning signs of domestic violence, such as stalking an intimate partner, controlling behaviour, alcohol or drug abuse, mistreatment of animals, "unwarranted aggression" or verbal abuse against civilians or fellow officers.

- **Support families**—Regularly check in with police families to provide information about domestic violence and support services.

- **Punish severely**—Enact "severe" discipline (up to dismissal) for officers who interfere with a domestic violence case involving themselves or a fellow cop or who intimidate survivors or witnesses.

- **Send a supervisor**—In a domestic violence call, send a supervisor of higher rank than the officer involved and make an arrest if there is probable cause. If no arrest is made, the supervisor has to explain why in a report.

The model policy has some important shortcomings.[152] For example, it does little to address the "blue wall of silence"—the problem of cops investigating their own. It recommends merely that investigations be conducted by a department's domestic violence unit or, if such a unit doesn't exist, the criminal investigations unit or detective division—or possibly an outside police agency. The door is still wide open to conflict of interest and "professional courtesy."

"You can't possibly investigate a member of your department the same way you investigate an average case," Vernon Geberth, a retired lieutenant-commander in the New York Police Department and author of a widely used text, *Practical Homicide Investigation*, told PBS in 2013. "Because people know each other as friends, you leave yourself open to criticism."[153]

The model policy also counts heavily on cops and families to ask for help if they have problems—even though it's clear most won't do so. "In our job,

---

[152] See Appendix D for a more detailed list of the policy's recommendations, discussion of its flaws and alternative guidelines.
[153] Sarah Childress and Alexander Hyacinthe, "How Should You Investigate a Death?" PBS *Frontline*, November 23, 2013, accessed March 21, 2015,
http://www.pbs.org/wgbh/pages/frontline/criminal-justice/death-in-st-augustine/how-should-you-investigate-a-death/.

admitting a personal weakness has always been tantamount to proclaiming yourself a member of the Wimp Squad," Renae Griggs, a former Florida major crimes detective, said in one article.[154]

The IACP guidelines also don't address the broader issue that policing appears to attract people with a desire for power and control over others—a key trait shared with abusers—or that it may implant that desire in cops. Current pre-hire screening obviously isn't fully effective; abusive officers continue to make headlines. And no systematic post-hire screening is suggested to identify cops who develop controlling behaviours on the job—apart from ad hoc monitoring by supervisors, who may be abusers themselves.

In fact, the model policy may in some ways make life harder for abused partners of cops. That's because it encourages police to work more closely with domestic violence advocates. This makes sense as a way to help other abused women, but when it comes to cops' spouses such efforts can "blur professional and personal boundaries resulting in the corruption and compromise of the advocates' role," retired abuse counsellor Diane Wetendorf warns.

"Many advocates have told me that their agencies shy away from assertively advocating for police victims due to fear of jeopardizing the agency's good relationship with the police; others say they fear retaliation against their programs and/or staff members. Victims sense this hesitancy."[155]

Yet, despite its flaws, the IACP model policy was a beginning and an important milestone. In an accompanying "concepts and issues paper," the IACP said domestic violence in police homes is "at least as common" as in the general population. It acknowledged that abused police spouses are "especially vulnerable. Police officers are usually well known within the criminal justice community and may be well respected in law enforcement circles. Victims in these circumstances may feel powerless."[156]

One of the key reasons to take action, the IACP said, is to limit a police department's exposure to lawsuits from abused spouses or their estates if they are killed. Having a policy may help get a department off the hook because it can argue that at least it tried to do something. "The IACP believes

---

154 Gallo, "A Family Affair."

155 Diane Wetendorf, "Police-Perpetrated Domestic Violence: An Advocate's Pessimistic Historical Perspective," *Domestic Violence Report* 19, no. 3 (February/March 2014), accessed April 14, 2015,
http://www.abuseofpower.info/Wetendorf_Pessimist.pdf.

156 "Domestic Violence by Police Officers; Concepts and Issues Paper," International Association of Chiefs of Police, July 2003, accessed March 20, 2015,
http://www.theiacp.org/Portals/0/documents/pdfs/MembersOnly/DomesticViolenc ebyPolicePaper.pdf.

that the presence of a clearly delineated policy and adequate training positions a department to reduce risk for charges of liability."

That liability came into sharp focus in 2003 in the gritty industrial Pacific Northwest port city of Tacoma, Washington. At 3 p.m. on April 26, 2003, Crystal Judson-Brame was speaking with her mother Patty on a cell phone while walking from her car to the pharmacy in a shopping mall parking lot.

"I think I see David," she said referring to her estranged husband David Brame, the chief of the Tacoma Police Department. Brame had just pulled into the parking lot in another car with the couple's two children.

Crystal's father Lane Judson, at home with Patty, told his wife, "If she sees him [David], tell her to get the hell out of there."

But Crystal ended the call. "I gotta go, I gotta go, I gotta go," she said.

Patty Judson tried to call her daughter back seven times in the next 12 minutes, but there was no answer. In the parking lot, Crystal returned to her car. But David slipped past her into the driver's seat and sat with his feet on the ground, stopping her from getting into her vehicle. Witnesses heard raised voices.

"Oh no, don't. Don't!" Crystal was overheard saying.

David Brame suddenly pulled Crystal's head down—or she may have crouched to protect herself; it's not clear. The police chief drew his .45-calibre Glock service pistol and shot Crystal at point-blank range behind the left ear.[157]

---

[157] Martha Modeen, "Brame ends wife's hopes for a new life; When the police chief's private life became public, he made good on his threats," *The News Tribune* of Tacoma, September 16, 2003. This account also draws on "Tacoma Confidential: Did Keeping Secrets Lead to Murder?" CBS News *48 Hours*, September 25, 2003, accessed March 21, 2015, http://www.cbsnews.com/news/tacoma-confidential/; "Tacoma Confidential," CBS News *48 Hours*, June 9, 2004, accessed August 11, 2015, http://www.cbsnews.com/videos/tacoma-confidential/; and *The News Tribune*'s story archive on the tragedy: http://www.thenewstribune.com/search/?q=david+brame.

Two months before she was killed, Crystal petitioned to change her name from her married name, Crystal Brame, to her maiden name of Crystal Judson as part of her application to divorce David Brame, but the divorce was never finalized. The monument at her grave reads "Crystal DeEtte Judson." Out of respect for her name change request and her family's wishes, this book refers to her as Crystal Judson-Brame. See Lisa Kremer, "Haley, David tell teachers their last name is Judson," *The News Tribune* of Tacoma, September 5, 2003.

Crystal fell forward, a quarter turn to the right toward the rear of the car. David then shot himself in the right temple and fell backward while the couple's two young kids sat in the other car nearby.

The children ran to their parents, their eight-year-old daughter screaming, "Daddy shot mommy! Daddy hurt mommy!"

With attention nationwide focused on the terrible incident, Tacoma city officials at first said Brame had been a good police chief and that the murder-suicide was "completely unexpected." But evidence soon emerged that officials had covered up for Brame and refused to heed warning signs or take action that may have averted the tragedy.

Investigators quickly found that red flags were apparent even when Brame was first hired as a cop. As part of the screening, a psychologist recommended against his hiring. A second psychologist said Brame was "deceptive," "defensive" and a "marginal" applicant. Brame had also failed the behavioural portion of the entrance exam at another local police agency, the second psychologist noted.

The Tacoma Police Department ignored the concerns and hired Brame, the son of a cop, anyway. As a police officer, Brame was the subject of a rape complaint and an allegation that he had threatened a girlfriend with his gun, though investigations never led to charges. He rose through the ranks and eventually became chief of police.[158]

At home, David Brame was exceptionally controlling, checking on his wife's whereabouts and receipts and giving her $100 every two weeks for household expenses for the family of four, according to people who knew the couple. He reportedly called her "fat" and "ugly," saying no man would want her.[159]

"He would say, 'You know, I can choke you out so quickly or I can snap your neck,'" Crystal's mother Patty later said. He reportedly tried to badger Crystal into participating in threesomes and foursomes.

In a declaration she filed as part of a divorce application a month before she was murdered, Crystal said her husband had tried to choke her twice in the previous six months, said he could break her neck and pointed his service

[158] Stacey Mulick, "Brame got 2 thumbs down: 'Marginal applicant, prognosis poor,' psychologist said in '81," *The News Tribune* of Tacoma, May 10, 2003. See also Jeffrey M. Barker and Sam Skolnik, "Tacoma police knew Brame had been accused of rape," *Seattle Post-Intelligencer*, May 9, 2003, accessed March 21, 2015, http://www.seattlepi.com/news/article/Tacoma-police-knew-Brame-had-been-accused-of-rape-1114454.php. See also David Seago, "David Brame's worst enemy: himself," *The News Tribune* of Tacoma, April 27, 2003.
[159] "Tacoma Confidential," CBS News *48 Hours*.

gun at her saying, "Accidents happen." "I do remain very afraid of my husband," she said.

Around the time of this declaration, Crystal told Assistant Police Chief Catherine Woodard that David had threatened to kill her, investigators later learned. Instead of reporting the allegation or starting an investigation, Woodard turned her notes about the conversation over to David Brame.

Woodard then surprised Crystal by tagging along with Brame when he went to pick up the couple's kids. Woodard reportedly acted in an aggressive and intimidating manner toward Crystal, who felt so daunted she later called 911 to report the troubling incident. A group of police officers learned of Woodard's visit and sent an anonymous note to then-city manager Ray Corpuz Jr. calling for an investigation. Corpuz rejected the idea.[160]

Stories about the abuse allegations came out in local media in the days before Crystal was murdered. Instead of taking any action, Corpuz defended the police chief. "I'm not interested in investigating any civil proceedings that he [Brame] is going through at this time," he told Tacoma's *News Tribune* newspaper, saying Brame was "doing a great job." Tacoma Mayor Bill Baarsma also dismissed the allegations as a "private matter," calling Brame an "outstanding chief." Also unheeded was a recommendation from city human-resources officials that Brame's gun and badge be taken away.[161]

Crystal's parents and other family members filed a $75-million wrongful-death suit against the city of Tacoma and the local county, saying officials failed to deal with Brame's behaviour and protect Crystal. In 2005, Tacoma agreed to settle the suit by paying the couple's orphaned children and Crystal's estate $12 million. As part of the settlement, the city also pledged to improve police procedures and declare April 26 each year Domestic Violence Awareness Day. In a separate settlement, the county agreed to create the Crystal Judson Family Justice Center, which offers free food, help and shelter to domestic violence survivors.

---

[160] Sean Robinson, "Woodard's silence broke city rules," *The News Tribune* of Tacoma, March 1, 2005. See also Sean Robinson, "Investigators condemn Woodard's judgment," *The News Tribune* of Tacoma, November 18, 2003; Sean Robinson, "Woodard notes tell of Crystal complaints," *The News Tribune* of Tacoma, June 29, 2003; and "Call to Review Police Chief Who Killed Was Unheeded," Associated Press, May 24, 2003, accessed March 21, 2015, http://www.nytimes.com/2003/05/24/national/24TACO.html.

[161] Ruth Teichroeb, "Tacoma police chief's wife says he pointed a gun at her," *Seattle Post-Intelligencer*, April 24, 2003, accessed March 21, 2015, http://www.seattlepi.com/news/article/Tacoma-police-chief-s-wife-says-he-pointed-a-gun-1113191.php. See also Sean Robinson, "10 years later: Looking back at former Tacoma Police Chief David Brame," *The News Tribune* of Tacoma, April 21, 2013.

Also in 2005, Tacoma settled a second lawsuit stemming from David Brame's behaviour. It paid $750,000 to Tacoma police Detective Mary Herrman, who said Brame had sexually harassed her and offered to promote her if she agreed to a threesome with Brame and his wife. Others in the police department knew of the harassment, but no one did anything, investigations later established.

Crystal's parents also took their campaign to the state legislature. As his daughter lay dying in the hospital after the shooting, Lane Judson, a retired U.S. Navy chief petty officer and former manager at Boeing, had promised her he'd do everything he could to prevent such crimes from happening to others. In 2004, the Judsons' campaign convinced the state of Washington to adopt a law requiring all police agencies to have a strict policy on domestic violence involving police officers. Police must:

- Screen new hires for domestic incidents.
- Respond immediately to reports of domestic violence by cops and conduct independent investigations.
- Share those reports with other concerned agencies (since officers may live in a different jurisdiction than where they work).
- Remove weapons from accused cops.
- Discipline problem officers.

But the Judsons knew the problems went beyond their state. They continued their campaign on the national level and scored another breakthrough in 2005 when they convinced Congress to vote to create the Crystal Judson Brame Domestic Violence Protocol Program as part of legislation to extend the Violence Against Women Act.

The measure, signed by President George W. Bush into law in 2006, gave law enforcement agencies access to a grant fund (currently worth about $220 million annually) that they could use to create programs to stop police officers from committing domestic violence, sexual assault and other crimes and to help survivors of such crimes.

"We just were so happy. It was the best Christmas present you could ever get," Lane Judson told *The News Tribune* newspaper. "Law enforcement agencies should be setting an example, and there's a serious problem nationwide," then-Representative Norm Dicks, whose congressional district covered most of Tacoma, told *The News Tribune*.[162]

---

[162] Paul Sand, "Congress passes Crystal Judson bill to stop abuse," *The News Tribune* of Tacoma, December 19, 2005.

The Judsons' campaign didn't stop there. They've continued to speak across the U.S. and beyond about domestic violence in police and other homes, often bringing audiences to tears with their emotional account of the impacts on their family.[163]

The Brame shooting finally stirred some cops to change attitudes about spousal abuse in their ranks. David Thomas is a retired police officer from the Montgomery County Police Department in Maryland, who developed the department's domestic violence unit, the first in the state. Thomas toured the U.S. on behalf of the IACP to educate police about the group's model policy on police domestic violence after it was adopted in 1999.

Before the Brame tragedy, cops were generally unreceptive to his message. "They were incredibly resistant. There was a lot of push-back. It was almost to the point of, 'You have the audacity to believe officers would do such a thing?'" Thomas said in an interview.

But after Brame, Thomas noticed more openness at his education sessions. "The Brame case was a watershed. That's when you had people say, grudgingly, 'You have a point. I hadn't looked at it like that.' They realize they've been duped when taking the side of an individual who's been involved in criminal activity," he said.

During his initial years in law enforcement starting in the 1980s, Thomas said he himself failed to act when responding to domestic calls at officers' homes. "There was a lot of pressure on you not to do anything," he said. "You'd be ostracized if you do something. You'd be clearing the call without so much as taking a report, especially if there was an officer involved. If there was no injury, you were often just leaving them right there. That individual [the abused person] was never going to call us again."

Now retired from the police due to a service injury, Thomas heads the domestic violence education program for public-sector administrators at Johns Hopkins University. He is also helping the IACP update its model policy on police domestic violence. "I want to make it political suicide for an agency not to address this," he said. "Agencies can't just say, 'Well, I didn't know about this issue.' The policy has been out since 1999. The courts will say wilful ignorance is not an excuse. Ignorance is what it rises to."

Still, the problems endure. Even after the Johnson and Seng studies, the LAPD investigation, the IACP model policy and Brame, many police officials remain oblivious. In 2000, 39 of 50 police chiefs at small U.S. police depart-

---

[163] Lane and Patty Judson also maintain a website devoted to Crystal's memory and police domestic violence: http://www.lanejudson.com.

ments (or 78 percent) said they had no knowledge of police domestic abuse in departments where they had served, according to a study by psychologist Michael Campion published in the FBI's *Domestic Violence by Police Officers* report.[164]

The police chiefs, averaging 23 years in law enforcement, were asked where they ranked domestic violence by cops among problems in their department. "At the bottom. I don't know of any in 30 years," one said. "It is not a high priority because I don't see it as being a problem. In other words, I am not aware of any problems currently," said another. A third chief said: "Extremely low because we've had no allegations."

In 1995, only 9 percent of 123 U.S. police departments surveyed said they had different or higher standards for how to handle officers involved in domestic violence.[165] Nearly 20 years later, in 2013, the situation was only somewhat improved. Only a quarter of 56 large U.S. police departments had a distinct policy for officers accused of domestic violence, according to the joint investigation by *The New York Times* and PBS in 2013. And only one, Nashville, had adopted the IACP model policy in its entirety.[166]

What's more, as Philip Stinson's "Fox in the Henhouse" study found, the Lautenberg Amendment is widely ignored or flouted. Most officers convicted of domestic violence misdemeanours aren't terminated. "Many of the police convicted of misdemeanor domestic assault are known to be still employed as sworn law enforcement officers who routinely carry firearms daily even though doing so is a violation of the Lautenberg Amendment prohibition punishable by up to ten years in federal prison," the study said.

"Equally troubling is the fact that many of the officers identified in our study committed assault-related offenses but were never charged with a specific Lautenberg-qualifying offense. In numerous instances, officers received professional courtesies of very favorable plea bargains where they readily agreed to plead guilty to *any* offense that did not trigger the firearm prohibitions of the Lautenberg Amendment."[167]

In fact, in Florida, a cop has more chance of keeping his job if he is accused of domestic violence than for almost any other misconduct, *The New York Times* reported as part of its joint investigation with PBS. The newspa-

---

164 Michael A. Campion, "Small Police Departments and Police Officer-Involved Domestic Violence: A Survey," in *Domestic Violence by Police Officers*, 123-131.
165 Boyd et al., "Domestic Assault Among Police."
166 Cohen, Ruiz and Childress, "Departments Are Slow to Police Their Own Abusers."
167 In addition, the lack of a central registry of people convicted of misdemeanour domestic violence makes it harder to ensure officers are in compliance with the gun prohibition, the study said.

per used Florida's progressive freedom-of-information law to analyze thousands of arrests and misconduct allegations involving police and corrections officers. Those accused of domestic violence had four times more chance of keeping their job than cops accused of theft and 28 times more than cops who failed a marijuana test.[168]

Florida isn't unique. In Los Angeles, even after the Victor Ramos murder and Inspector General Katherine Mader's investigation, the police department still has a dismal record today. In 2013, the latest year for which records are available, officers faced far lighter discipline for domestic violence than for making false statements or getting in an off-duty altercation, LAPD discipline records show. Only 13 percent of those with a sustained domestic violence complaint in 2013 lost their job—versus 33 percent of cops involved in an off-duty altercation and 77 percent of those who made a false statement. For domestic violence, the most common punishment was an official reprimand or admonishment.[169]

Remarkably, LAPD officers may face even less strict treatment today than when Katherine Mader did her investigation in 1997. Only 23 percent of domestic violence allegations were sustained in 2011-13, LAPD records show—far less than the 40 percent that were sustained in 1990-97. In other words, the department has in some ways actually gone backwards.[170]

"In many areas of law enforcement in general, we've been moving with jet-like speed," David Thomas, the retired Montgomery County, Maryland,

---

[168] Cohen, Ruiz and Childress, "Departments Are Slow to Police Their Own Abusers."

[169] Los Angeles Police Department, "Discipline Report 2013," accessed May 12, 2015, http://www.lapdonline.org/discipline_report_2013. LAPD records also suggest severe underreporting or biased investigations of officer-involved domestic violence. LAPD officers were subject to only 15 sustained complaints on average per year from 2011 to 2013. In fact, if the LAPD's 8,000 male cops reflect the 4-percent abuse rate that U.S. women report, then 300 assaulted their spouse in the prior year. And if they reflect the 28-percent abuse rate that Albert Seng reported in his 1992 study, over 2,000 LAPD cops abused their spouse in the prior year. The latter figure is over 100 times the number of sustained complaints.

[170] Another example of continuing problems: In the Philadelphia Police Department, of 164 officers accused of domestic abuse in the previous five years, only 11 officers were charged with a crime and fired, according to a *Philadelphia Daily News* investigation. Just three were successfully prosecuted. Most of those who were fired got their job back. See David Gambacorta and Dana DiFilippo, "Domestic terrors," *The Philadelphia Daily News*, September 11, 2014, accessed November 28, 2016, https://web.archive.org/web/20160706140754/http://articles.philly.com/2014-09-11/news/53775430_1_police-officer-police-families-philadelphia-police-department. And as we saw in Chapter 6, the Puerto Rico Police Department today has an abysmal record of disciplining abusive cops, with the vast majority of those arrested multiple times for domestic violence still on the force.

police officer and domestic violence educator, told PBS in 2013. "But with respect to violence against women and in particular OIDV [officer-involved domestic violence], we're still moving at a horse-and-buggy pace."

Thomas dismissed the police claim that cops investigate each other impartially. "In theory they do, but in practice they don't. As law enforcement, we have a great deal of discretion. Time and time again you see people say, 'You're going to ruin this guy's career over this incident.' You continually hear this attempt to lessen what the individual has done. With other criminal activity, we don't do that."[171]

As if to remind us the problems haven't gone away, tragedy continues to strike. Case in point: In 2009, in Utica, New York, police Investigator Joseph Longo Jr. killed his estranged wife, Kristin Palumbo-Longo, stabbing her more than a dozen times in their home, then stabbed himself to death. One of the couple's four children discovered the horrifying scene on coming home from school that afternoon.

In an eerie repeat of events in Tacoma, Utica's then-Police Chief Daniel LaBella said the killing was completely unexpected—an incident "no one could have prevented or predicted." But Kristin's family filed a $100-million wrongful-death suit against LaBella, the Utica Police Department, the city of Utica and Mayor David Roefaro, saying they didn't do enough about Longo's troubling behaviour before the tragedy.

Kristin had contacted police at least five times in the weeks before she was murdered, saying she feared her husband might kill her and their kids, but police supervisors discouraged her from making reports or seeking a protection order, the lawsuit said. In a preliminary ruling, a federal judge agreed that the police actions may have "enhanced the danger to Kristin and amounted to deliberate indifference." The city settled the suit in 2013, paying the couple's children $2 million.[172]

---

[171] Sarah Childress, "A Systemic Failure," PBS *Frontline*, November 26, 2013, accessed March 21, 2015, http://www.pbs.org/wgbh/pages/frontline/criminal-justice/death-in-st-augustine/a-systemwide-failure/.

[172] Courtney Potts and Rocco LaDuca, "Utica police, LaBella sued in Longo murder-suicide," *Utica Observer-Dispatch*, December 28, 2010, accessed June 23, 2015, http://www.uticaod.com/article/20101228/NEWS/312289916. See also Rocco Laduco, "Judge upholds alleged LaBella, Roefaro links in Longo lawsuit," *Utica Observer-Dispatch*, March 1, 2011, accessed April 9, 2015, http://www.uticaod.com/article/20110301/News/303019900; and "City board approves $2 million settlement in Longo lawsuit," *Utica Observer-Dispatch*, December 18, 2013, accessed April 9, 2015, http://www.uticaod.com/article/20131218/NEWS/131219382/10287/NEWS.

While the U.S. has made some improvements, it clearly still has a long way to go. Meanwhile, in most other countries, progress has yet to even start. That includes Canada.

Canadians like to think of themselves as being ahead of the U.S. on social justice issues. But when it comes to spousal abuse in police homes, Canada—like most other countries—is actually back in the Stone Age. Canada's example is a case study showing just how much catching up police worldwide have to do.

CHAPTER 8

Meanwhile, in Canada...

Just before dawn on a bitterly cold January morning in 2000, a police tactical team took up positions outside a bungalow in the Ottawa suburb of Aylmer, Quebec. Heavily armed officers smashed in the front door with a battering ram and charged in with a squad of plainclothes police. Inside was Pierre Daviault, a 24-year veteran constable in the Aylmer Police Service.

Daviault, a sixth-degree black belt in karate, was arrested on 10 criminal charges for allegedly assaulting and drugging three ex-girlfriends between 1984 and 1999. He eventually pleaded guilty to five charges—three counts of assault, one count of administering drugs with the intent to commit a criminal act and one count of possessing a firearm. He resigned from the police a few days later.

Daviault was sentenced to three years' probation, with no jail time. "In the case of Mr. Daviault, we must privilege rehabilitation and not detention," Quebec Court Judge Jules Barrière said before pronouncing the sentence.[173]

The light penalty shocked one of Daviault's ex-girlfriends. Anne Berard, who had left Daviault in 1999 after a two-year relationship, went into hiding after he was arrested. She told *The Ottawa Citizen* newspaper she was "dis-

---

[173] Jean-Michel Gauthier, "L'accusé continue de clamer son innocence," *Le Droit*, September 22, 2000.

gusted" with the weak sentence. "I've lost everything. I'm so scared and stressed out."[174]

One of the women Daviault pleaded guilty to assaulting, a mother of four, first met him at the police station after her son had some trouble with the law, the CBC reported. "He called me at home, [and] asked me out for a bike ride. I kept saying no, but my children and my sister kept saying he's such a nice man," the woman said.[175]

The woman and her kids eventually moved in with Daviault. She said she often woke up covered in bruises, wondering what had happened to her. Her daughter eventually told her Daviault was drugging her and then physically abusing her, but the woman didn't initially believe it. She said she phoned police after Daviault lost his temper and got out of control with one of the children. "To me he's a very, very sick man, and I don't know how he got away with it for so long. I'm lucky to be alive," the woman said.

Daviault was unrepentant even after he pleaded guilty, saying he did so only because he couldn't afford to pay for his defence and dismissing the three women's "allegations" as a "pack of lies." "I am an authoritarian man. You can speak about it with my two sons," he was quoted saying. "But I am not a violent man."[176]

It wasn't Daviault's first conviction for domestic violence. In 1992, he was charged with assault with a weapon and destruction of property after he attacked his then-wife of three years. He pleaded guilty to a reduced misdemeanour charge of assault with a weapon and was fined $1,000, but served no jail time. He was only briefly suspended from the force, then afterward continued to respond to domestic violence calls.

After Daviault's more recent arrest, Captain Jacques Sabourin of the Aylmer police told me he had no concerns about Daviault answering abuse calls following his first conviction. "When this person was on duty, he was a good police officer," Sabourin said. "Why would there be a concern?"

In an article in *The Ottawa Citizen* newspaper, Aylmer Police Chief André Langelier also defended Daviault, saying he was "a good policeman," while

[174] Don Campbell and Aaron Sands, "Ex-officer gets three years' probation," *The Ottawa Citizen*, September 22, 2000, C1.
[175] "Officer pleads guilty to 10 domestic abuse charges," CBC.ca, June 15, 2000, accessed March 22, 2015, http://www.cbc.ca/news/canada/officer-pleads-guilty-to-10-domestic-abuse-charges-1.239754. (Note that this article stated incorrectly that Daviault pleaded guilty to 10 charges.)
[176] Gauthier, "L'accusé continue de clamer son innocence."

the department's Sergeant Robert Saumure said, "The charges against him have nothing to do with his work as a police officer."[177]

The stories of Pierre Daviault and RCMP Constable Jocelyn Hotte show that police domestic violence is not just a U.S. problem. How common is it in Canada and other countries outside the U.S.? No one has done a study, but a few Canadian police officers are concerned and have taken the bold and risky step of speaking out. They believe Canada is on par with the U.S. when it comes to the prevalence of abuse in police homes.

Sergeant Amy Ramsay, a senior policy analyst at an Ontario police force, was one of the first police officers I interviewed on the problem in 2000. "The Canadian side is not that much different from the American. But it is kept quite quiet. Most police forces in Canada are very, very, very reluctant to give out information on that," she told me.

Ramsay was president of the International Association of Women Police and the founder and first president of the group Ontario Women in Law Enforcement. Before joining her current agency, where she has now worked for 20 years, Ramsay spent eight years with the Peel Regional Police, in the Toronto suburbs of Mississauga and Brampton.

"More than a couple" of the officers there openly boasted about beating up their wives, she said. "The guys talked about it in the report room and laughed about it. It was a joke to them. I never saw anyone take it seriously. It's been swept under the rug for years."

I later got back in touch with Ramsay to ask if she'd speak about her concerns on the CBC-TV investigative program *Disclosure*, where I worked as a researcher and associate producer. She agreed. "Abusers tend to be dominating and possessive," she said on the program in 2002. "That draws them more to a field like policing, where there's the authority, the gun, the badge and the power that goes along with that. It's kind of a perfect situation for an abuser to gain more control and authority.

"No police service anywhere wants it to get out that they have a serving officer who has been convicted of domestic violence. A lot of people refer to it as police's dirty little secret because so much of it is swept under the carpet and has been for years."[178]

---

[177] Aaron Sands and Gary Dimmock, "Aylmer police officer charged with assault: Man faces 10 charges; three women say they were drugged," *The Ottawa Citizen*, January 29, 2000, C1/Front.

[178] Amy Ramsay, interview, "Dirty Little Secret," CBC News: *Disclosure*, March 12, 2002.

Ramsay paid a price after speaking out. In her contribution in Appendix A of this book, she recounts how a supervisor told her, "Amy, you will never be promoted further... because you carry too much baggage. You speak up on things like police spousal abuse, and the police don't like that." Indeed, she never did get any further promotions. This, despite accumulating seven university degrees, including two PhDs (one in criminal justice and a second in management and organization) and two master's degrees in education and criminal justice, and having taught at the Ontario Police College.

"I never forgot those words," Ramsay writes, "because I always wondered if they would seal my fate. It turns out: They did." But she adds, "I have absolutely no regrets. I think that I at least introduced the topic."

Today, 16 years after we first spoke, Ramsay believes police in Canada have not made any progress on the question. "I wish I could say I have witnessed an improvement—no matter how small," she writes. "I cannot."

I also talked to Margaret Shorter, a RCMP staff sergeant who trained Mounties in ethics and management skills. In a 2003 story for *The Georgia Straight*, a Vancouver weekly, she told me she was "blown out of the water" when she first heard of the high rates of police domestic violence in the U.S. Shorter was one of the first women to join the RCMP and the first to become a noncommissioned training officer in British Columbia.

"Statistically, they [abusers] have to be here [in the RCMP]. That's the part that alarms me," she said. "It's not talked about anywhere. It's back in the places where other issues were decades earlier. It's very much a whispers-on-the-grapevine thing."

Now retired after 36 years on the force, Shorter is president of the International Association of Women Police. She told me the problems haven't gone away. "Considering the data on abuse in the population at large, abusers must exist in police agencies as they do everywhere else. The added challenges for the victim of an abuser who is also part of the police fraternity would seem insurmountable. No wonder it is not talked about," she said.

Another officer I spoke to early on was Inspector Rita Westbrook of the Waterloo Regional Police Service in Ontario. She was at the time the longest-serving woman on the force and was later promoted to superintendent. (She has since retired after 35 years as a cop.) "We are probably reflective of what's going on in the U.S. [with police domestic violence] because our cultures are similar," she told me. "We differ in a lot of ways, but we are more similar than we are different."

Albert Seng, the Arizona cop, agreed. "I think the job itself is pretty similar throughout North America—pretty much the same stressors, same pressures.... I would think the figures would be very, very similar [in Canada]."

And just like in the U.S., Canadian cops have time after time gotten away with domestic violence, facing only token punishment. Except in extreme cases, even a convicted officer rarely loses his job, hardly ever sees the inside of a prison cell and very often doesn't end up with a criminal record. Here are some notable stories.

2000

The RCMP promoted Rex Brasnett, an officer with a domestic violence conviction, to sergeant and put him in charge of the force's general-investigations section in Alberta, which handles serious crimes including domestic assaults.

In 1991, Brasnett was convicted of assault causing bodily harm to his wife, also an RCMP officer. His wife testified that Brasnett, who outweighed her by 40 kilograms, hit her head half a dozen times on the kitchen floor, struck her face and choked her unconscious, while using his free hand to take $200 from her purse. Brasnett admitted choking his wife but said she never lost consciousness. He said she had borrowed the $200 from him.

Judge Ross McBain called the woman's injuries "relatively minor" and sentenced Brasnett to just a single day in jail, a $2,000 fine and a weapons prohibition. Brasnett successfully appealed the weapons restriction.

In the decade after his conviction, he was promoted twice. Defending the second promotion, RCMP Superintendent Dennis Massey said in 2000 that Brasnett had paid his dues. "He made a mistake, and I don't know the circumstances, so it's not fair for me to comment," he said. "I do not believe this is relevant today."[179]

2000

Eight female officers in the Toronto Police Service said they were abused in relationships with fellow cops, but when they complained to police, they were stigmatized while their abusers were protected. Several of the women met then-Police Chief Julian Fantino to discuss their complaints and seek a zero-tolerance policy on police domestic violence. They said other police-women had similar complaints.[180]

---

[179] Lisa Gregoire, "RCMP officer with record to head crimes division," *The Calgary Herald*, March 10, 2000, A1.

[180] Alex Roslin, "Violent Secrets; They're women in uniform married to cop husbands who beat them and get away with it," *NOW*, December 7, 2000, accessed March 22, 2015, https://nowtoronto.com/news/violent-secrets/. Julian Fantino was later elected as a Conservative Member of Parliament and appointed as the Associate Minister of National Defence.

"I feel betrayed because I'm part of that brotherhood," one of the officers told me in 2000. "I do a good job—I'm a good copper. I, too, wear a uniform, and I'm very proud. But to know these sons of bitches are still there, that's hard to take. It was all covered up. Nothing was done. I thought he was going to kill me. How can you let him keep his gun and stay on the street?"

The eight officers said police investigations into their complaints were bungled and key evidence was lost, that they themselves were subjected to investigations, that their confidentiality wasn't upheld and that other officers interfered to protect the abuser.

When the women filed complaints about the abuse to police, they said investigating officers often deliberately derailed the case. Some of the women faced pressure from other officers to drop complaints. "They don't investigate as much as they would for another citizen," one of the officers told me. "If they can destroy evidence, they will. [The accused officers] know what it takes to build a case, and that's how they slip through the cracks. They can be very sneaky."

In a document outlining their concerns, the women said police investigations and court proceedings "only served to further victimize the victim." The police department's inaction left the officers feeling powerless and worried about their safety and that of their families. "I live in a state of hyper-alertness. I have to, for my own safety," one of the women told me. "I literally left my life. I feel like I was imprisoned in my home."

"I was treated like a troublemaker because I was trying to assert my rights. I'm very disturbed about the way the department handled it," another officer said. Her colleague agreed: "The common theme is that all of our careers are affected, while most of the men didn't suffer any career repercussions. Some got promoted."

The meeting with Chief Fantino was the second in three years. In 1998, several of the same policewomen met with the previous police chief, David Boothby, to try to get action on the concerns, but they said there was no improvement. One of the female officers who set up the meeting with Fantino later said the effort was a mistake and that the chief just gave the women "lip service," making no substantive changes.[181]

---

[181] In response to the women officers' concerns, the Toronto Police Service did an internal review in September 2000 that recommended a number of fairly anodyne policy changes that fell far short of the model policy of the International Association of Chiefs of Police. As it happened, most of the recommendations didn't end up being implemented because the department determined they were already being followed or needed to be reworded, according to freedom-of-information documents obtained by CBC-TV's *Disclosure* program, which aired an investigation of police domestic violence in 2002 that I helped research. The review also found 160 Toronto officers on

2007

Toronto police officer Richard Wills was convicted of the 2002 murder of his mistress Linda Mariani, whose body remained hidden in his basement for four months before it was found. His job at the time was to follow up on domestic abuse complaints.

Prosecutors said Wills was possessive and grew enraged when Mariani wouldn't leave her husband. He hit Mariani in the head with a baseball bat, strangled her with a skipping rope, then put her body in a garbage can and hid it behind a false wall in his basement, prosecutors said. Wills was sentenced to life in prison with no chance of parole for 25 years.

During the trial, Wills interrupted proceedings with outbursts, swore at his lawyers, court officials and the judge, urinated in a police car bringing him to court, threatened to punch the prosecutors and defecated in his pants in the courtroom in protest. He went through 10 defence lawyers.[182]

In 1984, Wills had previously been found guilty by a police complaints tribunal of striking a man two or three times while other cops pinned the man to the ground. He was docked 12 days of pay.[183]

2008

Ottawa police Constable Jeffrey Gulick, a detective in the spousal assault unit, was subdued with a Taser when he assaulted four Ottawa police officers and tried to escape from custody after a domestic dispute.

---

average each year approached the department's employee and family assistance program for help with "domestic issues" (a broad category that included domestic violence). The figure represented one third of all problems presented to the program. See Toronto Police Service, Domestic Violence Task Team, "Domestic Violence: A Review of Service Policy and Procedure as it applies to Members of the Toronto Police Service" (September 2000); and Sergeant Nadia Horodynsky, "A Report to the Domestic Violence Review Advisory Committee" (Toronto Police Service, November 28, 2001). As discussed later in this chapter, Toronto police didn't respond to requests for comment for this book and failed to reply to a freedom-of-information request.
[182] "Ex-Toronto cop guilty of murdering mistress," CTVNews.ca, October 31, 2007, accessed March 22, 2015, http://toronto.ctvnews.ca/ex-toronto-cop-guilty-of-murdering-mistress-1.262251. See also Peter Edwards, "Killer cop disgusts even Paul Bernardo," *The Toronto Star*, March 20, 2012, accessed March 22, 2015, http://www.thestar.com/news/crime/2012/03/20/killer_cop_disgusts_even_paul_b ernardo.html.
[183] Estanislao Oziewicz, "Constable faces murder charge," *The Globe and Mail*, June 18, 2012, accessed March 22, 2015, http://www.theglobeandmail.com/news/national/constable-faces-murder-charge/article1024097/.

Police came to Gulick's home after a neighbour called 911. Gulick was angry about failing a police test on restraining suspects and argued with his wife, overturned furniture, stabbed a couch and walls with a butcher knife and broke a phone. He threatened to kill responding officers, punched two in the face, kicked two others and reached for one officer's gun. Officers took him to a hospital where he escaped and was again subdued with a Taser.

Gulick pleaded guilty to assaulting a police officer, uttering threats to cause bodily harm, escaping custody and mischief. But his sentence was surprisingly mild: only a suspended sentence and two years' probation. He was later fired from the department after being found guilty of discreditable conduct in a disciplinary hearing. The Ottawa Police Association, the union representing the department's cops, said Gulick shouldn't have been dismissed and that the incident was just his "cry for help."

At the disciplinary hearing, one of the arresting officers, Sergeant Holly Watson, testified that fellow cops shunned her after the arrest and made her feel like an outcast. She also said that, unlike Gulick, she got no support from the police union.

"[There] was never any support for the four of us who were assaulted [by Gulick]," she said. "I used to have a fair number of friends in the partner assault unit. Now, I have to be aware of my surroundings because I don't know who I will bump into.... It was, poor Jeff this, poor Jeff that. No mention of the victims involved."

Another arresting officer, Sergeant James Heaphy, testified that the arrest quickly became a "life-or-death struggle" and that he later went on leave after being diagnosed with post-traumatic stress disorder. "I feel betrayed. I'm a strong believer that we have a brotherhood and we are there to support each other," he said. [184]

2011

RCMP Staff Sergeant Owen Wlodarczak pleaded guilty to assault and careless use of a firearm after hitting his former wife eight to 10 times in front of their two children, *The Kelowna Capital News* newspaper reported. He later put his police-issue gun to his head and told his wife, "You did this to me, woman."

---

[184] Meghan Hurley, "Officer's arrest leads to shunning; Disciplinary hearing told of fallout from domestic incident," *The Ottawa Citizen*, January 12, 2010, B1. See also Scott Taylor, "Violent cop acted 'superhuman,'" QMI Agency, January 12, 2010, accessed March 22, 2015, http://cnews.canoe.ca/CNEWS/Canada/2010/01/12/12428306-qmi.html; and Hurley, "Partner-assault unit rife with stress."

Instead of prison, he was sentenced to three years' probation and a conditional discharge (meaning no criminal record if he didn't violate probation rules) and was required to turn in his handgun at the end of work. An RCMP disciplinary panel decided not to fire Wlodarczak, citing his "outstanding" record, and instead demoted him to sergeant.

"They [the RCMP] created a monster," Wlodarczak's wife was quoted saying outside the courthouse after the sentencing. "With what he's seen and what he's been through... they need to do more. They need to take into account what's happening with their members."

She said it "wasn't the first time he's flipped out.... We can't force him to... go into a treatment centre because he doesn't think there's anything wrong with him."[185]

2012

Kevin Gregson, an RCMP officer, was found guilty of first-degree murder in the stabbing death of Ottawa police Constable Eric Czapnik four days after Christmas 2009. At the time of the murder, Gregson was suspended from the RCMP without pay due to a series of disciplinary violations. The RCMP had also taken away his police gun.

Before the murder, Gregson had argued with his ex-wife, who had accused him of raping a 10-year-old girl. The Mountie went in the bathroom and tried to commit suicide by stabbing himself in the throat. When that failed, he put on two bulletproof vests and headed out at night with his knife to find a random police officer and take his gun, hoping to use it to commit suicide. He stole a car and drove around Ottawa until he came upon Czapnik, a father of four, outside a hospital. Gregson killed Czapnik in a struggle for his gun. He was sentenced to life in prison with no chance of parole for 25 years for the murder.[186]

In a separate later case, Gregson was also found guilty of four counts of sexual assault causing bodily harm for repeatedly raping a 10-year-old girl.

---

[185] Kathy Michaels, "Kelowna cop gets conditional sentence for beating estranged wife," *The Kelowna Capital News*, August 9, 2011, accessed March 22, 2015, http://www.kelownacapnews.com/news/127280158.html. See also Andy Ivens, "Three years probation for RCMP officer who beat wife," *The Vancouver Province*, August 10, 2011, A4; and "Mountie demoted for attacking ex," *The Victoria Times Colonist*, December 22, 2011, A8.

[186] Gary Dimmock, "Gregson's jailhouse interview: 'I am a bit of a villain,'" *The Ottawa Citizen*, March 12, 2012, accessed August 13, 2015, http://www.ottawacitizen.com/Gregson+jailhouse+interview+villain/6294468/story.html.

He was sentenced to 10 years in prison to be served concurrently with the murder sentence.

The RCMP had a veritable avalanche of red flags about Gregson, including a tortuous history of run-ins with his superiors and a previous confiscation of weapons from his home—two shotguns, two rifles and a bow and arrows.[187]

In 2007, Gregson pleaded guilty to uttering a death threat after he pulled a knife on a Mormon bishop. He received a conditional discharge. The bishop agreed to testify in the case if Gregson got counselling. But despite several suspensions, including due to investigations for alleged domestic abuse and firearms violations, the RCMP never ordered the Mountie to get sustained counselling, *The Ottawa Citizen* reported.

In a statement to police, Gregson's first wife said he often intimidated her and others to get his way, according to *The Citizen*.[188] She said he forced her to have sex and once choked her in a rage. Gregson reportedly choked his second wife when she was pregnant until she blacked out and threatened to burn her parents' house down with her in it if she ever left him, *The Citizen* said.

Their children required therapy for their violent home life. Gregson reportedly once kicked his six-year-old daughter down the stairs, *The Citizen* said. On another occasion, he was said to have come home in uniform and pointed his service gun at his mother-in-law's head. "I am the authority in this house," he reportedly told her.

When his second wife said she wanted a divorce, he apparently dragged her up the stairs, threw her on the bed, choked her until she started to black out, then pulled out his police gun and pointed it at her saying he would kill her, *The Citizen* reported. He finally went to sleep in their children's bedroom with the loaded weapon.

In testimony at his murder trial, Gregson said he had difficulty coping with job stress and that this led to the breakup of his second marriage. "That's when I learned I was good at violence," he was quoted saying in *The National Post* newspaper.[189] He also testified about his previous work as a

---

[187] Chris Cobb, "Kevin Gregson: Lost in the line of duty," *The Ottawa Citizen*, April 22, 2010, accessed June 26, 2015, http://www.ottawacitizen.com/news/Kevin+Gregson+Lost+line+duty/2943869/story.html.

[188] Gary Dimmock, "The trouble with Kevin," *The Ottawa Citizen*, March 14, 2012, A1.

[189] Chris Cobb, "Accused Kevin Gregson explains the death of Ottawa police officer: 'I killed him, but I didn't murder him,'" *The National Post*, March 8, 2012, accessed March 22, 2015, http://news.nationalpost.com/2012/03/08/accused-kevin-gregson-explains-the-death-of-ottawa-police-officer-i-killed-him-but-i-didnt-murder-him/.

psychiatric hospital orderly where, *The Citizen* said, "he liked to provoke the most violent patients."[190]

2012

Former Toronto police officer Nebojsa (Ned) Maodus pleaded guilty to uttering a death threat against his wife and received a suspended sentence and probation for a year. "He indicated he was going to take his fist and punch hard enough so that it would go to the back of her skull," a prosecutor told the court. The Crown withdrew 11 other charges related to allegations of assault and threatening behaviour, *The Windsor Star* newspaper reported.[191]

In an earlier incident related to his ex-wife, Maodus was sentenced in 2007 to a year of house arrest and overnight curfew after pleading guilty to assault causing bodily harm, threatening and pointing a firearm. He was forced to resign from the Toronto police afterward.

Prior to these incidents, Maodus was one of five Toronto police drug-squad officers charged in 2004 as part of what then-RCMP Chief Superintendent John Neily called "the largest police corruption scandal in Canadian history." After a long court battle, the men were finally convicted in 2012 of attempting to obstruct justice (with Maodus and two others also convicted of perjury) and given conditional sentences of 45 days to be served at home. A jury acquitted them of more serious charges of theft, assault and extortion. An appeal court in 2015 dismissed their appeals of the convictions.[192]

2014

Former RCMP officer Chad Haggerty pleaded guilty to domestic assault against his ex-wife, also a veteran RCMP officer, *The Edmonton Journal* reported. Instead of prison time, he received a conditional discharge with three years' probation (meaning no criminal record if he sticks to the conditions) and was ordered to get counselling and perform community service.[193]

---

[190] Dimmock, "The trouble with Kevin."

[191] Craig Pearson, "Ex-cop hopes to turn page," *The Windsor Star*, August 30, 2012, A3.

[192] Timothy Appleby and Shannon Kari, "No jail time for convicted former Toronto drug squad officers," *The Globe and Mail*, January 4, 2013, accessed June 27, 2015, http://www.theglobeandmail.com/news/toronto/no-jail-time-for-convicted-former-toronto-drug-squad-officers/article6939338/. The appeal court sided with the Crown, agreeing with its suggestion of three-year prison sentences for the five officers, but then stayed the longer sentences because so much time had passed since the original sentences.

[193] Otiena Ellwand, "Former RCMP officer pleads guilty to assault," *The Edmonton Journal*, September 27, 2014, A11.

The assault occurred in 2004, but the case dragged through court for 10 years. "It speaks to the chaos in these systems and the value that we have on this issue that it would take this long to resolve," University of Calgary professor Lana Wells, a domestic violence expert, told *The Edmonton Journal*.

During the trial, the Crown prosecutor said two prior wives and a common law partner had all reported that their relationships with Haggerty ended because he was abusive going back to 1995.[194]

Haggerty was also involved in a series of other incidents. He was disciplined informally by the RCMP in 1998 for an off-duty fight, suspended in 2004 for using excessive force on two separate occasions and responsible for mishandling a drug case leading to charges being dropped against two people. He resigned from the RCMP in 2011.

Also in 2011, he pleaded guilty to assaulting a former girlfriend during an argument about how loudly he snored. In that case, he received a two-year suspended sentence and a 60-day jail term to be served intermittently (i.e. piecemeal on weekends).

What are Canadian police departments, governments and courts doing to prevent such cases? Not a heck of a lot, it seems. The inaction persists even after RCMP officer Jocelyn Hotte made national headlines for shooting his ex-girlfriend and her three companions in 2001. Hotte's high-profile murder trial should have been a clear wakeup call to Canadian police forces and governments about domestic violence in the ranks. As we saw in Chapter 2, every side in Hotte's murder trial—the judge, the prosecutor, the survivors, the police investigator, Hotte's defence and even Hotte himself—agreed that police should have done more before the Mountie went on his murderous rampage. The judge in the civil suit won by the three survivors said so, too. Yet, nothing changed.

Canada's do-nothing record endures also despite the various U.S. developments: the studies showing high rates of abuse among cops; the model policy of the International Association of Chiefs of Police adopted in 1999; the FBI's landmark conference on the problem and *Domestic Violence by Police Officers* report; and the high-profile David Brame murder-suicide in Tacoma, Washington, which sparked reform attempts across the U.S.

---

194 Jonathan Milke, "RCMP officer gets stiff sentence for domestic abuse," *Fort Saskatchewan Record*, April 26, 2012, accessed March 22, 2015, http://www.fortsaskatchewanrecord.com/2012/04/26/rcmp-officer-gets-stiff-sentence-for-domestic-abuse.

And despite Canada's mostly stricter gun legislation and a law-and-order Conservative government in Ottawa from 2006 to 2015, Canada still lags about 20 years behind the U.S. in keeping guns out of abusers' hands.[195]

To get an idea of how police in the U.S., Canada and other countries respond to abusive officers, I sent a survey in December 2015 to 178 police forces in 10 countries, including 68 in the U.S., 58 in Canada, 27 in the UK, 12 in France and eight in Australia. Most of my questions were drawn almost verbatim from the 1995 survey of U.S. departments done by the Arlington Police Department (see Chapter 4). No one had ever updated those results or asked them in other countries. In fact, as a sign of how little research exists on the issue, my questionnaire is the first survey ever done outside the U.S. on the police response to abusive cops. I am revealing the results for the first time here in the second edition of this book.[196]

In the U.S., only 38 percent of responding departments said they typically terminate an officer if a court or internal investigation finds they committed domestic violence. And just 33 percent have a specific policy on how officers should handle abuse allegations involving fellow cops. Not one department had adopted the IACP model policy on the issue. The results, albeit not great, were still an improvement over the 1995 survey results, which found that a mere 6 percent of departments normally terminated abusive cops, while 9 percent had different or specific rules on the issue.

---

[195] The Canadian government adopted new gun-control legislation, Bill C-42, in 2015 that prohibited firearm possession by anyone convicted of an indictable offence involving violence against a current or former intimate partner, their child or parent. Previously, a gun possession ban was automatic only for those convicted of an indictable violent crime eligible for a prison sentence of at least 10 years and certain gun-related offences. (Police officers aren't exempt from the old or new prohibitions.)

In contrast, as noted in Chapter 7, the U.S. banned gun possession back in 1968 by those convicted of any felony (the U.S. equivalent of an indictable offence) and in the mid-1990s extended the ban to anyone convicted of a domestic violence misdemeanour (the U.S. version of a summary offence), with retroactive application, and to violators of some domestic violence protection orders. While police officers and other government employees were exempted from the U.S. gun prohibitions for felons and protection order violators, they were subject to the ban for domestic violence misdemeanants. Canada's new law thus in some ways does not even catch up to the U.S. of the mid-1990s since it doesn't apply to summary domestic violence offenders or protection order violators, nor does it have retroactive application.

[196] See additional survey results in Appendix E. I am grateful to Gregory Smith, director of the Institute for Law Enforcement Administration at the Center for American and International Law in Plano, Texas, for permission to replicate questions from the 1995 survey.

The situation is much worse in Canada. In fact, Canadian police are at around the same retrograde level as U.S. police were back in 1995. Only 9 percent of Canadian police departments said they typically fire a cop after a domestic violence conviction or sustained complaint. Just 9 percent have a specific policy on the issue. Like in the U.S., none have adopted the IACP model policy. (In fact, as I report below, not a single abusive police officer was terminated in recent years at four of Canada's largest police forces, according to documents I got through access-to-information legislation.)

My survey also included a question asking how spousal abuse by cops ranks as a priority for the department. "Low to nonexistent. We don't have a high volume of this at all," said spokesperson Sergeant Lori Magee of the Saint John Police Force in New Brunswick. The Regina Police Service offered a similar reply: "Very low.... Domestic violence is not a systemic issue." Montreal Police Service spokesperson Anna-Claude Poulin told me: "The need for a policy isn't there. We are handling it fine."

The Vancouver Police Department, for its part, refused to answer the survey. "The questions themselves are written with inherent bias," spokesman Sergeant Randy Fincham said in an email. When told that the questions were largely based on an earlier survey led by a cop, Fincham didn't respond.

But as bad as the Canadian response was, at least there were answers. In the eight other countries surveyed, very few police departments bothered even to reply. While about one in three departments in the U.S. and Canada answered the questions, just four did so out of 52 police forces contacted in the other countries (or 8 percent)—two of 27 in the UK, one of 12 in France and one of eight in Australia. None at all responded in Ireland, South Africa, Jamaica, the Bahamas or Trinidad and Tobago.

Of the four departments that responded outside North America, just one normally terminated officers involved in domestic violence (the Metropolitan Police Service of London, England). And only one had a specific policy on handling police spousal abuse (Australia's Northern Territory Police Force).

In Canada, disinterest in the problem starts right at the top. At the 1,000-member Canadian Association of Chiefs of Police, knowledge about police domestic violence is virtually nil. "I can't honestly say from my perspective that it's a particular problem in our profession. Not that it doesn't exist, but I don't see that," Edgar MacLeod, then-chair of the association's crime prevention and community policing committee, told me in 2000.

MacLeod also told me he hadn't heard of the model policy of the International Association of Chiefs of Police on police domestic violence. (MacLeod later went on to become president of the Canadian police chiefs' group and is now executive director of the Atlantic Police Academy, in Prince Edward Island, which trains police and corrections officers and cadets.)

More recently, nothing has changed. Fifteen years after the IACP came out with its model policy, the Canadian Association of Chiefs of Police still hadn't endorsed it or made any recommendations to members on how to handle police domestic violence, spokesperson Tim Smith told me in 2014. "We've never studied that. We haven't adopted anything nationally within this area.... It's just something they haven't covered off."

Another missed opportunity occurred when the police chiefs' association released a 48-page report in November 2016 outlining best practices for how police should handle domestic violence in the general population. The report was developed over two years in collaboration with several academics, but devoted just a single sentence to cases involving cops. It called vaguely on departments to outline "steps to be followed" in such cases, giving no further suggestions. No mention was made, for example, of the IACP model policy.[197]

Meanwhile, I didn't get any reply to phone calls or an email requesting comment from the 50,000-member Canadian Police Association, whose board is made up of the heads of Canada's major police unions and associations.

Many Canadian police departments simply have no idea how many of their officers commit domestic violence. The data isn't compiled. "We're aware that, yes, it has happened in the past," said Heather Russell, a spokesperson for the RCMP's "F" Division, which covers Saskatchewan and includes over 1,000 Mounties. But she said her division did not keep any statistics. "We don't break it down," she told me in 2002.

Corporal Pierre Lemaitre, an RCMP spokesperson at "E" Division covering British Columbia, which employs over 7,000 Mounties, told me in 2003 he didn't have information on rates of domestic abuse by RCMP officers in the province either. "I can't track anything down here," he said.

Little had changed by the time I was writing this book and asked for an update from the RCMP, Canada's largest police force by far, with over 18,000 officers and another 10,000 civilian and public servant employees. No one was available for an interview, Mountie spokesperson Corporal Laurence Trottier told me. She responded to questions only in writing by email.[198]

---

197 *National Framework for Collaborative Police Action on Intimate Partner Violence*, Canadian Observatory on the Justice System's Response to Intimate Partner Violence and the Canadian Association of Chiefs of Police, March 2016, accessed December 7, 2016, https://cacp.ca/index.html?asst_id=1200.
198 Laurence Trottier, email to the author, May 14, 2014.

She said an RCMP officer convicted of domestic assault (or another crime) isn't automatically fired: "It is dependent on the case and is not automatic." The force rejects job applications from anyone involved in domestic violence, but only if the incident happened in the previous three years. The RCMP does, however, have the power to "mitigate" even this restriction and still consider the applicant.

The RCMP has compiled data on officers disciplined for domestic violence since the early 2000s, but Trottier said the information could only be obtained with a written access-to-information request. When I filed the request, the RCMP demanded an astonishing $29,280 fee to search for the information.

Trottier didn't answer a question about whether the RCMP changed any policies or training after Mountie Jocelyn Hotte killed Lucie Gélinas in 2001. She did say the RCMP had not adopted the IACP model policy on police domestic violence and had no specific policy on handling abusive cops.

Other Canadian police forces seem similarly blasé. "We don't have situations in the Vancouver Police Department where that has occurred," Vancouver police spokesperson Constable Sarah Bloor told me in 2003. "I have no reports on file currently of any officers who have been charged, nor do I have any over the last five years."

Nothing had changed when I approached the Vancouver police again more recently. "We don't really see domestic violence in police relationships as a problem here, in that we don't see incidents often," Vancouver police spokesperson Sergeant Randy Fincham told me. "Honestly, I can't remember the last time I heard of such an incident."

Like the RCMP, the Vancouver police have no distinct policy on handling domestic violence incidents in cop homes, don't give officers any special training on the issue and don't automatically fire officers convicted of domestic assault or another crime, Fincham said.

A recent domestic assault conviction "would drastically hinder your chances" of getting hired at the department, but it wouldn't necessarily eliminate an applicant, he said. "Depending on the circumstances of the assault conviction, it would be discussed to see if it has a bearing on employment."

Vancouver police also have no arrangements with neighbouring police jurisdictions to be informed if a member living outside the city is charged with domestic violence. And even if the department had data on domestic violence incidents among its officers, "I wouldn't be able to disclose that," Fincham said.

Meanwhile, I couldn't get any comment for this book from the Toronto Police Service, Canada's second-largest police force with 5,300 officers and 2,400 civilians. I left several messages via phone, email and the department's website seeking an interview with spokesperson Mark Pugash and other media relations staff. At one point I managed to reach Pugash and speak briefly with him. He said he'd get back to me but never did.

All this jives with the findings of University of Guelph sociology PhD student Danielle Sutton in her 2015 study on lenient sentencing of abusive cops in Canada (see Chapter 5). "The first step to addressing OIDV in Canada should be to make an OIDV policy *mandatory* for all departments to implement and enforce," she wrote.

Yet, she said, "departmental policies [on police domestic violence], or publically accessible versions, are non-existent in large police departments (i.e., Toronto, OPP, RCMP, Calgary, Vancouver, Ottawa, etc.)

"More progress is required.... Departmental policies designed to address OIDV should recognize that the behaviour is cultivated within the department and further fuelled by exposure to critical incidents, alcohol, authoritarian spillover and job burnout."[199]

Some provinces, recognizing the "professional courtesy" that officers extend to each other when investigating fellow cops, have created independent civilian-led agencies to handle some criminal investigations of officers. But such bodies aren't always an improvement. They often have a mixed investigative record, tend to be dominated by ex-cops and usually have a limited mandate that excludes all but the most severe domestic violence.

In Ontario, for example, an independent civilian-led body, the Special Investigations Unit, probes deaths, sexual assault and serious injury involving police—but just incidents that occur on-duty. It can investigate off-duty incidents only if the officer used police equipment or property or identified himself as a cop during the incident. The restricted mandate effectively excludes almost all domestic violence in police homes.

Even if the SIU can get involved, its record is dubious. In an investigation in 2008, Ontario Ombudsman André Marin slammed the SIU for its "impotent stance" and letting police control its investigations. "We heard repeatedly from SIU staff and members of the public alike that the SIU was essentially 'toothless,'" Marin said.[200]

[199] Sutton, "News Coverage of Officer-Invoved Domestic Violence," 117, 118.
[200] André Marin, *Oversight Unseen: Investigation into the Special Investigations Unit's operational effectiveness and credibility* (Ombudsman of Ontario, September

It turned out the SIU wasn't actually very independent at all. Its executive officer, all of its supervisors and three-quarters of investigators and forensic investigative technicians were former cops—mostly "white males in their 50s and older, who have retired from policing," Marin wrote.

The SIU was "so steeped in police culture" that many of its ex-cop investigators openly wore police watches, ties and rings. Some investigators confided that they'd "never charge a police officer," told police officials not to worry about cases under investigation and used derogatory police lingo, such as "shit rats" to describe anyone with a criminal record or "Jamaicans" for "anyone black assumed to have a criminal record," Marin said. He proposed 46 recommendations to boost the SIU's independence.

But despite the damning report, a *Toronto Star* investigation two years later found the SIU had actually gotten worse, not better. The portion of ex-cop investigators had risen to nearly 90 percent, *The Star* found. The consequences were plain enough in the SIU's miserable results. Out of 3,400 investigations since 1990, just 95 led to criminal charges and only 16 police officers were convicted of a crime. A mere three saw any jail time.[201]

Incredibly, those rates were even lower than the abominable performance uncovered in Inspector General Katherine Mader's investigation of the Los Angeles Police Department in 1997. In the LAPD's case (where cops investigated each other), prosecutors laid charges in 8 percent of investigations, while 1.8 percent resulted in convictions. Meanwhile, at Ontario's SIU, charges were laid in just 2.8 percent of investigations, while only 0.5 percent led to convictions. Ironically, cops investigating each other actually did far *better* than a supposedly independent civilian agency—with about a three times greater rate of charges laid and convictions.

But even after the ombudsman's report and the *Toronto Star* investigation, nothing had changed at the SIU by the time Marin did a follow-up review in 2011. He found that the Ontario Ministry of the Attorney General

---

2008), accessed March 22, 2015,
http://www.ombudsman.on.ca/Files/sitemedia/Documents/Investigations/SORT%2
0Investigations/siureporteng.pdf.
[201] David Bruser and Michele Henry, "Are these cops above the law?" *The Toronto Star*, October 28, 2010, accessed March 22, 2015,
http://www.thestar.com/news/gta/2010/10/28/are_these_cops_above_the_law.ht
ml. Then-SIU chief Ian Scott, who used to be a prosecutor, noted in a presentation before he joined the SIU that cops accused of using excessive force had a less than one-in-five chance of facing the same level of justice as a civilian accused of a similar crime, *The Star* said.

had ignored his recommendations and even "deliberately undermined" the SIU's attempts to reform.[202]

"In the past three years, the SIU has identified problems with police co-operation in more than one third of the cases formally investigated.... It is long past due for the SIU to be provided with the necessary powers and authority to carry out its mandate effectively, credibly and transparently," Marin said.

In Nova Scotia, the province created the Serious Incident Response Team in 2012 to handle criminal investigations of both on- and off-duty officers involving death, serious injury, sexual assault, domestic violence or "matters of significant public interest," according to the SiRT website.

The body has yet to be subject to an outside investigation, but it appears to be vulnerable to the same bias as Ontario's SIU. Its four-person investigative team is made up of two active-duty officers seconded from the Halifax Regional Police and RCMP, plus two retired Mounties who work as civilian investigators.[203]

In addition, police in Nova Scotia still have leeway to decide if a case should be referred to SiRT. "If an allegation is made, we need to validate the evidence, and if we come to believe there was an assault, it is referred to SiRT," said Jean-Michel Blais, chief of the Halifax Regional Police.

The Halifax police, like the RCMP and Vancouver Police Department, also don't automatically fire officers found guilty of a criminal offence, Blais said. "It depends on the severity of the file. It's case by case," he said. "We don't want our members to be so traumatized that they leave. We want to be able to discipline so the individual doesn't repeat and it is a deterrent, but we also want to ensure this person doesn't lose their fire to do their job." The Halifax police also have yet to adopt any kind of distinct policy on handling abusive officers, such as the IACP's model policy.[204]

---

[202] André Marin, *Oversight Undermined: Investigation into the Ministry of the Attorney General's implementation of recommendations concerning reform of the Special Investigations Unit* (Ombudsman of Ontario, December 2011), accessed March 22, 2015,
http://www.siu.on.ca/pdfs/ombudsmans_report_2011_oversight_undermined.pdf.
[203] "About SiRT," SiRT, accessed March 22, 2015, http://sirt.novascotia.ca/about. See also David Jackson, "Independent police investigators ready to take on complaints," *The Chronicle Herald* of Halifax, April 20, 2012, accessed March 22, 2015,
http://thechronicleherald.ca/novascotia/88680-independent-police-investigators-ready-to-take-on-complaints.
[204] Some other provinces have civilian agencies that investigate police, but their mandates generally exclude most officer-involved domestic violence. In Quebec, the civilian-led Bureau des enquêtes indépendantes investigates deaths, serious injuries

Faced with official nonchalance or an outright wall of silence, I filed requests in 2014 under freedom-of-information laws with five of Canada's largest police forces—the RCMP and city police in Toronto, Montreal, Vancouver and Halifax—for records on domestic violence incidents involving their officers. The response—or rather, nonresponse—was highly revealing.

The RCMP said it didn't compile the data in a "readily accessible" format and demanded an outlandish $29,000 search fee, while the Vancouver Police Department said it doesn't track abusive cops at all. The Toronto Police Service (again) didn't even bother to respond.

Only two police forces, the Montreal Police Service and Halifax Regional Police, provided even limited data. In both cases, this was merely a rudimentary one-page table listing cases and a perfunctory notation on how each was resolved. Though sparse, the never-before-released records confirm that police departments likely catch only a minuscule fraction of domestic violence in officers' homes, while the very few abusive cops who are nabbed seem to get more lenient treatment than civilians.

The Montreal Police Service sent data on 18 allegations of domestic or intrafamily violence against its officers in 2013 and the first half of 2014:[205]

- Four of the 18 allegations were deemed "unfounded"—leaving 14 allegations that were at least partially sustained.
- The most common result was no action (i.e. no discipline or criminal charges). This happened in seven cases (or 39 percent of all the complaints). The records don't say why no action was taken. (Chief Inspector Dominique Wérotte, head of the Montreal police internal affairs division, told me in these cases there wasn't enough evidence

---

and sexual assault allegations stemming from police operations or custody—a mandate that doesn't include most domestic violence.

In British Columbia, the civilian-led Independent Investigations Office conducts criminal investigations of police officers for off- and on-duty incidents involving death or "serious harm" (i.e. an injury that may lead to death, serious disfigurement or substantial impairment of the body, a limb or an organ)—again, excluding most domestic violence.

In Alberta, the civilian-led Serious Incident Response Team conducts criminal investigations of police officers for off- and on-duty incidents involving death, serious injury or "serious or sensitive allegations of police misconduct." Domestic violence is probed only if it involves aggravated or sexual assault or the discharge of a firearm at the victim.

[205] Montreal Police Service, "Statistiques 2013 et 2014 pour les policiers du SPVM qui ont fait l'objet d'allégation en matière de Violence conjugale et/ou Violence intrafamiliale," access-to-information release to the author, June 12, 2014. See Appendix E to view the data in table form.

for discipline or charges, but the officers were referred to the department's integrity unit for possible counselling or other intervention.)

- A criminal charge was filed in only four cases (or 22 percent of the total complaints).[206] That portion is less than a third of the Canadian public's arrest rate in the case of an accusation of domestic violence. (Seventy-one percent of police complaints about intimate-partner violence led to charges in Canada in 2013.[207])

- Four of the 18 complaints led to discipline for the officer, but no specifics are given on the punishment.

The Montreal police records show disturbing inaction on police domestic violence and paltry disclosure of information. Not included are details such as officer rank and unit, specifics of incidents and discipline meted out.[208] The records are also troubling because they show just how little police domestic violence is reported to the department: only about nine sustained cases per year on average, just three of them leading to criminal charges. They're implausibly low numbers that suggest extraordinary underreporting.

To put that in perspective, if Montreal's 3,200 male cops reflect the same abuse rate as Canadian women report, 60 male officers actually committed domestic violence in the previous year.[209] And if male Montreal cops reflect the 28-percent abuse rate that police reported in Arizona cop Albert Seng's 1992 study, 900 assaulted their spouse or girlfriend in the prior year. But with only three cops charged each year, that may mean only about one in 300 officers who are abusive actually ever face a judge.

Chief Inspector Dominique Wérotte, the man in charge of nabbing these cops, isn't worried. The internal affairs chief argued that the low number of cases is actually positive because it likely means his department is successfully screening out abusers during hiring. "It doesn't trouble me. I think it's good there aren't more," he said. But he acknowledged an alternative explanation could be that the department is catching only a fraction of abusive

---

[206] An additional fifth charge was withdrawn after a pledge to not disturb the peace.

[207] Statistics Canada, *Family violence in Canada: A statistical profile, 2013* (Ottawa: 2015), 36, accessed May 7, 2015, http://www.statcan.gc.ca/pub/85-002-x/2014001/article/14114-eng.pdf.

[208] Such specifics are available, for example, in the Los Angeles Police Department's discipline reports, which were discussed in Chapter 7. The LAPD's highly detailed quarterly reports are each about 60 pages long and are released online (i.e. without need for a freedom-of-information request).

[209] In 2009, 1.9 percent of Canadian women said they experienced domestic violence in the previous year, as we saw in Chapter 2.

officers. "It's possible. Like with all criminality, you never know the real number."

He said the Montreal police don't automatically fire cops convicted of domestic violence[210] and don't have a special policy on how to handle officers accused of abuse to reduce the chance of cops covering for each other. "It doesn't concern us. We have no cases on file of an officer voluntarily interfering with an investigation. I can't say it's a problem."

The situation is similarly sobering in the Halifax Regional Police. As in Montreal, Halifax police records show lax punishment and dismal information disclosure. The Halifax police only sent data on domestic violence complaints that resulted in discipline against an officer (with nothing about cases that were deemed unfounded or didn't result in discipline). Nine discipline cases were divulged from 2010 to 2014:[211]

- The most common result (in five cases) was in-house discipline alone, with no criminal charge. Apart from a cursory notation (i.e. "reprimand," "fine," "informal resolution"), no details are given on the discipline—for example, the amount of the fine.
- A criminal charge was laid in four cases (or 44 percent of the total).
- Halifax didn't disclose the total number of complaints, but even without this total, Halifax's 44-percent rate of laying charges is still much lower than the Canadian arrest rate of 71 percent when a member of the public is accused of committing domestic violence.[212]

As in Montreal, the minuscule number of cases in Halifax—about two officers disciplined per year, and just under one charged with a crime on average—suggests extreme underreporting. For comparison, if Halifax's 420 male cops reflect the same abuse rate as Canadian women report, eight of them committed domestic violence in the previous year. And if male Halifax police reflect the abuse rate in Albert Seng's study, 120 officers assaulted

---

[210] As explained in Chapter 5, under Quebec's Police Act an officer is fired automatically only if convicted of an indictable offence. In the case of an offence that could have been prosecuted as either an indictable or summary offence (such as assault or uttering threats), an officer can keep his job if he can show that "specific circumstances justify another sanction."

[211] Halifax Regional Police, "Appendix 1," freedom-of-information release to the author, June 19, 2014.

[212] The actual charging rate for Halifax officers would no doubt be lower if rejected and nondisciplined cases were included.

their intimate partner in the prior year. That suggests as few as one in 150 abusive cops may ever get charged.

But at least Montreal and Halifax disclosed a modicum of data, however trifling. The Toronto Police Service, in contrast, took nearly three months to reply to my freedom-of-information request and then did so only to ask for clarification about what I wanted. The department never did release any information in response to this request. (Ontario law gives organizations 30 days to complete an access request or notify the requestor that a time extension is required. No such notice was made.)

Meanwhile, at the Vancouver Police Department, an official said no data is compiled on abusive cops and that no disciplinary information about officers can be disclosed. "The Department does not retain or categorize police investigative records in a manner that would allow for ready identification of the police reports you seek.... The Department has no reasonable manner to compile the information you seek," Darrin Hurwitz, the department's freedom-of-information coordinator, said in an email. [213]

Hurwitz acknowledged the department "may have investigated specific allegations involved members," but he refused to release any details, saying the records are exempt from British Columbia's freedom-of-information law.

As for the RCMP, I followed spokesperson Corporal Laurence Trottier's advice and filed an access-to-information request for data on officers disciplined for domestic violence. Trottier had told me the RCMP has compiled such data since the early 2000s.

But when I filed a request for the data, the RCMP had a new line. It said it does not actually compile any information on officers disciplined for domestic violence and demanded $29,280 to do a manual search of human resources records going back 100 years. The RCMP acknowledged that "basic statistics" on discipline have been compiled for the past decade, but nothing "in a readily accessible way" specifically on domestic violence, so a manual search of each discipline file was needed. [214]

"We probably don't have the proper equipment to do this request," Romy Mounzer, an RCMP access to information analyst, told me. "We don't have a database that captures this information."

---

[213] Darrin Hurwitz, email to the author, June 26, 2014.
[214] RCMP, note in letter to the author, June 20, 2014.

After the run-around from the RCMP, I dug around on the force's website and was surprised to find the very data I had requested—available for free. Most of it was removed from the RCMP site shortly after and transferred to the government of Canada's web archives, which aren't as easily accessible.[215]

The RCMP's annual discipline reports show Canada's iconic police force does much worse than even the Montreal and Halifax police at catching abusive officers—even after Mountie Jocelyn Hotte's murder of Lucie Gélinas. And cops who do get caught mostly get very light punishment. In fact, the RCMP punishes officers for domestic violence less severely than for theft or making a false statement, the records show.

Just 10 RCMP officers faced formal discipline for domestic violence from 2008 to 2013.

- The RCMP meted out harsher discipline to Mounties who made a false statement (11 percent of whom were dismissed or ordered to resign) or committed theft (half were dismissed or made to quit) than those involved in domestic violence (none were dismissed or told to resign).
- The most common punishment for domestic violence was a reprimand and pay forfeiture (6.8 days of lost pay on average). Officers were docked more pay if they made a false statement (7.9 days on average) or committed theft (8.5 days).
- Only three of the 10 domestic violence cases, or 30 percent, led to a criminal charge. That's less than half of the 71-percent Canadian public's arrest rate for a domestic violence accusation. The RCMP doesn't reveal the total number of allegations against Mounties, so its actual charging rate is very likely even lower.[216]

---

[215] "Management of the RCMP Disciplinary Process: Annual Reports," RCMP, accessed March 23, 2015, http://www.rcmp-grc.gc.ca/pubs/adj/ann-report-rapport-eng.htm. As of July 2015, the RCMP site linked only the 2011-12 and 2012-13 reports. Three earlier reports have been moved to the government of Canada's web archives: https://web.archive.org/web/20141123074945/http://publications.gc.ca/collections/collection_2010/grc-rcmp/PS61-17-2009-eng.pdf (2008-09 report); https://web.archive.org/web/20141123074930/http://publications.gc.ca/collections/collection_2010/grc-rcmp/PS61-17-2010-eng.pdf (2009-10 report); and https://web.archive.org/web/20141114175549/http://publications.gc.ca/collections/collection_2012/grc-rcmp/PS61-17-2011-eng.pdf (2010-11 report).
[216] The RCMP rejects an extraordinarily high portion of complaints made against its officers, a *Toronto Sun* investigation found in 2014. It rejected 90 percent of 12,400 formal written complaints made against Mounties from 2010 to 2014. See Giuseppe Valiante, "RCMP rejects 90% of formal complaints," *The Toronto Sun*, October 27,

The numbers work out to a stunningly low two abusive Mounties disciplined per year on average—and 0.6 officers charged annually. When adjusted for the size of the RCMP, those rates are dramatically lower than the already abysmal rates of the Montreal and Halifax police for disciplining and charging abusive cops.

To put the RCMP's implausibly low number in perspective, if the force's 14,400 male officers have the same abuse rate as Canadian women report, about 275 Mounties actually abused their intimate partner in the prior year. And if male RCMP officers reflect the abuse rate in Albert Seng's study, over 4,000 Mounties assaulted their partner in the previous year.

The numbers may mean as few as one in 6,500 abusive Mounties is charged for their crime.

After the first edition of *Police Wife* was published in 2015, I filed a new set of access-to-information requests to the same five Canadian police forces. This time, the Toronto police and RCMP finally did cough up some information. It was, however, about as skimpy on details as the rudimentary one-page tables I got once again from the Montreal and Halifax police. Vancouver police, again, refused to release anything.

The documents, never previously disclosed, show that not a single abusive cop had been terminated from their job at any of the four police forces in recent years—even when the officer was convicted of a domestic violence criminal offence or disciplined for assaulting a domestic partner. [217]

Only one in five complaints of domestic violence led to discipline. The most common punishment was being suspended from work, in many cases with pay. Just 4 percent of complaints led to a criminal conviction.

What has Canada learned since Jocelyn Hotte killed Lucie Gélinas? Pretty much nothing, it appears.

2014, accessed March 24, 2015, http://www.torontosun.com/2014/10/27/rcmp-rejects-90-of-formal-complaints.

[217] Montreal Police Service, "Statistiques de 2013 à 2015 impliquant policiers SPVM qui ont fait l'objet d'allégation et/ou accusation en matière de Violence conjugale et/ou Violence intrafamiliale," access-to-information release to the author, March 7, 2015; Toronto Police Service, "5 year data for Domestic Violence and Domestic related arrests," access-to-information release to the author, May 27, 2016; Royal Canadian Mounted Police, untitled document, access-to-information release to the author, January 22, 2016; Halifax Regional Police, "Appendix 1," freedom-of-information release to the author, December 16, 2015.

CHAPTER 9

The Surprising Truth Behind Police Domestic Violence

We are all affected when a police officer abuses his family. He breaks the law with impunity and yet has extraordinary power and discretion to enforce the law on others, deprive them of freedom and even take their life. It isn't hard to see the problem.

But police domestic violence isn't simply about a few badly behaving cops. It is by all evidence a rampant, systemic problem—a serious job hazard for many police officers—rooted in the very nature of law enforcement and likely existing in any society where police have a similar structure. It thus requires systemic solutions.

Even a zero-tolerance police policy on officer-involved domestic violence does little to tackle the underlying causes of the abuse: power and control, anti-woman attitudes and impunity. The strictest policy will deal mostly with symptoms, not the deeper structural problems.

Without deep changes, the abuse epidemic thus appears inevitable in any country where police exist in the same form. It is likely to persist so long as and wherever police carry on as an institution focused on power and control, predictably attracting abusive men who shield each other from punishment and strive to maintain a male-dominated police culture. "Without fundamentally changing the cultural context within which police officers do their jobs, intimate partner abuse among officers is unlikely to decrease," said University of Maryland law professor Leigh Goodmark.[218]

Yet, it is hard to imagine our communities functioning very smoothly without police officers imposing their authority. Our society depends on a coercive police presence. This means police domestic violence is rooted in the very nature of our society. The question we are left with is this: Why do we need police to forcibly keep people in line?

Professional policing is a fairly recent human invention. The first large modern-day professional police forces emerged in the 1800s in Europe and North America as industrialization transformed farmers into factory workers in quickly growing cities. The social upheavals forced governments to create the "broad historical project of police," which had as its mission "fabricating a social and economic order," according to a study co-authored by Carleton University professor George Rigakos.[219]

"The police project, therefore, has a long history, emerging as a civilizing 'science'... and eventually as an essential system of order maintenance for the discipline of the indigent, the poor and the working classes."

Police play a similar role today. "Police power assumes its most formidable aspect when cops deal with the underclass. This is the group they've been pressured, implicitly, to control," said Anthony Bouza, the former New York Police Department commander and ex-police chief of Minneapolis. "When cops deal with the poor (blacks, Hispanics, the homeless and street people), the rubber of power meets the road of abuse.... The underclass must be kept in its place or the chief will lose his or her job. Cops are the cleaners of society's charnel houses." Instead of addressing racism in society and other problems that create an underclass, "the usual answer is to get the police to clean up society's failings," Bouza said.[220]

---

218 Goodmark, "Hands Up at Home," 41.
219 George S. Rigakos and Aysegul Ergul, "Policing the industrial reserve army: An international study," *Crime, Law and Social Change* 56, no. 4 (November 2011): 329-371.
220 Bouza, *The Police Mystique*, 4, 7, 93. Bouza also noted: "The fact that they [police] think of their precincts as embattled fortresses in alien lands reflects, at once, their problems with the minorities they've been sent to police and their resentment toward an overclass that has issued the *sub rosa* marching orders" (p. 6). In a later book, Bouza put it like this: "There is a clear, yet subliminal, message being transmitted that the cops, if they are to remain on the payroll, had better obey. The overclass—mostly white, well-off, educated, suburban, and voting—wants the underclass—frequently minority, homeless, jobless, uneducated, and excluded—controlled and, preferably, kept out of sight." See Bouza, *Police Unbound*, 13.

Statistics back up this view. The number of police officers per capita in the U.S., Canada and other countries is closely correlated with unemployment, income inequality and economic marginalization, particularly among women, African Americans, First Nations people and youth. The more inequality and marginalization, the more cops we tend to find.

For example, in 22 developed countries, including the U.S. and Canada, the per-capita number of police officers has a statistically significant correlation with the level of women's economic inequality and the unemployment rate, especially among youth.[221]

- **Unemployment**—A strong 58-percent correlation exists between the per-capita number of cops and the unemployment rate. In other words, the more unemployment, the more cops there tend to be.
- **Youth unemployment**—The correlation is even stronger—63 percent—for youth unemployment.
- **Women in the workforce**—A 46-percent *negative* correlation exists between police per capita and women's participation in the labour force. In other words, the more women stay home and don't work, the more police there tend to be. (One possible explanation is that employment empowers women and gives them more options to escape domestic violence. That in turn may mean fewer police officers are needed since, as we've seen, domestic violence is one of the main reasons for calls to police.[222])

---

[221] A correlation shows how much two sets of data fluctuate together. It doesn't prove one thing causes the other, but it can point to predictive relationships worthy of attention. When a correlation is statistically significant, it's very unlikely to be a random coincidence.

[222] The unemployment and labour force participation data is from the United Nations Development Programme, *Human Development Report 2014; Sustaining Human Progress: Reducing Vulnerabilities and Building Resilience* (New York: United Nations Development Programme, 2014), accessed July 18, 2015, http://hdr.undp.org/en/2014-report/download. I focused on the 22 developed countries for which I obtained data on the number of police officers per capita from "Most Heavily Policed: Countries," Bloomberg.com, last updated August 15, 2013, accessed March 24, 2015, http://web.archive.org/web/20141206083021/http://www.bloomberg.com/visual-data/best-and-worst//most-heavily-policed-countries. The female labour force participation rate may also correlate with police levels because gender economic inequality can exacerbate domestic violence. "Women's poverty has an enormous impact on women's experience of violence and their ability to leave it. Many poor women decide to stay in an abusive relationship because they cannot imagine how they could survive if they left," Ontario lawyer and domestic violence expert Pamela

In Canada, police levels also correlate very closely with unemployment among Aboriginal people (which is telling in light of police indifference to missing First Nations women, discussed in Chapter 6).

- **Aboriginal youth unemployment**—In 13 of Canada's largest cities, a strong 69-percent correlation exists between the number of police officers per capita and Aboriginal youth unemployment. In other words, the more young Aboriginal people are jobless, the more cops there tend to be.
- **Aboriginal male youth unemployment**—An even stronger 76-percent correlation exists with unemployment among Aboriginal young men.[223]

The patterns have a parallel in the U.S., where policing levels correlate with income inequality and economic discrimination against African Americans. It's not hard to see how such conditions would spark the Black Lives Matter movement.

- **Income inequality**—A 38-percent correlation exists between the number of police officers per capita in each state and income inequality (as measured by the portion of total income going to the top 10 percent of income earners). In other words, the more income is concentrated in a few hands, the more officers there tend to be.
- **Black unemployment**—Police per capita in each U.S. state also has a 42-percent correlation with the ratio of black to white unem-

---

Cross wrote in her paper "It Shouldn't Be This Hard," 56. In the U.S., female labour force participation in 132 large cities is negatively correlated with the rate of male-on-female homicides, which mostly occur in domestic situations, according to Ismail Nooraddini in "Gender Inequality and Female Victimization," Analytical Paper, January 7, 2012, accessed May 6, 2015, https://www.academia.edu/1576766/Gender_Inequality_and_Female_Victimization . "Full-time employment can often empower the victim to take charge and leave dangerous situations," Nooraddini wrote, noting that the finding supports the idea that "gender equality should lead to an environment less conducive to male on female violence."

[223] All of the Canadian correlations are statistically significant. For Aboriginal unemployment rates, see Statistics Canada, "2006 Aboriginal Population Profiles for Selected Cities and Communities," accessed July 6, 2015, http://www5.statcan.gc.ca/olc-cel/olc.action?ObjId=89-638-X&ObjType=2&lang=en&limit=0. The data for Aboriginal people includes both First Nations and Métis people.

ployment. In other words, the more African Americans are unemployed compared to white people, the more cops.

- **Black male unemployment**—The correlation is even stronger—55 percent—between police per capita and the ratio of black male versus total white unemployment.[224]

It's of course simplistic to say police exist only to mishandle calls about abused or missing women and oppress the marginalized. But the correlations do support Chief Bouza's claim that policing the "underclass" is a central part of a cop's life. A key tacit function of the police seems to be to preserve order in the face of the disruptive impacts of women's inequality, poverty, economic marginalization, discrimination and subjugation of First Nations people. By so doing, police in effect help to preserve these injustices.

This unofficial police role was alluded to by William Bratton, commissioner of the New York Police Department, after the first Black Lives Matter protests started in 2014 against a series of police killings of African Americans. Bratton blamed the protests on "pent-up frustrations. You need to understand this isn't just about policing. This goes to much larger issues. We're the tip of the iceberg at the moment. This is about the continuing poverty rates, the continuing growing disparity between the wealthy and the poor. It's still about unemployment issues. There are so many national issues that have to be addressed that it isn't just policing, as I think we all well know," he said.[225]

---

[224] The U.S. correlations are all statistically significant. Data on the number of law enforcement officers per capita in each state is from Federal Bureau of Investigation, Criminal Justice Information Services Division, "Crime in the United States 2013," accessed July 7, 2015, https://www.fbi.gov/about-us/cjis/ucr/crime-in-the-u.s/2013/crime-in-the-u.s.-2013/tables/table-77/table_77_full_time_law_enforcement_employess_by_state_2013.xls. State-level income inequality for 2012 is from Mark W. Frank, "U.S. State-Level Income Inequality Data," accessed July 16, 2015, http://www.shsu.edu/eco_mwf/inequality.html. Unemployment rates are from the U.S. Bureau of Labor Statistics, Local Area Employment Statistics, "Employment status of the civilian noninstitutional population by sex, race, Hispanic or Latino ethnicity, marital status, and detailed age, 2013 annual averages," accessed May 8, 2015, http://www.bls.gov/lau/table14full13.pdf.
[225] William Bratton, interview with Chuck Todd, *Meet the Press with Chuck Todd*, NBC, December 28, 2014, accessed November 28, 2016, http://www.nbcnews.com/meet-the-press/meet-press-transcript-december-28-2014-n279436.

Greg O'Connor, head of the 1.5-million-member International Council of Police Representative Associations, which speaks for police unions worldwide, made similar comments, saying politicians "should perhaps be asking the harder questions, about why 'the system' they preside over delivers, for far too many of its citizens, the social conditions that breed crime."[226]

Of course the remarks by Bratton and O'Connor were partly self-serving and meant to deflect responsibility from police for their actions. But they still made a valid point.

The data on correlations tells us an ugly truth about policing in our society—and in turn about what's really needed to stop police domestic violence. The family troubles of police officers are inextricably connected to the marginalization present in a highly unequal, divided society. In a different kind of society, we can imagine guiding people with abusive traits toward help and supporting anyone they hurt. In our society, too many of them get handed a gun, badge and uniform and taught to impose power and control more efficiently over others, then society looks away when some turn on their own families.

And far from getting easier, the burden on law enforcement to preserve order is growing. Since the financial crisis of the last decade, wealth disparity has risen to levels unseen since the 1920s, unemployment for African Americans and youth has gone up, and female participation in the labour force has declined in the U.S. and Canada.[227]

---

[226] "International police body responds to NYPD officer murders," International Council of Police Representative Associations press release, December 23, 2014, accessed March 24, 2015,
http://www.icpra.org/sites/default/files/Documents/E-news/icpra_media_release_re_brooklyn_shootings_dec_14_3.pdf.

[227] For wealth disparity data, see Emmanuel Saez, "Striking It Richer: The Evolution of Top Incomes in the United States (Updated with 2012 preliminary estimates)," September 3, 2013, accessed April 27, 2015,
http://eml.berkeley.edu//~saez/saez-UStopincomes-2012.pdf; and "Income Inequality," Conference Board of Canada, January 2013, accessed April 27, 2015,
http://www.conferenceboard.ca/hcp/details/society/income-inequality.aspx. For African American unemployment data, see U.S. Department of Labor, Bureau of Labor Statistics, "Household Data, Annual Averages, Employment status of the civilian noninstitutional population by age, sex, and race," accessed July 18, 2015, 2007 data, http://www.bls.gov/cps/aa2007/cpsaat3.pdf, and 2014 data,
http://www.bls.gov/cps/cpsaat03.htm; see also Aaron Morrison, "Black Unemployment Rate 2015: In Better Economy, African-Americans See Minimal Gains," *International Business Times*, March 8, 2015, accessed July 7, 2015,
http://www.ibtimes.com/black-unemployment-rate-2015-better-economy-african-americans-see-minimal-gains-1837870. For youth unemployment data, see "Canada

Inequality and economic hardship are fuelling growing social unrest in North America and worldwide. Expressions of this include the Black Lives Matter movement and the rise of reactionary and far-right movements in the U.S. (where they helped Donald Trump win the presidency), Europe and elsewhere. As the unrest grows, the best efforts of reform-minded police officers are likely to be swamped by the primary burden of law enforcement—to maintain law and order.

In service of this burden, police in many areas have already entrenched by becoming more militarized, adopting military-style equipment, training and tactics. In the U.S., police are likely to get even more entrenched if they take up Trump's call for stop-and-frisk police tactics and if the Trump administration scales back justice department efforts to investigate discrimination and misconduct in local police departments. And all these impulses favouring more police coerciveness mean domestic violence in officers' homes could actually get worse, not better.

If problems like inequality, joblessness and subjugation of Native Americans somehow disappeared, would the need for police vanish too? Such a scenario is hard to imagine and would require a drastically different society. But it's reasonable to think that any significant improvement in those areas would likely mean far fewer police officers and less coercion among those who remain. And that in turn could make a real difference for curtailing police domestic violence—and obviously impact lives far beyond law enforcement families, too.

Those who hope for a more just society would do well to make police domestic violence a key priority. The issue is a critical fulcrum for the entire system. That means abused police wives hold a key to sweeping social change. They are a terrorized and powerless underclass, literally at the heart of power and without voice, with the massive might of the state arrayed against them. Their conditions are so atrocious and precarious that not only

---

Youth Unemployment Rate, 1976-2015," TradingEconomics.com, accessed July 7, 2015,
http://www.tradingeconomics.com/canada/youth-unemployment-rate. For female labour force participation data, see TD Economics, "Falling Female Labour Participation: A Concern," October 24, 2014, accessed July 7, 2015,
https://web.archive.org/web/20160420204102/https://www.td.com/document/PDF/economics/special/FemaleParticipation2014.pdf; and U.S. Department of Labor, Bureau of Labor Statistics, "Labor Force Statistics From the Current Population Survey, Household Data, Historical, Employment status of the civilian noninstitutional population 16 years and over by sex, 2005 to date," last modified July 2, 2015, accessed July 7, 2015,
http://www.bls.gov/web/empsit/cpseea02.htm.

do they almost never speak out in their own name, but they also can't usually join other women and advocates to work together to improve their collective situation.

Most other disadvantaged groups collaborate publicly to build lasting social movements. Not police spouses. They usually wage their survival struggle utterly alone, in anonymity, with little or no help or knowledge of others in the same situation, each woman reinventing her struggle anew. Their unique position is why their condition is so little known and why improving their lives is so difficult. Real improvement can't happen without deep social changes on many levels.

But despite the powerlessness of abused police spouses, they do hold great power in their hands over not only their own fate, but also the entire social order. Because of the resilience and resourcefulness of the human spirit, police spouses like Amy Morrison and Dottie Davis do break free and speak out, and they do so more and more. In their titanic struggle, their accumulating voices are not only testimony to the horrors they personally overcame, but also to some of the most extreme conditions of inequality and injustice existing in our society—an indictment of a social order that makes their condition inevitable.

Very few of us ever see the personal impacts of police work on officers and their families, in large part because of the silence about police family violence. But we still feel the impacts.

Abused women feel the impacts when they call 911 and get an abuser at their door who mishandles the call or sexually harasses them. We as taxpayers feel the impacts when governments have to pay millions to settle lawsuits because police failed to protect a woman from violence or didn't act on sexual harassment in the ranks. We also pay when abusers engage in mass shootings when better police intervention early on may have prevented the tragedy. The families of missing women feel the impacts when police fail to investigate properly. African Americans, First Nations people, the homeless and others pay a price when a derelict officer singles them out on the street. Young women drivers feel the impact when a predatory cop harasses or abuses them at a traffic stop.

Not the least of the impacts is the corruption that is bred when public servants hired to enforce the law systematically engage in and cover up massive law-breaking that violates human rights and constitutional guarantees of equal protection. In this sense, the police home is the front line of a battle for our civilization's soul. As philosopher Hannah Arendt wrote, "The nation-state cannot exist once its principle of equality before the law has broken down.... The greater the extension of arbitrary rule by police decree, the more difficult it is for states to resist the temptation to deprive all citizens of legal status and rule them with an omnipotent police."[228]

And we are all impacted by the marginalization and gender, racial and other inequalities in our society, which police coercion helps stabilize and thus defend.

We must also weigh the critical impacts on police officers, their families and the community—on people like Lucie Gélinas, her children, Jocelyn Hotte and the three men Hotte shot; Crystal Judson-Brame, David Brame, their children and Crystal's parents; Amy Morrison and her daughters and husband; Dottie Davis and her daughter. Apart from the horror of domestic violence, the impacts on police families also include job stress, burnout, shortened lifespans, heart disease, obesity and divorce.

Police families pay a steep price for being on the frontline of upholding our uneven social order. Maybe in full knowledge of all these impacts, we may still feel the cost is fair and reasonable. After all, no one forces people to work as cops. Perhaps some lives do not matter as much as others, after all.

But perhaps we would balk at the terrible sacrifices required to maintain our social and economic system—particularly the epidemic of terror unleashed on police spouses and children, who are the unwilling collateral casualties of the defence of our social inequalities. It is a sacrifice that virtually no one honours these families for or is even aware of—a sacrifice the families themselves do not willingly make.

We may decide such a sacrifice is so outrageous and disgraceful that it calls into question the society that necessitates it. We may conclude that a social order must be reexamined if it compels systematic criminality and human rights violations—not to mention the far-reaching impacts beyond police families.

In order to assess if such sacrifices—and the costs to the rest of us—are what we want, we at least have to know about them. That is the ultimate truth of police domestic violence. It is a mirror reflected back on ourselves.

---

[228] Hannah Arendt, *Imperialism: Part Two of The Origins of Totalitarianism* (New York: Harcourt Brace & Company, 1994), 170.

APPENDIX A

Police and Other Voices

NO REGRETS

By Amy Ramsay

Amy L. Ramsay is a sergeant and senior policy analyst with a police service in Ontario, Canada, and has been a police officer for 28 years. She was president of the International Association of Women Police and the founder and first president of the group Ontario Women in Law Enforcement. She has seven university degrees, including a PhD in criminal justice and a PhD in management and organization, along with master's degrees in education and criminal justice. She is a part-time professor in the Bachelor of Human Services (Police Studies) program at Georgian College in Barrie, Ontario, and has taught at the Ontario Police College.

I loved your book. I found it both very sad and very inspiring... sad because of what these women have endured and inspiring because they came forward and told their story regarding police spousal abuse—and inspiring that author Alex Roslin never lost interest in the subject over the years.

This is a book that should be given to the wife or girlfriend of every single male police officer.

About 12 years into my career, I was told by my supervisor some words that I never, ever forgot: "Amy, you will never be promoted further (I was a sergeant then) because you carry too much baggage. You speak up on things like police spousal abuse, and the police don't like that."

I never forgot those words because I always wondered if they would seal my fate. It turns out: They did. That person went on to occupy a very high position within the police agency. I am two years from retirement—and I have never been further promoted, despite accumulating some 18 degrees, diplomas and professional designations (including two PhDs).

Speaking up about spousal abuse cost me advancement in rank. However, I have absolutely no regrets. I think that I at least introduced the topic, and I counted on survivors (as difficult as it is) to speak out and make this terrible abuse known to the public. God bless the women who have done so.

As I near the conclusion of my career, I wish I could say I have witnessed an improvement—no matter how small—in the way police spousal abuse is handled. I cannot. Nothing has changed. Few survivors have the courage (or resources) to speak up. The women in this book are a rare exception—but look at the cost they bear.

The situation will not change until an outside agency becomes accessible to the survivors of police spousal abuse. Right now, these women have no place to turn. They cannot go to the police for all the reasons listed in this book. It is very apparent that neither the police nor the courts are willing to deal with the problem.

What will it take to change that? I wish I knew the answer.

WE MUST DO BETTER

BY DOTTIE DAVIS

Deputy Chief Dottie Davis, Retired, was a police officer for 32 years with the Fort Wayne Police Department in Indiana. She co-authored the department's protocol on domestic violence and authored its protocols on officer-involved domestic violence and crisis intervention. She served as chair of the Indiana Governor's Council for the Prevention and Treatment of Family Violence, and the Indiana Coalition Against Domestic Violence named her its Indiana Law Enforcement Officer of the Year in 1998.

She has been an instructor and lecturer on domestic violence at numerous law enforcement agencies and conferences in the U.S. and Canada. Her testimony as a court-recognized expert witness on domestic violence in over a dozen criminal and civil trials has helped victims' estates and families win millions of dollars in jury awards due to inadequate police protection of abuse victims.

Amy Morrison's story mirrors mine in so many ways. Like her, I lived in fear for my personal safety and my life for years. Like her, I experienced violence at the hands of a police officer who was my intimate partner. Like her, I felt trapped in a system that would protect the perpetrator because of the badge he carried.

But unlike Amy, I too carried that badge. I too was a police officer sworn to protect and trained to defend myself.

For some, my profession blurs how they view the abuse I endured. They find it difficult to understand how a police officer skilled with weapons and self-defence could be a victim.

However, I never acted as a law enforcement officer in the privacy and sanctity of my home. I acted as the wife of a man who took an oath of marriage with me and who professed to love me even as he nearly took my life. I also acted as a woman trying to hold a marriage together while feeling her spirit dying through this abuse and through five miscarried pregnancies.

I was a woman who escaped this horrific life not because of my badge, but because of the birth of a baby girl who gave me back my spirit and provided me with the determination to protect both of us.

This book clearly demonstrates that police officers are not exempt from being perpetrators of violence in their own homes. Nor are they exempt from being victims of such violence. Because our stories are being told, recognition of the issue is growing and we are seeing changes in the industry. And in the many years I wore that badge and since, I've grown more and more hopeful about how my industry has evolved in understanding police-perpetrated domestic violence. We have made progress, and we must also recognize that we still have a long way to go.

I spent more than three decades in law enforcement serving in a myriad of capacities, including many years training other officers and in a command position in my agency. I have seen the men and women who serve from all angles. And I remain devoted to the belief that law enforcement is a noble profession.

I also realize that everyone employed in this noble profession is human, that we come from the general population at large and that batterers are attracted to professions in which they can have power and control over others. After all, power and control are the root cause of domestic violence.

I believe that those in law enforcement must be held to at least the same standard as everyone else, which is that an arrest will be made if probable cause exists that a crime has been committed. All of us associated with this profession must make it clear that domestic violence will not be tolerated in our ranks by enforcing the same standard on our co-workers. We cannot allow the focus of the investigation to shift from a criminal matter to one of how do we save his career.

I believe that the future of policing can truly change as we recognize that police-perpetrated domestic violence exists and we look at solvability factors to alter the systemic culture.

To do that, law enforcement agencies must self-police from the beginning. Starting with recruitment they must conduct extensive background investigations that include face-to-face interviews of the applicant, spouse or significant other, as well as the mother of any children belonging to the applicant, neighbors and current and former employers.

Psychological examinations should include more than a written examination. Also needed is an individual interview with the psychologist or psychiatrist, who has been provided any follow-up questions from the background investigator and his or her summary findings. A voice stress or polygraph test should then be done with each prospective recruit.

Acknowledging that there is no specific exam that will identify someone as a perpetrator of intimate partner violence, the more information an expert can access the better choices a department can make in selecting the best candidate for employment.

An agency can demonstrate intolerance for domestic violence in its ranks from the start of the officer's employment and throughout his or her career. Some ways this can be done:

- In the training academy, recruits should receive extensive training on the dynamics of domestic violence, common myths and prejudices surrounding the subject, the Power and Control Wheel used in the Duluth Model and the Lethality Assessment Program devised by Johns Hopkins School of Nursing professor Jacquelyn Campbell, an eminent and pioneering domestic violence researcher.

- Each recruit in the academy should receive instruction on police-perpetrated domestic violence, including the agency's written protocols, requirements to report should they have knowledge of an officer involved in domestic violence, early warning signs, methods of conducting an investigation, effecting an arrest of a fellow officer when probable cause exists and referral sources.

- Agencies should periodically review and update policies and procedures regarding police-perpetrated domestic violence.

- Annual in-service training on issues surrounding police-perpetrated domestic violence should be presented to all law enforcement, police dispatchers, police chaplains and victim advocates.

- Spouses and intimate partners of police officers should be offered sessions on police-involved domestic violence, not classes on stress in the family.

- Families should have access to victim advocates who are not paid by the law enforcement agency and not housed in the agency.

- Pamphlets should be created and made readily available to family members and loved ones of police officers on the topic of police-perpetrated domestic violence.

The community can also play a role in policing our law enforcement agencies. Civilians can form committees and receive training from the National Association for Civilian Oversight of Law Enforcement, which works to establish and improve oversight of police officers in the United States.[229]

Community members can volunteer to serve on interview panels for law enforcement applicants, civilian review boards and task forces overseen by the mayor's office. They can use their voice to ask questions and strive for transparency within agencies on police-involved domestic violence cases and written policies and procedures.

I have been involved in this subject matter for almost 30 years—from the 1980s as a victim experiencing pain and emotional devastation, to the 1990s when I found my voice and regained my strength to be able to tell my story

---

[229] Note from the author: The Canadian equivalent is the Canadian Association for Civilian Oversight of Law Enforcement.

and became an advocate, to the 2000s when I find myself testifying in criminal and civil trials against law enforcement officers, who find themselves as defendants along with their agency and their municipality or county.

In a recent court case where I provided expert witness testimony, I listened to a 27-minute audio of an officer charging his semiautomatic handgun then placing it to his girlfriend's head and then into his mouth while threatening to murder her and commit suicide in the presence of his three- and six-year-old children. I watched the faces of the rows of officers who came to support their comrade while they listened to the audio. I watched their heads bow and their eyes water as he was sentenced to serve eight years in prison for each of three felonies and one year for misdemeanor domestic battery (all to be served concurrently).

Much like Amy and me, the victim in this case is alive. Each of us is lucky to be. The same cannot be said for a police officer in the Indianapolis Metropolitan Police Department who was murdered in 2014 by her ex-husband, a sergeant in the same agency, who then killed himself. She had told her department that her ex-husband was harassing and intimidating her. Just weeks before she was killed, she obtained a protection order telling the court she was "extremely afraid" for her life.

Could more have been done to stop this horrific tragedy? It is too late for these two police officers, but other lives can be saved if agencies and the community take serious action. The time is overdue.

UNACCEPTABLE COST OF INACTION

By Leanor Johnson

Leanor Johnson is a professor emeritus of sociology at Arizona State University and founder of the university's African and African American Studies Department. She was the researcher who discovered high rates of spousal abuse in police families. She was a member of a Federal Bureau of Investigation advisory board on police stress and family violence that counselled the FBI on the planning of a landmark conference on police domestic violence in 2000. She is co-author of the pioneering book Black Families at the Crossroads: Challenges and Prospects, *an associate editor of the* Journal of Family Relations *and a fellow of the National Council on Family Relations.*

Kudos and gratitude to Alex Roslin for speaking on behalf of the too-often silenced voices in abusive police families. This book needs to be widely circulated.

From a survivor's perspective, pages of testimonies capture their experience. Moreover, this book empowers those who perceive that officers lack accountability. Survivors can do something. They can turn to the impressive appendices that serve as an easy-to-read handbook for guidelines, online resources and publications.

Tools for family and friends (Appendix C) provide not only invaluable information on how to identify abuse signs, but also guidelines for supporting victims within the unique police culture—a culture that functions to both protect officers on the street and potentially endanger those most dear to them in their private lives.

Unveiling the unique situation of abused police spouses allows family and friends to understand that what may aid victims in non-police families may increase the danger for victims in police families. Bravo for this revelation!

From a policy maker and administrator's perspective, the author provides substantial evidence establishing the existence and prevalence of police domestic violence, the difficulties in administering an effective policy and the best practices. Progressive administrators can glean within a historical context the unacceptable human and societal cost of not taking proactive measures against domestic violence. The author's citation of flaws in existing policies challenges administrators to seek alternatives and creative measures in addressing the problem within their departments.

This book transforms the police wife's private agony into a public issue, provides a plethora of recommendations for effecting change and powerfully concludes that both private and public players share responsibility in liberating and empowering survivors.

CONNECTING THE DOTS

By Margaret Shorter

Margaret Shorter is a retired staff sergeant of the Royal Canadian Mounted Police and president of the International Association of Women Police. Shorter was one of the first women to join the RCMP and the first to become a noncommissioned training officer in British Columbia. During her 36-year career in the RCMP, she trained Mounties in ethics, conflict management, leadership and occupational health and safety.

Roslin's book spotlights a timely and relevant topic. Once we begin to understand the implications of officer-involved domestic violence, we start to connect the dots to other marginalized groups. We recognize the connections between the behaviour of police officers in their personal lives and their engagement in the broader social picture—such as Black Lives Matter.

Good writing provokes thought and discussion. Once readers open themselves to the possibilities, we then wonder whether there may be a correlation. Do the demands that a society makes on its officers have unexpected consequences? When we withdraw our respect and social support from those we depend on to protect "the lamb from the lion," are we contributing to our own vulnerability? Could it be that some of that pressure is released on other vulnerable parties... even in the invisible places in those officers' personal lives?

As the president of the International Association of Women Police, I wonder how the historically recent deployment of female officers is affecting front-line policing today. How do women police experience the pressures in today's society to solve our social ills? How are these women contributing to the experiences of social change such as Black Lives Matter? Is it possible they could mitigate those experiences? Investigation is difficult when the U.S., at 12 percent, has one of the lowest percentages of female police officers among countries in the developed (and perhaps even developing) world.

As police officers move into retirement, where robust "old boys' networks" support post-retirement work projects, could the addition of now-retiring women police also alter these dynamics? A retiring 25-year female police officer with a large Canadian municipal police force was recently courted to head a provincial insurance investigative unit. She was hired with the understanding that they wanted her experience *and* they wanted the unit purged of the very real perception that it was comprised of former officers whose group single-mindedness was predetermining the outcomes of their investigations. I was encouraged that a public organization had come to this insight independently and was clearly acting on it!

The details of Amy Morrison's story convince readers to suspend judgment and always reassess their first impressions. The subtlety, pervasiveness and accumulation of separate events, tied to many seemingly minor decisions she made while her courage wavered, paint the bigger picture of Amy's life. At the same time, I was disappointed in the number of professionals who did not adhere to their own policies or codes of ethics and conduct. These aspects suggest larger questions that need further exploration. I encourage you to continue the discussion. I'm sure these suggest larger questions that need research in several fields.

HOW ONE CITIZEN TOOK ACTION

By Alan Corbett

Alan Corbett is a retired former teacher and university lecturer who served eight years as a state legislator in New South Wales, Australia. He advocates for the welfare and safety of children and has campaigned in Australia against corporal punishment. His pioneering research into police spousal abuse in Australia was highlighted in a 2016 government inquiry into domestic violence, which recommended that police investigate how spousal abuse is handled in the ranks.

He was built, as we say in Australia, like a brick shithouse, and I wasn't going to argue the point.

It was 2013, and I was at a community education event for Queensland's Domestic and Family Violence Prevention Month. He was a domestic violence police liaison officer—a sergeant whose duties included training and educating police officers about this issue.

As he towered over me, his power, authority and overall "presence" on display, he told me that he had hit each of his three children and that all parents should do the same.

His statement didn't make sense. Here was a police officer, a so-called expert in family violence, advocating that parents should hit their children.

My professional background is in education, and I had also spent eight years in the New South Wales state parliament advocating against the physical punishment of children and on other child safety issues. I knew there was solid research that said hitting and hurting kids could lead to a number of adverse outcomes, including aggression toward pets, siblings and intimate partners.

So I wanted to ask him: Do you really believe that hitting kids has no association whatsoever with later intimate partner abuse? Aren't parents modelling the very practices you want to prevent in adult relationships, namely the abuse of power and control over people who are vulnerable and unable to resist?

I went home confused and alarmed and Googled "police" and "domestic violence." I came across work by the U.S. author Diane Wetendorf and the tragic story of Crystal Judson-Brame in Tacoma, Washington, who was murdered by her police chief husband in 2003. Crystal's parents continue their advocacy today. And so my journey commenced.

At that time, there was absolutely no Australian research about what is referred to in the U.S. literature as officer-involved domestic violence (OIDV). In fact, almost all the literature was North American and dated to the early 1990s.

The absence of any Australian research was both exciting and daunting— the former because I could break new ground and the latter because I had no idea where to start. Besides, it was a bit nerve-wracking for a person without official police permission to examine one of the darker sides of police life, a phenomenon politicians and police were well aware of but had given scant attention to.

Nevertheless, I convinced myself that the vast majority of police officers would not tolerate the few who would harm their families and bring their profession into disrepute. I was also emboldened when I heard an advocate say, "The perpetrator is always responsible."

In early 2014, I made requests for information about OIDV to the state of Queensland minister for police, the police commissioner, the union and the head of the state police recruit training branch.

The reaction was not unexpected. I was politely told to obtain information through official channels, I was ignored by the minister (himself a former policeman with 19 years of service), and I was met with disbelief by others who were astonished that I would be investigating such a "personal" issue.

A right-to-information request also revealed that there were no available statistics and that the prevailing attitude was if an officer's behaviour did not impact on his or her operational duties or bring the organization into disrepute, it was not something of any real concern to politicians or the police hierarchy.

I understand now that these reactions are not unusual. Police organizations are by nature secretive, conservative and concerned about public image. Nevertheless, the lack of openness and transparency is unfortunate because it erodes the bedrock of police authority—that is, the public's trust and confidence in the police's ability and willingness to protect every member of the community, including the families of police members.

In late 2014, I also made a right-to-information request of every police force in the UK and Ireland for a copy of their policy on police who commit domestic violence-related offences. Each force emailed me its policy for free.

In 2014 and following the murder of 11-year-old Luke Batty by his abusive father, which galvanized Australia, the media started to shine a light into a dark corner of Australian life. Over the next two years, three official inquiries were held across Australia into domestic violence. I made a submission to each about OIDV, but only the 2016 state of Victoria's Royal Commission into Family Violence made reference to my submission and made a recommendation based on it. I suspect political sensitivities prevented the other two inquiries from addressing the issue.

To the readers of this award-winning book I say this: Alex has provided us with a wealth of information on the issue. He has laid the foundation for others to continue research, and he has provided the direction and means to do so.

Finally, whether you are interested in this or some other issue that needs attention, take heart because with patience, tenacity and a belief in your cause, you can and will make a difference.

APPENDIX B

What To Do If You're in an Abusive Relationship With a Cop

Abused women face great challenges in getting help and justice. If you are the intimate partner of a police officer, you probably face even bigger problems. Your abuser may be protected by fellow cops, he knows where women's shelters are, and his training and access can help him track you down if you leave. What's more, cops are armed and trained to use physical force.

Below are steps you can consider if you are in an abusive relationship with a police officer or are trying to decide if your partner's actions are abusive.[230]

---

[230] Although men commit most domestic violence, this advice also applies to women in same-sex relationships and men abused by women. Some of the information in this appendix is adapted from advice from these sources: counsellor Diane Wetendorf's website on police domestic violence (http://www.abuseofpower.info/), the National Network to End Domestic Violence (http://nnedv.org/), the Centre for Research & Education on Violence Against Women & Children (http://www.neighboursfriendsandfamilies.ca/eng/safetyplanningforwomen.php?q=how-to-help/safety-planning), the National Domestic Violence Hotline (http://www.thehotline.org/is-this-abuse/abuse-defined/), the Public Health Agency of Canada's family violence web page (http://www.phac-aspc.gc.ca/sfv-avf/info/ha-plan-eng.php), a 2013 PBS investigation into police domestic violence (http://www.pbs.org/wgbh/pages/frontline/criminal-justice/death-in-st-augustine/what-to-do-if-youre-a-victim-of-abuse/), the National Center for Victims of

KNOW THE SIGNS

Physical abuse can include pushing, slapping and hitting, throwing things and hurting a pet. You can also be abused in other ways, such as:

- Emotionally (name-calling, controlling behaviour, stalking physically or online, making threats, "gaslighting"[231]).
- Sexually (forcing you to have sex with him or other people, refusing to use contraception).
- Financially (denying access to money, ruining your credit, hiding assets).
- Legally (filing repeated harassing court actions).
- Through children (trying to manipulate them against you, teaching them abusive behaviours, threatening that if you leave he will claim you are a bad mother and seek full custody).
- Through pets (violence or threats against an animal to hurt or control you).

Abusers often engage in a combination of various kinds of behaviours. Or they may start with emotional abuse, then progress to other forms. Prolonged emotional abuse can also make a survivor think the violence is her fault. It may be hard to figure out where behaviours cross the line into abuse. An abuser may also have good qualities, a difficult past or ongoing hardship that make her confused about what to do.

Most abusers share a few common characteristics, according to the U.S. National Network to End Domestic Violence:[232]

- They want to jump into the relationship too quickly.
- They can be very charming and seem too good to be true.

Crime (https://www.marincourt.org/PDF/LethalityRisk.pdf) and WebMD (http://www.webmd.com/mental-health/tc/domestic-violence-signs-of-domestic-violence).

[231] Gaslighting is a form of emotional abuse in which the abuser frequently questions a partner's memory, instincts and perception of reality. The abuser may deny saying things or insist a partner's recollections are wrong when they aren't, eventually leading to inability to trust oneself and dependency on the abuser. See "What is Gaslighting?" National Domestic Violence Hotline, accessed April 16, 2015, http://www.thehotline.org/2014/05/what-is-gaslighting/.

[232] "Frequently Asked Questions About Domestic Violence," National Network to End Domestic Violence, accessed May 14, 2015, http://nnedv.org/resources/stats/faqaboutdv.html.

- They frequently put you down and criticize how you look.
- They want you to drop hobbies and stop seeing friends and family.
- They are highly jealous or controlling.
- They blame others for problems and don't take responsibility.

Other red flags can also signal abuse. Does your partner do any of the following?

- Call you names and insult you.
- Frighten you or lose control.
- Deny you access to money, pay or bank accounts.
- Pressure you to stop working.
- Listen in on your calls or tap your phone.
- Check your web browsing history, texts or phone records.
- Follow you.
- Demand to always know where you are.
- Constantly check up on you with phone calls or texts.
- Have a history of abusing people or animals or getting into fights on the job.
- Blame his exes for the failure of previous relationships.
- Use previous children to harass or manipulate an ex (e.g. constantly clashing over visitation, custody or family support; badmouthing the ex to the kids).
- Pressure you to use alcohol or drugs or have sex with him or others.
- Drive dangerously when you're in the car.
- Intimidate you with guns or other weapons.
- Tell you he could have you killed.
- Threaten to kill you, himself or others.
- Say other cops won't do anything if you call 911.
- Deny it or laugh it off when he hurts you.
- Throw or hit things when he's mad.
- Shove, slap, choke, kick, hit or spit at you.

Long-term abuse can leave you confused and doubting your instincts. Do you do any of the following?

- Often second-guess yourself or wonder if you're crazy.
- Have trouble making simple decisions.
- Frequently apologize to your partner.

- Make excuses for his behaviour or say things like: "He doesn't mean to hurt me—he just loses control," "He's scared me a few times, but he never hurts the children—he's a great father" or "He's always sorry afterward."[233]

If you are a female police officer and you are being abused, you likely face additional challenges. You may worry about repercussions from other officers or impacts on your career if you report abuse. On the other hand, depending on your department's policies, you may be disciplined if you don't disclose your own abuse. You may distrust outside advocates, leaving you feeling isolated. You may be afraid to put your spouse's police career at risk with a complaint. You might have fought back and be worried about being accused yourself. You may also feel shame about being an abuse survivor or excuse some behaviour because it's not clear if it crosses the line.

Other spouses also face unique challenges, such as:

- Those with children—They may fear for their children's safety as well as their own and, after leaving, sometimes face continued abuse with the children used as pawns, such as arbitrarily exercised visitations or harassing legal actions over custody and family support.
- Same-sex intimate partners of a cop—They may have to deal with police homophobia toward them or their partner if they disclose abuse.
- Intimate partners of racialized officers—They may be reluctant to expose yet another racialized person to a discriminatory criminal justice system.

REMEMBER IT'S NOT YOUR FAULT

No one deserves to be abused. Abusers often blame the victim for provoking mistreatment. They often try to undermine their partner's self-confidence and even their sense of reality.

If you have children, you can explain that abuse is never right, even when it's being done by someone they love. You can tell them what is happening

---

[233] Examples of excuses come from Bancroft, *Why Does He Do That?* Also see the Danger Assessment Instrument, a free 20-item online questionnaire that helps you determine your risk of being killed by an intimate partner: https://www.dangerassessment.org/, accessed June 15, 2015.

isn't their fault or yours and that when someone is being violent it is important to keep safe.

FIND WAYS TO INCREASE YOUR SAFETY

Whether or not you're planning to leave the relationship, here are ways that may help you increase your safety. Use your own judgment. You know best what is safe for you.

Computer and communications safety tips

Because technology changes so quickly, some of the advice and websites below may become outdated by the time you read this. Many domestic violence agencies offer up-to-date safety tips on their sites. See Appendix F for a list of agencies.

- **Activities can be monitored**—Police officers often have training and tools to access information about your activities. They may be able to access phone records, credit card and banking information, email and records from utility companies, schools, hospitals, transportation services, border crossings and the post office.
- **Deleting doesn't always work**—Deleting documents, emails or your internet browsing history and cache doesn't rid them completely from a computer or mobile device. Your abuser may know how to restore this information or track your computer activity. Deleted files can make him suspicious. One possible option is to use a web browser's do-not-track mode (for example, Google's incognito or guest modes), which limit the information that your computer stores about your web browsing. Be aware, however, that your browsing activity can still be tracked if software or a device is put on your computer that records what you type (known as a keystroke logger). [234]
- **Use another device**—A more secure option is to completely avoid using your home computer or mobile device to research domestic abuse or how to get away. For example, use a friend's computer or a public device in a library or hotel. Consider creating a new online account and password just for this purpose.

---

[234] Google's incognito mode still gives you suggestions based on your browsing history—which may arouse your abuser's suspicion—while guest mode does not. See more information here: https://support.google.com/chrome/answer/95464?hl=en.

- **Careful with your phones and other devices**—Don't make confidential calls using your cell phone or home phone. An abuser can check call records or may have tapped the line. He can also use a cell phone to monitor your location. He may even know how to remotely activate the microphone in your cell phone, laptop, voice-enabled home systems or vehicle emergency tracking system to secretly eavesdrop on conversations.
- **YouTube tracks views and searches**—If you use YouTube, remember that it tracks the videos you watch and search, records them in a history folder (which your abuser can access) and uses that to display similar recommended videos, even when you are not signed in to YouTube or Google (and even in Google's incognito mode). To disable this service, you can click "Pause watch history" on the page https://www.youtube.com/feed/history and "Pause search history" on the page https://www.youtube.com/feed/history/search_history. Also on those pages, you can click "Clear all watch history" and "Clear all search history" to delete your YouTube activities. Then close your web browser. Double-check that it worked by going back to YouTube and reviewing the recommended videos to see if they are based on your browsing history. When you're done your research, don't forget to turn these services back on by clicking "Resume watch history" and "Resume search history" so as not to arouse suspicion. Also keep in mind your abuser may question you if he notices your YouTube history is erased. As mentioned, it's safer to avoid using your own computer or device.
- **Avoid unusual changes**—Police officers are trained to notice anything out of the ordinary. Avoid causing suspicion with sudden or unusual changes—such as altering your daily routine, erasing your internet history, deleting email accounts or leaving your web browser in do-not-track mode.
- **Careful with online posts**—Avoid posting personal information or your abuse history on the internet, even using a false name.

Save evidence

Documentation can be very helpful. Save communications with your abuser, including email, phone messages and other correspondence. After an incident, ask someone to take photos of the scene and any injuries. (Note that it can take several days for maximum bruising to appear.) Do not take photos on your own cell phone as your abuser can find them or, if you delete them, may be able to restore them.

Keep a diary if you feel it is safe. You can use it to record details of incidents, including the date, time and names of any witnesses (writing them down as soon as possible afterward). A journal can also help you give voice to your feelings and make notes and plans.

Put copies of all this material in a safe place, such as with a domestic violence counsellor or lawyer or in a rented mailbox or safety deposit box. Ensure your abuser can't discover the existence of any mailbox or safety deposit box through bank or credit card records or by asking at the post office or bank.

Consider making a safety plan

- **Protecting yourself**—Plan where you and your kids would go in an emergency, how you would leave your house if needed and whom your kids would call. Discuss with your kids what to do if you or they are in danger. Tell your kids not to get between you and your partner if there is violence or potential for it. Plan a code word to tell them to leave or get help.

  In a violent situation, you can put your arms around each side of your head to try to protect your face and head. If an argument starts, consider moving to an area where you can exit the home quickly. Don't go where the children are. Try not to wear clothes or jewellery that could be used to strangle you. Seek medical attention if you or your children are injured. Ask for injuries to be documented.

- **Getting help**—Always remember you are not alone. People are out there who want to help you. Think about people you trust whom you can talk to and who can support you. It is normal to feel completely overwhelmed and paralyzed, but help can come from taking things one small step at a time.

  If you feel safe doing so, it can be a good idea to get to know a counsellor at a local domestic violence agency or help hotline (see Appendix F for a list). A counsellor can give advice and information, help you plan for your safety (including possibly getting a protection order) and safeguard documents. These services are usually confidential and anonymous, but keep in mind that in many jurisdictions a counsellor who is concerned that you or a child is at risk of harm may have to contact authorities and give them your contact information or, if you are using a chatline, your computer's Internet Protocol address (i.e. your computer's location). Check the agency's privacy rules or clarify with the counsellor before deciding what to disclose.

When you seek help, you may have to explain your unique situation to other people—and especially how police domestic violence is different from other abuse. Counsellors, social workers, lawyers, psychologists, police officers, friends and family members often won't understand what you're going through.

Try to maintain your composure when relating your experiences. This will help your credibility. On the other hand, don't minimize the severity of the abuse. Describe each incident clearly, with ample detail. Show your documentation.

If you are a female police officer yourself and disclose abuse by a fellow cop, think about how you will deal with possible repercussions at work, such as being ostracized or harassed. Your disclosure may be deliberately mishandled, and the union may side with your abuser. You will likely have to explain your unique situation to investigating officers. Familiarize yourself with all relevant department protocols. Associations of women police officers may be a good resource. You may also find support from other female officers in your department who are in the same situation. Never go to internal affairs without a witness or attorney.

- **If you or someone else calls 911**—If you, a child or a neighbour has called 911, ask that a supervisor attends the scene—or, if the abuser is the top-ranked local police officer, request the responsible government official. Provide a complete and truthful account. Again, don't understate the severity of the abuse. If your account changes over time, you will undermine your credibility. Ask to read the police report and/or criminal complaint to ensure it is accurate. If not, ask for it to be amended. Try to get a copy, and take down the report number and responding officers' names and badge numbers.

    If you have a safe opportunity to do so before 911 is called, familiarize yourself with your local police jurisdiction's policy on domestic violence (it should be on the department's website). Check if the department also has a specific policy on officer-involved domestic violence. Note any discrepancies in how responding officers deal with your case, follow up with the department, and consider filing a complaint if protocols weren't followed. Be ready for responding officers to pressure you to drop the complaint because it could get your spouse fired.

Be prepared for an abusive police officer to lie and try to undermine your credibility. That could include saying you assaulted him, abused the children or have mental health or substance-abuse problems.

- **Leaving the relationship**—Leaving an abusive relationship can be a dangerous time for anyone, but especially so for the intimate partner of a police officer.

    If you are considering leaving your home, think of places to go where he wouldn't look for you—to the home of an old friend or distant relative he doesn't know about; to another state or province. Local shelters for abused women are known to most cops in the community. You may have to go further away. If possible, keep some belongings with a friend or relative or in another safe place, including clothes, medication, copies of ID documents, school and medical records, kids' toys, money and valued possessions. But also be aware your abuser may be suspicious if he notices things are missing.

    Leave quickly and at an unexpected time, such as when it's calm and no argument has occurred. If possible, take important phone numbers, medication, a list of bank account numbers, ID and documents, school and medical records and valued possessions.

    Keep in mind a police officer may be able to track you via your vehicle GPS, phone calls, credit card and bank transactions, cell phone, hotel registration, plane tickets and border crossings (see "Computer and communications safety tips" above).

    If you stay in your home but your partner has left, consider installing steel or metal doors, outside lighting with motion detectors and security cameras. Be sure your house is equipped with smoke detectors and fire extinguishers.

    Don't meet your partner alone. Discuss a safety plan with your children and anyone else staying with you. If you have a restraining order, always keep it with you and inform family, friends, employers, neighbours and your kids' school or daycare provider, leaving them a copy.

    If possible, change your work hours and use a new cell phone. Also change your locks, phone number and social hangouts. Vary your route to and from work and school. Consider changing your children's school and getting a post office box for your mail. Carry a charged cell phone preprogrammed to dial 911.

- **Hold on to hope and get informed**—No matter how despondent or frightened you may feel, it can help to know you aren't alone and to inform yourself about resources available to you. This knowledge may open up new options for you and give you hope. Picking up this book was a step on the way. You can keep reading the appendices for more information and ideas.

Annotated Safety Plan for OIDV Survivors

By Diane Wetendorf
©1998, revised in 2014. Reprinted with permission.[235]

Standard suggestions for a safety plan may be problematic or even dangerous for women whose abusers are in law enforcement. The following takes a standard safety plan and includes additional safety considerations for officer-involved domestic violence.

SAFETY DURING AN EXPLOSIVE INCIDENT

Standard: *Try to avoid being trapped in a bathroom or the kitchen because there are objects that can be used as weapons.*

While this is good advice, your abuser may wear his service weapon all the time as well as have other weapons throughout your home. He also knows how to subdue a person using his body alone.

Standard: *Try to stay in a room with a phone so you can call 911, a friend or a neighbor.*

He may make it impossible for you to reach the phone or he will pull the phone from the wall, so try to keep your cell phone on your person. Again, his training may make him particularly effective at physically controlling you and preventing you from making a call.

Standard: *Call 911.*

This might only be a last resort for you. You know that he has a close working relationship with the dispatchers and responding officers. He may taunt you to "go ahead and call the police," because he is confident that his co-workers or colleagues will accept his version of the incident.

---

[235] Diane Wetendorf, "Annotated Safety Plan for OIDV Survivors" (2014), accessed April 2, 2015, http://www.abuseofpower.info/Tool_AnnotatedSafety.htm.

Standard: *Practice how to get out of your home safely. Visualize your escape route. Identify the best doors, windows, elevator or stairwell.*

Good advice but remain aware that your abuser is also aware of escape routes and may make sure you can't get to them. Again, he has been trained in a variety of tactics to stop someone who is trying to escape.

Standard: *Have a packed bag ready with any medications and other important items. Keep it hidden in a handy place in order to leave quickly. Consider leaving the bag elsewhere if your abuser searches your home.*

Your abuser may be hypervigilant and notice items that you would need are missing from their usual places. Consider buying duplicate items so that things remain as "normal" as possible.

Standard: *Ask a neighbor to call the police if they hear a disturbance coming from your home.*

You may not want neighbors to call the police. Is there anything else you would want them to do to intervene or create a distraction?

Standard: *Devise a code word to use with your children, grandchildren and others to communicate that you need the police.*

Again, you might use a code word to signal that you need help, but may not want them to call the police. Is there anything else you would want them to do to intervene or create a distraction? Give them specific instructions on when to notify the police.

Standard: *Decide and plan for where you will go if you have to leave home (even if you don't think you will need to).*

This must be somewhere the abuser would not think to look. Do not take your car if at all possible, since he has access to methods of tracking it down.

Standard: *Memorize all important phone numbers.*

This is a good safety measure.

SAFETY WHEN PREPARING TO LEAVE

Standard: *Open a credit/debit account in your own name to start to establish or increase your independence. Consider direct deposit of your paycheck or benefit check. Think of other ways to increase your independence.*

Abusers in law enforcement know how to track financial information and may have informants at your local financial centers. If at all possible, set aside cash rather than use savings/checking/debit accounts.

Standard: *Leave money, an extra set of keys, copies of important documents and extra clothes with someone you trust so you can leave quickly.*

Friends and close relatives are probably not your best choice. This should be someone who the abuser does not know or would not think of contacting. Ideally, this person would be someone whose name/number will not display on your phone, any bills, emails or other standard means of communication.

Standard: *Bring any medications, prescriptions, and glasses, hearing aids or other assistive devices you may need.*

Your abuser may be hypervigilant in watching for signs that you are preparing to leave him. He may notice if items that you would take with you are missing from their normal place. Keep things as "normal" as possible. Again, his professional training makes him tuned in to details.

Standard: *If you leave the relationship or are thinking of leaving, you should take important papers and documents with you to enable you to apply for benefits or take legal action. This includes Social Security cards[236] and birth certificates for you and your children, documentation of legal residency, your marriage license, leases or deeds, your checkbook, your charge cards, bank statements and charge account statements, insurance policies, proof of income for you and your spouse, and any documentation of past incidents of abuse.*

You may not have access to any of these documents because your abuser knows you will need them if you ever try to build a new life. Copies of these documents may not be legally accepted, but may help you with any authorities or advocates you contact.

Standard: *Determine who would be able to let you stay with them or lend you some money.*

Make sure this is someone the abuser would not think of.

Standard: *Keep the domestic abuse program number close at hand and keep some change or a telephone calling card with you at all times for emergency phone calls.*

---

[236] Note from the author: The Canadian equivalent could be a health insurance card.

Purchase a phone card or disposable cell phone rather than using your personal phone. Your abuser may have access to individual and electronic databases that can track telephone use.

Standard: *If you are 60 years old or older, contact your local elder adult service agency to learn about eligibility for public and private benefits and services such as Social Security, pensions, housing, transportation and medical insurance.*

If you are hiding, remember that accessing or even asking about public benefits will blaze a trail by which the abuser can find you.

Standard: *Review your safety plan as often as possible in order to plan the safest way to leave your abuser.*

Remember—*leaving can be the most dangerous time.* Do you think that your abuser will become obsessed with tracking you down if you "disappear?" If so, consider other options. Will you be safer if you stay more visible, either in the relationship or in your community?

SAFETY IN YOUR OWN HOME (IF THE ABUSER DOES NOT LIVE WITH YOU)

Standard: *Change the locks on your doors as soon as possible. Buy additional locks and safety devices to secure your windows.*

Replace wooden doors with steel or metal doors. Consider installing or increasing outside lighting with motion detectors. Consider cameras inside and outside the house. Install smoke detectors and purchase fire extinguishers. Remember that your abuser may know how to enter locked doors and windows. Consider installing locks that are especially difficult to open. Place obstructions in front of doors, windows and any entry points (but make sure you can easily escape in case of a fire).

Standard: *If you have young children, grandchildren or other dependents living with you, discuss a safety plan for when you are not with them and inform their school, day care, etc., about who has permission to pick them up.*

This is a good safety measure.

Standard: *Inform neighbors and your landlord that your abuser no longer lives with you and that they should call the police if they see your abuser near your home.*

Will the local police take action against your abuser? Consider what else people might do if they see your abuser near your home.

SAFETY WITH A RESTRAINING ORDER/ORDER FOR PROTECTION

Standard: *Keep your protective order with you at all times. (When you change your purse, this should be the first thing that goes into it.) If it is lost or destroyed, you can get another copy from the County Court office.*[237]

Will the local police enforce an order against your abuser?

Standard: *Call the police if your abuser violates the conditions of the restraining order. Learn what violations of the order require officers to arrest the abuser.*

You may have to demand that the responding officers call a supervisor.

Standard: *Think of alternative ways to keep safe in case the police do not respond right away.*

Think of what you will do if the responding officers refuse to take any action.

Standard: *Inform family, friends, teachers and neighbors that you have a restraining order in effect.*

This is a good safety measure.

SAFETY IN PUBLIC (SCHOOL, WORK, SOCIAL, RECREATIONAL OR VOLUNTEER ACTIVITIES)

Standard: *Plan how to get away if confronted by an abusive partner.*

This may be more difficult with a police officer abuser since he is trained to prevent people from getting away from him in a confrontation.

---

[237] Note from the author: In Canada, depending on the jurisdiction, you would go to the court or authority that issued the peace bond or restraining order.

Standard: *Decide whom you will inform of your situation. This could include your school, work location or residence security (provide a picture of your abuser if possible).*

Alert them that he is a police officer and may use his professional status or other police officers to gain access to you or your children. He may appear in uniform to mislead or intimidate them.

Standard: *Change your phone number.*

This remedy may be ineffective because police officers can easily get phone numbers.

Standard: *Screen calls; arrange to have someone screen your telephone calls, if possible.*

This is a good safety measure.

Standard: *Save and document all contacts, messages, injuries or other incidents involving the batterer.*

Your abuser is probably smart enough not to leave this type of evidence, or will word messages ambiguously/vaguely to create confusion or doubt as to intent; save and document them anyway. Taken together, they may provide useful evidence of stalking behavior or other abusive tactics.

Standard: *Devise a safety plan for when you are out in public. Have someone escort you to your car, bus or taxi. If possible, use a variety of routes to go home. Think about what you would do if something happened while going home.*

Civilian escorts may be afraid that they cannot protect you or themselves from a police officer.

YOUR SAFETY AND EMOTIONAL HEALTH

Standard: *If you are thinking of returning to a potentially abusive situation, discuss an alternative plan with someone you trust.*

This is a good safety measure.

Standard: *If you have to communicate with your abuser, arrange to do so in a way that makes you feel safer, whether by phone, mail, email, in the company of another person, through an attorney, etc.*

Be very aware of what you say to the abuser as he may record and save any communication with you.

Standard: *If you have to meet your partner, do it in a public place.*
This is a good safety measure.

Standard: *Decide who you can call to talk to freely and openly, and who can give you the support you need.*
Remember that no electronic communication is secure. Your abuser may be able to track your cell phone use, any email accounts, social media, etc.

Standard: *Plan to attend a victims' support group to learn more about yourself and abusive relationships and to gain support from others in similar situations.*
It might be safer to attend a group that meets away from your immediate area. However, few advocates are familiar with police-perpetrated domestic violence and they may not understand your unique situation.

Standard: *Call a shelter for battered women.*
It may be somewhat difficult for you to find a shelter that is equipped or willing to shelter you and your family since they work closely with the police.

Standard: *Avoid staying alone.*
This is a good safety measure.

Standard: *Vary your routine.*
This is a good safety measure.

APPENDIX C

Advice for Family and Friends

We are often reluctant to get involved or interfere if we think a friend or family member may be in a violent or abusive relationship. We may be scared, not know how to help or not want to make the situation worse. But your help may be critical for an abused person and her children. You may even save a life.

Keep in mind that any support you offer should aim to empower the survivor to help herself. When someone experiencing domestic violence is ready to talk or get help, this is a first step to freedom. Understand and acknowledge the courage it took to reach this point. Be a good listener. An abuse survivor may have a hard time trusting anyone, including you. Do not interrupt, assume or judge. Just having your ear may be of pivotal importance to her. Here is other advice:[238]

---

[238] Some of the information in this appendix is adapted from these sources: the National Domestic Violence Hotline (http://www.thehotline.org/help/help-for-friends-and-family/), counsellor Diane Wetendorf's website on police domestic violence (http://www.abuseofpower.info/Vict_HowHelp.htm), the Centre for Research & Education on Violence Against Women & Children (http://www.neighboursfriendsandfamilies.ca/how-to-help/helping-abused-women), Battered Women's Support Services (http://www.bwss.org/wp-content/uploads/2008/07/BWSS_Help-my-friend_2014.pdf), the Public Health Agency of Canada (http://www.phac-aspc.gc.ca/sfv-avf/info/ha-know-savoir-abus-eng.php) and Pandora's Project (http://www.pandys.org/articles/tipsforfriends.html).

- **Watch the signs**—Watch for signs that your friend or relative is being abused by her police husband or boyfriend (see Appendix B for more details). Does her partner insult her? Call her names? Dominate all conversation? Stop her from seeing family and friends? Control her money? Act very jealously? Does she act nervously around him, excuse his behaviour, try to cover up injuries—or seem sad, withdrawn and unable to concentrate well?

- **Get informed**—Review the information, resources and advice in this book, including the appendices, to inform yourself about the unique circumstances of police domestic violence. The risks for these women are substantially magnified. Advice for other abused people doesn't necessarily apply.

- **Be safe with emails and calls**—Be extremely careful about electronic and phone communications, which the abuser may be monitoring (see "Computer and communications safety tips" in Appendix B).

- **Ask what you can do**—Find a time and place to talk privately. Offer your support. Tell her she isn't alone. Assure her you'll always be there if she wants to talk. Ask if you can do anything to help her or if she wants to go somewhere safer. Offer to help her find someone to talk to. Explain what you see and that you are concerned.

- **Listen with respect**—Be prepared to listen. Do so respectfully without interrupting, blaming or assuming. Simply being heard may be critically important for her. Thank her for confiding. Don't demand to know all the details. Tell her she didn't cause the abuse and that she isn't crazy. Don't minimize the abuse, excuse the abuser or express disbelief. Don't ask her why she stays. Comfort her. Tell her what you think are her strengths. Offer to help take care of children and pets. Do not try to take over or argue with her decisions. Remember that the abused person knows better than you what will be safe for her and is best for her children.

- **Be patient**—If the person doesn't want to talk or denies the abuse, don't get frustrated or angry. Tell her you are available whenever she needs. If she has children, express concern about their safety and emotional well-being.

- **Avoid confronting the abuser**—Don't encourage her to confront the abuser. Don't confront the abuser yourself. Be careful not to say or do anything that could make him upset with her.

- **Gather resources**—Gather a list of agencies, information and professionals experienced in working on domestic violence to share

with her when she is ready to get help (see Appendix F). Try to locate professionals who know about police spousal abuse and are
willing to help a survivor.

- **Safety planning**—Offer to help her make a safety plan (see Appendix B). That may include offering a safe computer for her to use
  to research what to do, a phone to call a helpline or a place to safeguard her documents.

- **Learn police protocols**—Familiarize yourself with local police
  department policies on domestic violence, including any special policies on officer-involved domestic violence. (Check the department's
  website.)

- **Offer accompaniment**—Offer to accompany her to get help or to
  act as an intermediary with intervenors. Offer to help her explain
  her unique situation to advocates and other professionals unfamiliar
  with police domestic violence.

- **Consider your safety**—Be aware that the abuser may target you if
  he discovers your role. Consider ways to protect yourself. Ask an experienced advocate for advice.

- **Panic attacks and flashbacks**—If she has a panic attack or flashback (i.e. reliving an incident), gently remind her where she is. Ask
  her to sit, remind her to take deep breaths, and in the case of a
  flashback tell her it's not happening even though it feels real. Get to
  know her triggers. Explain that flashbacks can help the survivor
  work through what happened. Don't push her to talk. A hug, holding
  a hand or pat on the back may be welcome for some survivors; for
  others, not. Ask first.

- **Be aware of special circumstances**—Keep in mind that certain
  abused spouses may face special challenges, including those who
  have children, female officers, same-sex intimate partners of a cop
  and intimate partners of racialized officers (see additional details in
  Appendix B). Regardless of the survivor's background, listening
  without judgment and being sensitive to her unique circumstances
  and fears will increase the likelihood that you can empower her to
  make a decision that leads to safety.[239]

Finally, keep in mind that survivors of long-term abuse may be so despondent they feel paralyzed and unable to help themselves. They are often
faulted for not leaving or calling police, but years of abuse can leave a person

---

[239] Thank you to Leanor Johnson for suggesting the advice in this bullet.

with poor self-esteem, feelings of powerlessness and hopelessness, and mistrust of her instincts, memory and sanity.

The abuse may have started gradually, with putdowns and other emotional abuse that eventually progressed to physical violence. By that point the person may believe the mistreatment is their fault. The partner of a police officer often experiences these feelings even more strongly because of her abuser's powerful position.

Your intervention may mean the difference between life and death. Showing that you care and offering valuable support may be the very thing that turns a situation around and allows your friend or relative to believe she has choices and support. A survivor who believes she is not alone is one in whom hope can grow and action can follow.

APPENDIX D

Recommendations for Police, Governments, the Public, Advocates, the Media and Academics

RECOMMENDATIONS FOR POLICE

T he International Association of Chiefs of Police has produced the best-known set of recommendations for police departments on officer-involved domestic violence. The group issued a model policy on the issue in 1999 (updated in 2003 and, as of this writing, in the process of being updated once again) that it recommends for adoption by its 21,000 members in more than 100 countries.[240]

---

[240] "Domestic Violence by Police Officers Model Policy," International Association of Chiefs of Police. See also "Domestic Violence by Police Officers; Concepts and Issues Paper," International Association of Chiefs of Police. The IACP model policy isn't the only set of best practices available. The Chicago Police Department was reportedly the first in the U.S. to start developing a program and specific rules for officer-involved domestic violence in 1992 after four murder-suicides involving police officers and intimate partners (see more details here: http://www.ncdsv.org/images/Russell_DevelopingAPolicyToCombatOfficer-InvolvedDV_2011.pdf). The Washington state Attorney General's Office has produced a handbook for police agencies that gives a good overview of policies and experiences across the U.S.:

The IACP's guidelines have some important flaws (as we'll see below), but they are among the most comprehensive to be developed so far. Some key provisions:

Termination

- Law enforcement agencies shall fire officers convicted of a domestic violence crime, including assault or restraining an intimate partner, property damage, stalking, death threats, sexual battery and violating a court protection order. Officers shall also be fired if they are found through an internal administrative procedure to have committed domestic violence.
- Police departments should review records of officers to check if they have been convicted of a misdemeanour domestic violence crime or are subject to a protection order (both of which trigger a firearms prohibition under U.S. federal law), and if so, legal counsel and the city or county attorney should be consulted about continued employment or assignment.[241]

Hiring

- The department shouldn't hire an officer who has "a history that indicates a pattern of violence," including elder or child abuse, sexual assault or stalking, the IACP advises in its "Concepts and Issues Paper," a background document on the model policy. Pre-hire screen-

---

http://agportal-s3bucket.s3.amazonaws.com/uploadedfiles/Another/Supporting_Law_Enforcement/Domestic_Violence/Law_Enforcement_HB.pdf. Other policies include those of Tacoma, Washington (http://www.lanejudson.com/1_TACOMA_OIDV_POLICY.htm), and San Francisco (http://www.sf-police.org/Modules/ShowDocument.aspx?documentID=27436) and the model policy of the state of Florida (http://familyvio.csw.fsu.edu/wp-content/uploads/2010/05/FloridaModelPolicyonOfficerDV2010.pdf). See additional policy recommendations for police departments and governments in Marci L. Fukuroda, "Law Enforcement Response to Officer-Perpetrated Domestic Violence; Where Do We Go From Here?" in *Murder at Home: An Examination of Legal and Community Responses to Intimate Femicide in California* (California Women's Law Center, 2005), 138-150, accessed May 21, 2015, http://cwlc.org/web/wp-content/uploads/2014/03/Murder-at-Home-Report.pdf.

[241] See Chapter 7 for more details on the firearms restrictions. Police-issued weapons are exempted from the gun prohibition for people subject to a protection order.

ing should include a search for protection orders in areas where the applicant has lived.

- Departments shouldn't hire anyone with "a history of perpetrating violence" and should "strongly consider" not hiring an applicant who shows abusive tendencies in pre-hire psychological screening.
- When an officer is hired, the department should contact intimate partners and families to explain its policy on domestic violence committed by police officers and periodically get back in touch to give information on the policy and local support services.

Training, support and monitoring

- Officers should get continual training on domestic violence, including on warning signs that a fellow cop is abusive.
- Officers who ask for help or display warning signs should be offered counselling and other nonpunitive support before violence occurs.
- Supervisors should monitor and document any pattern of abusive behaviour that could indicate domestic violence, including physical or verbal aggressiveness, mistreatment of animals, stalking or inappropriate surveillance, monitoring or controlling a family member, disparaging a partner, tardiness, excessive absences and alcohol or drug abuse. An officer who engages in such behaviour should be referred for psychological screening, counselling and/or discipline.
- Departments should severely discipline any officer who fails to report knowledge of abuse by a fellow officer; who fails to cooperate with an investigation or interferes in a case; or who intimidates an abuse survivor or witness.
- Officers must inform supervisors if they are the subject of a criminal investigation or protection order proceeding in any jurisdiction.

Responding to calls

- In a domestic violence incident call, a supervisor of higher rank than the officer involved must be sent and assume command of the crime scene. An arrest should be made if there is probable cause (i.e. if officers believe a crime occurred). Photos and/or video should be taken of the parties and scene if equipment is available. The "dominant aggressor" should be arrested, not both parties. If no arrest is made, the supervisor must explain why in a report.

- The arrested officer's service weapons should be seized, as should other firearms if legally possible.
- The supervisor must inform the police chief and the officer's immediate supervisor or, if the officer works in another jurisdiction, the police chief there.
- The supervisor shall inform the abuse survivor about the department's policy on police domestic violence, how to get a protection order, victim compensation, how to contact domestic violence counsellors and advocates, and the availability of confidential transportation to a shelter.
- If the incident involves the police chief or commissioner, the supervisor must inform the district/state's attorney and the government official with direct oversight over the chief, such as the mayor.
- A member of the command staff must do a danger assessment of the accused officer and inform the abuse survivor and police chief. This commander will also act as a point of contact to inform the survivor about developments in the case and help the survivor and children with safety planning.
- An administrative investigation must be done even if there was no arrest. This should be done by the internal affairs department, or if such a unit doesn't exist, the police chief should appoint an experienced investigator or bring in an outside law enforcement agency.
- Departments should issue administrative orders of protection to control officer behaviour. Such orders can direct an officer to refrain from certain behaviour toward a specific person as a condition of employment.
- Criminal investigations must be handled by the department's domestic violence unit or, if such a unit doesn't exist, the criminal investigations unit or detective division. The chief can also ask an outside agency to handle it.

The IACP model policy was a step forward and an important milestone, signalling growing awareness of police domestic violence. But 17 years later, few police departments have adopted it. Only a quarter of 56 large U.S. city and county police departments had a specific policy for officers accused of domestic abuse, according to a *New York Times*-PBS investigation in 2013. And only one, Nashville, had adopted the IACP model policy in its entirety.[242]

In Canada, not a single police department appears to have adopted the IACP model policy, and the Canadian Association of Chiefs of Police still has

---

[242] Cohen, Ruiz and Childress, "Departments Are Slow to Police Their Own Abusers."

not endorsed or even reviewed it. And so far as I could discover, no Canadian law enforcement agency automatically fires an officer convicted of a domestic violence crime.

Flaws in the policy

The model policy has important flaws, as we saw in Chapter 7. Here are some of them, along with possible solutions. [243]

- **Conflict of interest**—Cops still investigate their own. The policy leaves unaddressed one of the main causes of unchecked police domestic violence: the notorious "blue wall of silence." An organization that investigates itself is obviously open to conflict of interest. A stronger policy would endorse an independent civilian-staffed and -led agency to conduct criminal investigations involving police (including for domestic assault, threats, stalking and sex-related crimes) and the need to beef up civilian oversight of police.
- **Hiring**—During hiring, the policy relies heavily on officers to report incidents in their own past. Pre-hire screening should also involve checks of civil and family court records for domestic violence complaints. The hiring process should include representation from domestic violence advocates and other community groups.
- **Training**—While officers are required to get training on domestic violence in general, no mention is made of training on the causes of police domestic violence, the difficulties of investigating it and how to assure survivor safety. Such training is essential.
- **Post-hire screening**—The policy relies heavily on supervisors to spot warning signs in subordinate officers. This ignores the fact that some supervisors may themselves be abusers or may not see the task as a priority. [244] Officers from the chief down should undergo regular post-hire psychological rescreening, akin to skills recertification.

---

[243] The same flaws are generally present in other policies on officer-involved domestic violence in place in the U.S. Some of the recommendations that follow for police and governments are mutually exclusive (such as recommendations to strengthen investigations of police internally and to transfer such investigations to an outside agency). They are offered to give administrators and others various options to consider.

[244] As ex-police chief Anthony Bouza noted: "Wrongdoing will rarely be reported or acted on by supervisors in daily contact with their subordinates.... The supervisor will be brought to intervene only if he or she believes the risks of failing to do so to be unacceptably high. In order to bring this about, harsh action needs to be taken against those who fail to report infractions." Bouza, *The Police Mystique*, 133.

Departments should closely monitor cops who do poorly in post-hire screening, investigate them for possible abuse, provide counselling, task independent advocates to reach out to their families and consider use of administrative orders of protection.

- **Compliance mechanisms**—The model policy lacks any systematic mechanisms to ensure compliance. Continual performance monitoring is needed using indicators and benchmarks. Departments should mandate internal affairs units and separate audit or inspection units (led by tough, pro-reform commanders) to do surprise inspections, audits, spot checks, surveys and other probes of how the department investigates and disciplines abusive officers and those accused of sexual misconduct, compliance with firearms prohibitions for abusive officers, how survivor safety is assured and how police investigate violence against women in general. The audit or inspection unit should also periodically examine the internal affairs unit's record of investigating officers. Creative approaches should be used, including:[245]
  - ✓ random tests of service and performance (e.g. sting operations using decoy officers in a controlled fashion to check police response at a staged 911 domestic violence call or traffic stop; having a decoy officer call the department claiming to be an abused police spouse and seeking help and information)
  - ✓ satisfaction surveys of survivors, shelters and advocates
  - ✓ audits of past investigations of officer-involved domestic violence (especially those involving cops who fail post-hire screening)
  - ✓ investigations of officers who fail post-hire screening tests (e.g. electronic surveillance, interviews with family members, neighbours, teachers)
  - ✓ cultivation of a network of officers who act as informants about police wrongdoing and report to the inspection unit
  - ✓ solicitation of anonymous complaints of wrongdoing to a hotline or directly to the chief
- **Firm action on misconduct**—Officers should be sent a strong message on misconduct via severe discipline, arrests, publicizing of

---

[245] Some of the recommendations in this bullet are adapted from suggestions in Bouza, *The Police Mystique*, 133, 263-5. "The key to control [of misconduct] is the development of tough, effective central units, whose commander and members have been carefully selected.... If the internal affairs unit does its job well, it will not only uncover wrongdoing but energize field supervisors into participating in the program." Bouza, *The Police Mystique*, 133.

results and commanders being held accountable (including discipline or reassignment) for unit performance during compliance monitoring.

- **Understaffing in domestic violence units**—The IACP model policy doesn't address the critical understaffing in some police domestic violence units. Underresourced units may be hard pressed to find extra resources for the potentially more complex investigation of police officers. Such investigations should be handled by a special internal affairs unit devoted solely to police spousal abuse. Police should adequately staff domestic violence units and also press governments to improve the community, legal, educational and health care response to domestic violence (see "Recommendations for Governments" below).

- **Independent advocates**—The policy encourages police to work more closely with domestic violence advocates. This may sound like a good idea when it comes to other abused women, but it can compromise one of the few outside sources of support for abused police family members and leave them more vulnerable. Survivors need access to confidential help from independent advocates.

- **Special situations**—The policy doesn't recognize or address the special challenges faced by certain abused spouses such as those who have children, female officers, same-sex intimate partners of a cop and intimate partners of racialized officers (see additional details in Appendix B). Departments should work with advocates to develop protocols specifically for such special cases—for example, not requiring female officers to report their own abuse (see below) and assigning a female officer of the same ethnicity to follow up with survivors.

- **Unions should support survivors**—Police unions and associations often support officers accused of domestic violence, but not the survivor, even if she is an officer herself. Unions should assist both abusers and survivors in law enforcement families, whether or not the survivors are cops. Officers who are survivors of domestic abuse or sexual harassment on the job should also have access to legal representation.

- **Transparency**—Departments should track and regularly disclose to the public detailed information on domestic violence complaints, disciplinary and criminal investigations and results of compliance monitoring.

- **Coordinated campaign**—A tough and efficient senior executive should be appointed to coordinate a zero-tolerance campaign on police domestic violence, with objectives, indicators and an action plan—all to be included in the agency's strategic plan. The executive should report directly to the chief and be held accountable for the campaign's success.

- **Power and problematic attitudes**—The policy doesn't address power and control and the derogatory anti-woman and other problematic attitudes that are behind police domestic violence and connected issues, such as mishandled police investigations of violence against women and missing women (particularly those of First Nations descent); police underrepresentation of women, black people, First Nations people and others; police sexual misconduct against female officers and women drivers in traffic stops; and mistreatment of black people, First Nations people and others. Such attitudes should be addressed at all points, including:
  ✓ police academies and police studies courses
  ✓ zero-tolerance messages from commanders and supervisors
  ✓ the hiring process (e.g. via mandatory employment equity, regular audits of compliance with equity targets and higher academic standards for recruits, particularly a university degree)
  ✓ more effective screening for controlling, anti-woman and racist attitudes in pre-hire evaluations, regular post-hire rescreening and tests for promotion and special unit assignment
  ✓ regular training (including on police domestic violence, sexism and cultural diversity)
  ✓ enactment of stringent, updated workplace discrimination and harassment policies and their strict enforcement
  ✓ investigation and discipline of misconduct

A large number of abusive people will no doubt continue to be drawn to law enforcement so long as police exist in their present form—as an institution rooted in power and control, with a mandate to impose order in the face of difficult underlying social problems.

Police departments can't do much directly to change the social issues, but they can speak publicly about them and how they impact police and communities. They can also enact internal reforms to reduce the impacts on officers, their families and the public and to combat wrongdoing in the ranks. Change is needed both inside police departments and beyond.

Protecting survivors

Some advocates say policies such as the IACP's are less about survivor safety than reducing liability to lawsuits from those targeted by abusive cops. A more survivor-oriented approach has been jointly put forth by retired abuse counsellor Diane Wetendorf and Dottie Davis, the retired Fort Wayne, Indiana, deputy police chief. They recommend:[246]

- **Hiring**—During pre-hire screening, departments should meet candidates face to face in their home and meet separately with any intimate partner. Family, friends and neighbours should be asked about current and prior relationships.
- **Training**—All officers and other staff should be required to attend training sessions on police domestic violence given by police instructors and survivor advocates. Training must include the message that sexism isn't acceptable in the police department.
- **Family orientation**—Orientation sessions for police families should not portray domestic violence as being due to the stresses of the police work, a viewpoint that excuses abuse.
- **Survivor information**—Survivors and witnesses should be informed about the complaint process and ensuing investigation. They should be told before any interview that their statements are not confidential and that the accused will have access to what they say.
- **Survivor safety**—Before the department takes any action against an abusive officer, the survivor should be told so she has time to take safety precautions in case he comes after her.
- **Female officers**—The requirement that officers report domestic violence in the ranks is problematic for a female cop who is being abused. It means she may be disciplined herself if she doesn't report being abused. Or she may not be able to disclose the abuse to an officer friend without putting that officer in the position of having to report the abuse. (As a solution, the policy on officer-involved domestic violence at the Tacoma Police Department in Washington exempts cops from reporting that they are being abused themselves.[247])

[246] Diane Wetendorf and Dottie L. Davis, "Developing Policy on Officer-Involved Domestic Violence" (2015), accessed April 17, 2015, http://www.abuseofpower.info/Wetendorf_DevelopPolicy2015.pdf.
[247] Tacoma Police Department, "Officer-Involved Domestic Violence Policy," Section III. G., accessed July 15, 2015,

- **Independent advocacy**—Survivors should be referred to independent advocacy services, not to advocates or social workers employed by the police department.
- **Specialized officer counselling**—If an officer is referred to counselling, it should be to someone specialized in domestic abuse, not a couples counsellor, police psychologist or chaplain. Inappropriate counselling by someone uninformed about domestic violence may place the survivor in greater danger because it could validate the abuser's excuses for violence.
- **Publicize data**—Departments should keep statistics on domestic violence complaints and make them public.

Also, in an important divergence from conventional advocacy on domestic violence, Wetendorf and Davis question so-called "pro-arrest" policies. Such policies, in place across Canada and much of the U.S., require police to automatically arrest a suspected abuser if there is evidence of violence, even if the survivor refuses to press charges. The goal is to induce sometimes-reluctant officers to arrest more often and to counteract batterers who pressure survivors to deny abuse.

While such a policy may help other abused women, it can endanger the spouse of a police officer and "rob her of her right to do what she believes is in her best interest," Wetendorf and Davis said. Criminal charges are likely to enrage an abusive officer further, without resulting in any likely benefit for the survivor because courts are generally apt to dismiss the case or, at most, impose only a token sentence such as probation or a conditional discharge.

Meanwhile, the abuser's lawyer will seek to discredit the survivor in court, "portraying her as a bad wife, a neglectful mother, a promiscuous woman, or a mentally unstable person who is lying about the abuse in an attempt to ruin her partner's career."

RECOMMENDATIONS FOR GOVERNMENTS

- **Get informed**—Familiarize yourself with police domestic violence (see resources in Appendix F) and the recommendations and advice in these appendices for other individuals and bodies, especially those for police departments above.
- **Mandate a policy**—Involve domestic abuse survivors, advocates and women police associations in developing a strict specific policy

http://www.lanejudson.com/1_TACOMA_OIDV_POLICY.htm.

for police departments on officer-involved domestic abuse, drawing on model policies and experiences in other jurisdictions. Mandate police departments to adopt the policy and internally monitor compliance with the policy, severely disciplining misconduct. Require departments to regularly report compliance results to the public.

- **Research**—Fund independent academic research on police domestic violence rates, police department compliance with policies on the issue, survivor safety perceptions, satisfaction with police service, police compliance with firearms prohibitions for domestic violence offenders, how police investigate domestic violence in general and police sexual misconduct against officers and civilians, including female drivers at traffic stops. Require police departments to cooperate with the research.

- **Investigate**—Order public inquiries and regular internal and outside audits into how police departments investigate and discipline abusive officers and those accused of sexual and other misconduct, compliance with firearms prohibitions for abusive officers and other relevant protocols, how survivor safety is assured and how police investigate violence against women in general. Create an independent inspector general with subpoena and prosecutorial powers to conduct inspections, audits, spot checks, surveys and other investigations of wrongdoing and how it is handled not only in police departments but also the entire criminal justice system.[248] Monitor and analyze the data, and release it regularly to the public.

- **Independent criminal probes**—Create an independent civilian-led and -staffed agency to handle criminal investigations of police officers, including for domestic violence and sex-related crimes. Ensure the agency has adequate resources and independence to conduct proper investigations, including staff free of past or current police affiliations. Mandate regular inquiries into the agency's performance by bodies such as the auditor general's office and ombudsman, and promptly implement recommendations.

- **Coroner's inquests**—Order coroner's inquests into police-involved deaths of intimate partners and other family members. Act promptly on recommendations.

- **Civilian oversight**—Create stringent civilian oversight over law enforcement through independent bodies such as police boards, police hiring boards and national and state/provincial civilian police

---

[248] This suggestion is adapted from a recommendation made in Bouza, *Police Unbound*, 260-1.

commissions empowered to demand accountability, with representation from domestic violence advocates, racialized people, First Nations, police reform proponents and other community groups.

- **Reform-minded chiefs**—Hire reform-minded police chiefs. Make their willingness to take tough action on police domestic violence a key hiring criterion. Give them the power to hire new commanders from outside the department (if they don't already have this ability).

- **Gun prohibitions for abusers**—Enact laws prohibiting gun possession to domestic abuse offenders, including those who commit felony/indictable offences, misdemeanour/summary crimes and anyone subject to a protection order, with no exemptions for police and other government employees. Apply restrictions retroactively.

- **Gun ban registry**—Create a national registry for those who commit offences triggering a gun ban, mandate checks of the registry during police pre-hire screening and all gun purchases, and create a mechanism for police departments to be automatically informed if an officer triggers the ban. Restrict easy restoration of gun rights via court application, pardon or other remedy.

- **Compile and release data**—Require departments to compile comprehensive data on allegations and investigations of police domestic violence and sexual misconduct, including disciplinary outcomes, and to make it public regularly.

- **Better screening**—Fund research to improve psychological screening techniques that police can use to weed out candidates with abusive tendencies or sexist or racist attitudes and to conduct regular post-hire rescreening for the same factors.

- **Review records**—Require police to review civil and family court records of potential new employees during the pre-hire check and to exclude anyone who has been involved in domestic violence.

- **Misconduct database**—Create a national database for police misconduct incidents, and require police to report incidents to the database and check the database as part of pre-hire screening.

- **Domestic violence units**—Study police department resourcing of domestic violence units, and require improvements if needed.

- **Improve domestic violence response**—Work with advocates to develop independent resources with no connection to law enforcement that police family members can access. Improve the community, legal, educational and health care response to domestic violence in the broader population. Problems include underfunding of women's shelters, lack of access to legal representation for impoverished

women in family court, poor training of judges, court staff and lawyers on violence against women, outdated family law legislation, the
ability of abusers to use courts to legally harass survivors and lack of
rehabilitation for abusers.[249]

- **Police power, impunity and anti-woman attitudes**—Study
  and enact other measures to constrain police power, impunity, derogatory attitudes toward women and related problems, such as
  mishandled police investigations of violence against women and
  missing women (particularly those of First Nations descent); police
  sexual misconduct against female officers and female drivers at traffic stops; police brutality and mistreatment of black people, First
  Nations people and other marginalized people; police underrepresentation of women, racialized people and First Nations; and workplace harassment and discrimination.
- **Underlying social problems**—Study and enact measures to address the underlying social problems that cops are tacitly mandated
  to police, including women's inequality, discrimination against black
  people, subjugation of First Nations, income inequality and unemployment, especially among youth.

RECOMMENDATIONS FOR THE PUBLIC

- Read about police domestic violence (see resources in Appendix F)
  and the recommendations and advice in these appendices for other
  individuals and bodies.
- Demand that police departments, governments, advocates, the media and academics act on the recommendations listed in these appendices. Emphasize the issues in protest actions, elections,
  municipal council meetings, social media, letters to the editor, conferences and other public events.
- Support local women's shelters. Ask them to address the special
  needs of abused police spouses. Pressure governments to increase
  shelter funding and other resources for domestic violence survivors.
  Volunteer, hold fundraisers, donate old cell phones. Organize events

---

[249] For a comprehensive list of recommendations, see *A Blueprint for Canada's
National Action Plan on Violence Against Women and Girls*, Canadian Network of
Women's Shelters & Transition Houses, February 18, 2015, accessed August 10, 2015,
http://endvaw.ca/wp-content/uploads/2015/10/Blueprint-for-Canadas-NAP-on-
VAW.pdf.

to commemorate your local domestic violence awareness day or month. If you don't have one in your area, ask local authorities to create one.

- When police domestic violence incidents arise, don't be silent. Express your views in letters to the editor, opinion pieces, social media posts, YouTube videos and online comments to news stories. Work with others to demand investigations of police handling of abusive officers, improved practices and protection of survivors. Highlight the systemic, mostly unchecked nature of the abuse epidemic. Make connections with other incidents and the underlying structural issues.

- Join others to start a group or campaign on police domestic violence. Create a citizen journalism investigation, wiki or mapping project.

- Initiate domestic violence awareness programs and discussion of gender inequality, sexual harassment and respect in your workplace, in schools, religious organizations and the community.

- Form or join groups active on issues of police power, impunity, derogatory attitudes to women and related problems, including domestic violence (e.g. underfunding of women's shelters, lack of access to legal representation for impoverished women in family court, poor training of judges, court staff and lawyers on violence against women, outdated family law legislation and lack of rehabilitation for abusers, access to firearms for abusers, the ability of abusers to use courts to legally harass survivors); mishandled police investigations of violence against women and missing women (particularly those of First Nations descent); police sexual misconduct against female officers and female drivers at traffic stops; police brutality and mistreatment of black people, First Nations people and other marginalized people; police underrepresentation of women, racialized people and First Nations; workplace harassment and discrimination; lack of independent criminal investigation of police officers; and lax civilian oversight over law enforcement.

- More broadly, also focus on the underlying social problems that cops are tacitly mandated to police, including women's economic inequality, discrimination against black people, subjugation of First Nations, income inequality and unemployment, especially among youth. Study the connections. Work for change.

RECOMMENDATIONS FOR ADVOCATES

Advocates must understand that intimate partners of police officers face very different challenges than other women. As abuse counsellor Diane Wetendorf put it, "When a victim says, 'You don't understand, he's a police officer; but this is different, he's a police officer; I can't DO that, he's a police officer,' she's expressing her frustration that no one understands the many ways in which her situation is different."[250]

Complicating matters, many domestic violence programs work closely with police—sharing information, accompanying police to survivors' homes, inviting police officials to events. Police spouses are aware of this collaboration and may find it hard to trust some advocacy agencies.

"It's easy to understand how victims may think we're part of the criminal justice system," Wetendorf wrote. "If we even appear to be a part of the criminal justice system, the victim of an officer will not trust us. Our independence can be compromised—or appear compromised—by the close working relationships that accompany efforts to build coordinated community response and inter-agency collaboration. Victims are often left more alone, more isolated and more at risk."

Some of the advice below is adapted from various sources, including Wetendorf's tips to advocates. (Be aware this isn't a complete list of her suggestions. For comprehensive advice, please refer to her website abuseofpower.info and her guide for advocates.[251])

- Familiarize yourself with the unique challenges of dealing with police domestic violence. Study the resources in Appendix F and the recommendations and advice given in these appendices for other individuals, especially abused police spouses (Appendix B).
- Research how local police handle complaints about their employees, including any special protocols for investigating domestic violence.
- If your agency is contacted by a police spouse, assign an experienced advocate who has worked with a wide variety of women, has an excellent understanding of available options and doesn't let her personal views dominate the survivor's wishes. "Many advocates have strong feelings about police officers who abuse their intimate partners," Wetendorf said on her web page. "They may believe these bat-

---

[250] Diane Wetendorf, "Advocates' Role," accessed July 16, 2015, http://www.abuseofpower.info/Adv_Role.htm.
[251] Wetendorf, *When the Batterer Is a Law Enforcement Officer: A Guide for Advocates.*

terers have no right to be police officers and want the victims to co-operate with attempts to hold the officers accountable. An advocate's desire to get an abusive officer off the streets can make it hard to remember that it is not the victim's responsibility to see that the law is enforced or to reform the police department. As always, our first commitment is to support *her* wishes and decisions."

- Shelter staff should get legal advice on what to do if police arrive in search of an officer's spouse. A procedure should be in place before a crisis occurs, Wetendorf suggested. "If the board and staff cannot agree on how to handle a conflict with law enforcement or if local political realities require avoiding conflicts with the police, it may be best to refer victims of police officers to another agency."

- Help the survivor explore her options and a safety plan (see Appendix B for safety planning information).

- Validate her experience and feelings. Assure her she is not alone or "going crazy."

- Advise her to save documentation and keep it in a safe place. Offer to do so at your agency if you can be certain it will be secure.

- Be aware of the heightened dangers when an officer faces investigation or the survivor is in the process of leaving the relationship.

- Advocate for the survivor and her family in the legal and other community systems. Help her tell her story clearly and with adequate detail. Give her information on how the justice system works.

- Be aware of the added challenges for certain abused spouses, such as those with children, female officers, same-sex intimate partners of a cop and intimate partners of racialized officers (see additional details in Appendix B).

- Lobby police and governments to investigate how police handle abusive officers and those involved in sexual misconduct, improve police practices and enhance survivor protection.

- Conduct surveys of survivors, shelter workers and advocates about police response to domestic violence incidents. Publicize the results.

- Connect with journalists, other advocates, community groups and unions to publicize the challenges of police domestic violence and press for change.

- Work with groups that campaign on police power, impunity, derogatory attitudes to women and related problems, such as domestic violence (e.g. underfunding of women's shelters, lack of access to legal representation for impoverished women in family court, poor training of judges, court staff and lawyers on violence against women, outdated family law legislation and lack of rehabilitation for abusers, access to firearms for abusers, the ability of abusers to use courts to legally harass survivors); mishandled police investigations of violence against women and missing women (particularly those of First Nations descent); police sexual misconduct against female officers and female drivers at traffic stops; police brutality and mistreatment of black people, First Nations people and other marginalized people; police underrepresentation of women, racialized people and First Nations; workplace harassment and discrimination; lack of independent criminal investigation of police officers; and lax civilian oversight over law enforcement.

- More broadly, also focus on the underlying social problems that cops are tacitly mandated to police, including women's economic inequality, discrimination against black people, subjugation of First Nations, income inequality and unemployment, especially among youth. Make the connections.

RECOMMENDATIONS FOR THE MEDIA

- Familiarize yourself with the issues by reviewing previous media investigations, background resources (see Appendix F) and the recommendations and advice in these appendices for other individuals and bodies.
- In stories on police domestic incidents, mention the broader context of widespread, largely unchecked abuse in law enforcement families. Get reactions and context from domestic violence advocates, abused police spouses and former and active cops who know the issues.
- Follow up breaking stories with broader context items on police domestic violence. Include prior incidents and developments in other areas.
- Investigate law enforcement agencies in your city, province/state and nationally, including officer-involved domestic violence rates, discipline outcomes, disclosure practices, policies on officer-involved domestic violence (or lack thereof) and compliance with policies and firearms prohibitions.
  - ✓ Compare discipline outcomes for officer-involved domestic violence against other misconduct, such as making a false statement, theft, off-duty altercations or use of controlled substances.

- ✓ Compare discipline outcomes for police officers (number of complaints, portion of sustained complaints, arrest ratios, etc.) to figures for the wider population.
- ✓ Investigate how well police, governments and academics follow the recommendations in these appendices.
- ✓ Use freedom-of-information legislation to obtain records from police department and responsible government agencies.
- ✓ Review past media stories to investigate disciplinary and court outcomes for officers. Use Google News alerts to monitor ongoing issues.
- ✓ Check criminal, civil, traffic and family court records of individual police officers, including commanders and those involved in high-profile cases or wrongdoing.
- ✓ Investigate whether police departments report misconduct to a central registry and whether they use such a registry for pre-hire screening of candidates. If not, why not?
- ✓ Examine the effectiveness of police pre-hire and post-hire screening practices to identify officers who have committed abuse, display or develop abusive tendencies and have discriminatory attitudes.
- ✓ Check court records for lawsuits against police agencies and unions to find story ideas, interesting records and sources.
- ✓ Investigate how law enforcement agencies and governments use (or misuse) grants available for domestic violence programs, training and prosecution, such as Violence Against Women Grants Office funds from the U.S. Department of Justice.
- Develop stories and bring them to life with accounts from abused police spouses, active-duty and former cops, women's shelter staff, domestic violence researchers and advocates, associations of women police officers, counsellors of abused people and abusers, staff at hospital domestic violence programs and lawyers involved in court actions related to mishandled police investigations of violence against women or police sexual misconduct. Some of these people can help you find abused police spouses, as can scanning past media stories for keywords like "police" and "domestic violence." Women police associations may be able to refer you to female officers abused by fellow cops.
- Take extra care to ensure source confidentiality and safety.
- Pursue related stories about police power, impunity, derogatory attitudes to women and related problems, such as:

✓ Poor government response to domestic violence in the wider population—including underfunding of women's shelters, lack of access to legal representation for impoverished women in family court, poor training of judges, court staff and lawyers on violence against women, outdated family law legislation, lack of rehabilitation for abusers, access to firearms for abusers and the ability of abusers to use courts to legally harass survivors.

✓ Mishandled investigations involving violence against women and missing women (particularly those of First Nations descent). For example, survey survivors, shelter workers and advocates about police response to domestic violence in the general population.

✓ Police sexual misconduct against female officers. Contact women police associations for story ideas.

✓ Police sexual misconduct against young female drivers at traffic stops. For example, survey female drivers using traffic court records.

✓ Police brutality and mistreatment of black people, First Nations people and other marginalized people.

✓ Police underrepresentation of women, racialized people and First Nations.

✓ Workplace harassment and discrimination.

✓ Lack of independent criminal investigation of police officers.

✓ Lax civilian oversight over law enforcement.

✓ The underlying social problems that cops are tacitly mandated to police, including women's inequality, discrimination against black people, subjugation of First Nations, income inequality and unemployment, especially among youth.

RECOMMENDATIONS FOR ACADEMICS

• Familiarize yourself with police domestic violence by reviewing past research and media investigations, background resources (see Appendix F) and the recommendations and advice in these appendices for other individuals and bodies.

• Research police domestic abuse rates (including type and severity of abuse, lifetime and past-year frequency of incidents, whether the abuse was reported and the outcome) and potential correlates such as gender, age, marital status, years of police service, rank, shift and work assignment (e.g. uniform, narcotics, traffic).

- Research police discipline disclosure, policies on officer-involved domestic violence (or lack thereof) and compliance with policies and firearms prohibitions. Also research:
  - ✓ Discipline outcomes for domestic violence versus other police misconduct, such as use of controlled substances, making a false statement, theft or off-duty altercations.
  - ✓ Discipline outcomes for police officers (number of complaints, portion of sustained complaints, arrest ratios, etc.) versus the figures for the wider population.
  - ✓ How well police, governments and journalists follow the recommendations in these appendices.
  - ✓ Whether departments report misconduct to a central registry and use such a registry for pre-hire screening of candidates.
  - ✓ The effectiveness of police pre-hire and post-hire screening practices to identify officers who have committed abuse, display or develop abusive tendencies and have discriminatory attitudes. Also, research more effective screening methods.
  - ✓ How law enforcement agencies and governments use (or misuse) grants available for domestic violence programs, training and prosecution, such as Violence Against Women Grants Office funds from the U.S. Department of Justice.
- Use freedom-of-information legislation and court records to obtain research material.
- Develop research ideas through contacts with abused police spouses, active-duty and former cops, women's shelter staff, domestic violence researchers and advocates, associations of women police officers, counsellors of abused people and abusers, staff at hospital domestic violence programs and lawyers involved in court actions related to mishandled police investigations of violence against women or police sexual misconduct.
- Take extra care to ensure source confidentiality and safety.
- Research related topics involving police power, impunity, derogatory police attitudes to women and related problems, such as:
  - ✓ Poor government response to domestic violence in the wider population—including underfunding of women's shelters, lack of access to legal representation for impoverished women in family court, poor training of judges, court staff and lawyers on violence against women, outdated family law legislation and lack of rehabilitation for abusers, access to firearms for abusers and the ability of abusers to use courts to legally harass survivors.

- ✓ Mishandled investigations involving violence against women and missing women (particularly those of First Nations descent). For example, survey survivors, shelter workers and advocates about police response to domestic violence in the general population.
- ✓ Police sexual misconduct against female officers and female drivers at traffic stops.
- ✓ Police brutality and mistreatment of black people, First Nations people and other marginalized people.
- ✓ Police underrepresentation of women, racialized people and First Nations.
- ✓ Workplace harassment and discrimination.
- ✓ Lack of independent criminal investigation of police officers.
- ✓ Lax civilian oversight over law enforcement.
- ✓ The underlying social problems that cops are tacitly mandated to police, including women's economic inequality, discrimination against black people, subjugation of First Nations, income inequality and unemployment, especially among youth.

APPENDIX E

Statistics

H ere are selected statistics cited in this book, in most cases with full citations included again for ease of reference.

DOMESTIC VIOLENCE IN POLICE FAMILIES

Percentage of 728 officers who admitted to sociologist Leanor Johnson that they had "gotten out of control and behaved violently" toward their spouse or children in the previous six months: 40 [252]

Percentage of 385 male cops who admitted to Arizona cop Albert Seng and his team that they were violent toward their spouse at least once in the previous year: 28 [253]

Percentage of 115 female police spouses of male cops who told Seng their husband had been violent to them in the prior year: 25

Percentage of cops in their 20s who reported domestic violence: 64

Percentage of divorced or legally separated cops who reported domestic violence: 66

---

[252] Leanor Boulin Johnson, Prepared statement before the U.S. House of Representatives Select Committee on Children, Youth and Families (Washington, D.C.: May 20, 1991), 32-48, accessed March 18, 2015,
http://files.eric.ed.gov/fulltext/ED338997.pdf.

[253] Peter H. Neidig, Harold E. Russell and Albert F. Seng, "Interspousal Aggression in Law Enforcement Families: A Preliminary Investigation," *Police Studies: International Review of Police Development* 15 (Spring 1992), 30-38.

Percentage of U.S. and Canadian women who reported physical or sexual
assault by an intimate partner in the previous year: 1.5 to 4[254]

POLICE RESPONSE AROUND THE WORLD

The results in the table below (discussed in Chapter 8) are from a survey I
sent in December 2015 to 178 police forces in 10 countries: the U.S., Canada,
the UK, France, Australia, South Africa, the Bahamas, Ireland, Jamaica, and
Trinidad and Tobago. The "international" column's figures are weighted
equally by responding country and include the data for the U.S. and Canada.

	U.S.	Canada	Interna-tional
# of police dep'ts contacted	68	58	178
% of dep'ts that answered	31	38	26
% of dep'ts that typically fire a cop after 1st sustained domestic violence complaint	38	9	19
% of dep'ts that typically fire a cop after 2nd sustained domestic violence complaint	48	14	22
% of dep'ts that have a specific policy on domestic violence by officers	33	9	28
% of dep'ts that have adopted the IACP model policy on domestic violence by officers	0	0	0

POLICE DISCIPLINE IN THE U.S.

Out of 227 investigations of LAPD officers for domestic violence from 1990 to
1997, number of upheld abuse complaints: 91[255]
Number that led to a criminal charge: 18

---

[254] See Chapter 3 for references for this bullet point.
[255] Katherine Mader, *Domestic Violence in the Los Angeles Police Department: How
well does the Los Angeles Police Department police its own? The Report of the
Domestic Violence Task Force to the Board of Police Commissioners* (Office of the
Inspector General, Los Angeles Police Department, July 22, 1997).

Number that led to a conviction: 4

Number of cops who were fired: 1

Most common discipline: suspension of one to four days or admonishment

Portion of abusive cops who had no mention of the sustained complaint in their performance records: over three-quarters

Percentage who got a promotion after a sustained complaint: 29

Out of 123 U.S. police departments responding to a survey about discipline for domestic violence, percentage that normally terminated an officer for a first sustained domestic violence incident: under 6[256]

Percentage that said termination was appropriate after a second sustained incident: 19

Percentage of U.S. cops convicted of misdemeanour domestic assault who lost their job: 32[257]

Number of officers in the Puerto Rico Police Department still on active duty after two or more domestic violence arrests: 84 out of 98 (or 86 percent)[258]

Number still on active duty after three or more domestic violence arrests: 11 out of 17 (or 65 percent)

Percentage of U.S. cops charged with a criminal offence who were convicted: 33[259]

Percentage of the U.S. general public charged with a criminal offence who were convicted: 68

Percentage of U.S. cops convicted of a criminal charge who were incarcerated: 36

Percentage of the U.S. general public convicted of a criminal charge who were incarcerated: 70

---

256 Larry Boyd et al., "Domestic Assault Among Police: A Survey of Internal Affairs Policies" (Southwestern Law Enforcement Institute and Arlington Police Department, 1995), accessed March 18, 2015, http://www.cailaw.org/media/files/ILEA/Publications/domestic_99.pdf.

257 Philip M. Stinson and John Liederbach, "Fox in the Henhouse: A Study of Police Officers Arrested for Crimes Associated with Domestic and/or Family Violence," *Criminal Justice Policy Review* 24 (2013), accessed March 20, 2015, http://scholarworks.bgsu.edu/cgi/viewcontent.cgi?article=1005&context=crim_just_pub.

258 U.S. Department of Justice, Civil Rights Division, *Investigation of the Puerto Rico Police Department* (September 5, 2011), 16-17, accessed May 21, 2015, http://www.justice.gov/crt/about/spl/documents/prpd_letter.pdf.

259 David Packman, *2010 NPMSRP Police Misconduct Statistical Report —Draft* (National Police Misconduct Reporting Project, Cato Institute, April 5, 2011), accessed December 7, 2016, http://www.policemisconduct.net/2010-npmsrp-police-misconduct-statistical-report/.

POLICE DISCIPLINE IN CANADA[260]

	Montreal police	Halifax police	RCMP
# of officers on the force	4,600	520	18,400
Avg annual # of complaints against officers for domestic violence	12	not disclosed	not disclosed
Avg annual # that were at least partially sustained	9.3	not disclosed	not disclosed
Avg annual # that led to discipline	2.7	1.8	2
Avg annual # that led to criminal charges	2.7	0.8	0.6
# of male cops who committed domestic abuse in the prior year, if we apply the 28% abuse rate in the 1992 Albert Seng et al. study	900	120	4,000
Portion of abusive male cops who got charged, if the 28% abuse rate applies	1 in 300	1 in 150	1 in 6,500

Percentage of RCMP officers disciplined for domestic violence who were dismissed or ordered to resign (2008-2013): 0

Percentage of RCMP officers disciplined for making a false statement who were dismissed or ordered to resign: 11

Percentage of RCMP officers disciplined for theft who were dismissed or ordered to resign: 50

Average number of days of docked pay for Mounties disciplined for domestic violence: 6.8

Average days of docked pay for Mounties who made a false statement: 7.9

Average days of docked pay for Mounties disciplined for theft: 8.5

Percentage of officers at four large Canadian police forces who were terminated from their job after being convicted of domestic violence or disciplined for assaulting a domestic partner: 0

---

[260] See Chapter 8 for references for the data in this table and section. The Toronto Police Service failed to respond to an initial freedom-of-information request for data, while the Vancouver Police Department said data wasn't available or compiled.

Percentage of Canadian cops convicted of domestic violence who were sentenced to prison: 7[261]

Percentage of the Canadian general public convicted of comparable domestic violence offences who were sentenced to prison: 49

POLICING: A MAN'S WORLD

Percentage of U.S. cops who are women: 12[262]

Percentage of U.S. cops who said they'd be equally comfortable with a female or male boss: 7.2[263]

Percentage of U.S. cops who agreed that "women are just as capable of thinking logically as men": 7.1

Percentage of Canadian cops who are women: 21[264]

POLICE OFFICER HEALTH

Portion of police spouses who wanted departments to offer cops and families alcoholism treatment and stress reduction programs: over three-quarters[265]

Percentage of cops who said they felt worried or guilty about excessive alcohol use: 36

---

[261] Danielle Sutton, "News Coverage of Officer-Invoved Domestic Violence (OIDV): A Comparative Content Analysis," a thesis presented to the University of Guelph in partial fulfillment of requirements for the degree of Master of Arts in Criminology and Criminal Justice Policy (Guelph, Ontario: August 2015), accessed November 28, 2016, https://atrium.lib.uoguelph.ca/xmlui/bitstream/handle/10214/9099/Sutton_Danielle_201508_MA.pdf?sequence=1

[262] U.S. Department of Justice, Office of Community Oriented Policing Services, "Women in Law Enforcement," *Community Policing Dispatch* 6, no. 7 (July 2013), accessed March 21, 2013, http://cops.usdoj.gov/html/dispatch/07-2013/women_in_law_enforcement.asp.

[263] Amy Dellinger Page, "Judging Women and Defining Crime: Police Officers' Attitudes Toward Women and Rape," *Sociological Spectrum* (July 2008), 389-411, accessed April 23, 2015, http://libres.uncg.edu/ir/asu/f/page_2008_judging_women.pdf.

[264] Hope Hutchins, *Police resources in Canada, 2014* (Ottawa: Statistics Canada, 2015), 14, accessed June 28, 2015, http://www.statcan.gc.ca/pub/85-002-x/2015001/article/14146-eng.pdf.

[265] Boulin Johnson, Prepared statement before the U.S. House of Representatives Select Committee on Children, Youth and Families.

Percentage who reported suicidal thoughts: 30

Divorce rate of cops in large U.S. cities: nearly 75 percent[266]

Life expectancy of U.S. while male cops compared to the American white male average: 21.9 years lower[267]

How long a U.S. white male cop can expect to live after the average police retirement age of 57: six years

How long the average U.S. white male can expect to live after age 57: 31 years

THE ROLE OF POLICE

What is the role of police in society? Numbers tell part of the story. Below are correlations between the number of police officers per capita and measures of inequality. The higher the correlation, the more closely policing numbers are tied to each measure:[268]

In 22 developed countries
Correlation with total unemployment: 58 percent

... youth unemployment: 63 percent

... women's participation in the labour force: negative 46 percent

In the U.S.
Correlation with income inequality in each state: 38 percent

... the ratio of black to white unemployment: 42 percent

... the ratio of black male to total white unemployment: 55 percent

In Canada
Correlation with Aboriginal youth unemployment in Canadian cities: 69 percent

... Aboriginal male youth unemployment: 76 percent

---

[266] Vincent Van Hasselt and Donald C. Sheehan, introduction to *Domestic Violence by Police Officers*, ed. Donald C. Sheehan (Quantico, Virginia: Behavioral Science Unit, FBI Academy, 2000), 2.

[267] John M. Violanti et al., "Life Expectancy in Police Officers: A Comparison with the U.S. General Population," *International Journal of Emergency Mental Health and Human Resilience* 15, no. 4 (2013), 217-228.

[268] See Chapter 9 for data sources and discussion. All correlations are statistically significant.

APPENDIX F

Resources/Bibliography

T he resources below are intended to help abuse survivors, family members, police officers, advocates, perpetrators, government officials and others learn more about police domestic violence and abuse in general. This appendix is also a selected bibliography for the book.

If you are experiencing abuse, before getting started please consider the computer and communications safety tips in Appendix B. Note that website addresses listed here and elsewhere in this book may change after publication. Their inclusion in this book doesn't imply endorsement.

RESOURCES ON POLICE DOMESTIC VIOLENCE

Counsellor Diane Wetendorf's police domestic violence website
http://www.abuseofpower.info

Life Span: Chicago-based non-profit providing info, counselling, legal help and a 24-hour crisis line to domestic violence and sexual assault survivors, including specialized support for intimate partners of police officers
http://life-span.org/

Police domestic violence website of Lane and Patty Judson, the parents of Crystal Judson-Brame, who was murdered by her husband Police Chief David Brame of Tacoma, Washington, in 2003
http://www.lanejudson.com

Author Alex Roslin's blog on police domestic violence
http://policedomesticviolence.blogspot.com

Police Officer-Involved Domestic Violence Network's Facebook page
https://www.facebook.com/PoliceDomesticViolence

Behind The Blue Wall, blog devoted to police domestic violence
http://behindthebluewall.blogspot.ca/

"Police Family Violence Fact Sheet" from the U.S. National Center for
Women & Policing
http://www.womenandpolicing.org/violenceFS.asp

"A Death in St. Augustine": *New York Times*-PBS joint investigation of police
domestic violence in 2013
http://www.pbs.org/wgbh/pages/frontline/death-in-st-augustine/

Police domestic violence web page from Vancouver-based Battered Women's
Support Services
http://www.bwss.org/police-officer-involved-domestic-violence-2/

"Domestic Violence by Police Officers Model Policy": by the International
Association of Chiefs of Police, July 2003
http://www.theiacp.org/MPDomesticViolencebyPO

"Domestic Violence by Police Officers; Concepts and Issues Paper": by the
International Association of Chiefs of Police, July 2003
http://www.theiacp.org/Portals/0/documents/pdfs/MembersOnly/Domesti
cViolencebyPolicePaper.pdf

National Prevention Toolkit on Officer-Involved Domestic Violence: by
Florida's Law Enforcement Families Partnership
http://nationaltoolkit.csw.fsu.edu/

*Handbook for Developing, Implementing, and Administering Local Pro-
grams to Address Domestic Violence Involving Law Enforcement Personnel*: by the Washington State Office of the Attorney General
http://agportal-
s3bucket.s3.amazonaws.com/uploadedfiles/Another/Supporting_Law_Enfo
rcement/Domestic_Violence/Law_Enforcement_HB.pdf

Officer-Involved Domestic Violence Training Pilot, Executive Summary: by
the Washington State Office of the Attorney General, June 2004
http://www.atg.wa.gov/training-materials

GENERAL DOMESTIC VIOLENCE RESOURCES IN THE U.S.

National Coalition Against Domestic Violence
http://www.ncadv.org/
https://www.facebook.com/NationalCoalitionAgainstDomesticViolence/

National Domestic Violence Hotline: warning signs of abuse and other
resources
1-800-799-SAFE (7233)
http://www.thehotline.org/is-this-abuse/abuse-defined/

National Network to End Domestic Violence (U.S.)
http://nnedv.org/

DomesticViolence.org: tips and resources
http://www.domesticviolence.org/

DomesticShelters.org: searchable shelters database, 24/7 hotline and other
resources
https://www.domesticshelters.org/

Domestic Violence Survivors: Facebook page
https://www.facebook.com/DomesticViolenceSurvivors/

WomensLaw.org: state-by-state legal information, tips and support from the
National Network to End Domestic Violence, including custody issues, state
gun laws and restraining orders
http://www.womenslaw.org/

Danger Assessment Instrument: free online questionnaire assessing your risk
of being killed by an intimate partner
https://www.dangerassessment.org/

NoMore.org: campaign against domestic violence and sexual assault—events and resources
http://nomore.org/

The Verbal Abuse Site: information, resources and discussion forums by author Patricia Evans
http://verbalabuse.com/

Domestic violence shelters that accept pets: from lawyer Allie Phillips, director of the National Center for Prosecution of Animal Abuse
http://alliephillips.com/saf-tprogram/saf-t-shelters/

Myths and facts about domestic violence from the Clark County, Indiana, Prosecuting Attorney's Office
http://www.clarkprosecutor.org/html/domviol/myths.htm

Domestic violence safety planning advice
http://www.clarkprosecutor.org/html/domviol/plan.htm

Pandora's Project: support and resources for survivors of rape and sexual assault
http://www.pandys.org/articles/tipsforfriends.html

Stalking Resource Center: tips, handbook for victims, resources
http://www.victimsofcrime.org/our-programs/stalking-resource-center

Center for Policing Equity
http://policingequity.org/

National Association for Civilian Oversight of Law Enforcement
http://www.nacole.org/

GENERAL DOMESTIC VIOLENCE RESOURCES IN CANADA AND OTHER COUNTRIES

Canada: Canadian Network of Women's Shelters & Transition Houses
http://endvaw.ca/

Canada: Centre for Research & Education on Violence Against Women & Children
http://www.neighboursfriendsandfamilies.ca/eng/safetyplanningforwomen.php?q=how-to-help/safety-planning

Canada: "How to plan for your safety"—family violence web page of the Public Health Agency of Canada
http://www.phac-aspc.gc.ca/sfv-avf/info/ha-plan-eng.php

Ontario: Assaulted Women's Helpline
http://www.awhl.org/

Ontario: Legal rights information related to family violence
http://yourlegalrights.on.ca/resource-legal-topic/1

Ontario: Voisin-es, ami-es et familles—une campagne de sensibilisation du public aux signes avertisseurs de la violence faite aux femmes
http://voisinsamisetfamilles.ca/

Ontario: Kanawayhitowin—campaign on woman abuse in Aboriginal communities
http://www.kanawayhitowin.ca/

Quebec: Women Aware/Femmes Averties—domestic violence support by survivors
http://www.womenaware.ca/

British Columbia: Domestic violence fact page from Battered Women's Support Services
http://www.bwss.org/resources/information-on-abuse/numbers-are-people-too/

Canada: Kids' Help Line—resources and free anonymous, bilingual and confidential phone and 24-7 web advice for kids and teens
http://www.kidshelpphone.ca/

Canada: Cut It Out—Salons Against Domestic Abuse
http://cutitoutcanada.com/

Canada: Women and Pets Escaping Violence—from the Canadian Federation of Humane Societies
http://cfhs.ca/athome/human_animal_violence_connection#link_twelve

Canada: Military Family Violence Support—resources from a Halifax-based agency
http://militaryfamilyviolencesupport.ca/

Canada: Canadian Association for Civilian Oversight of Law Enforcement
http://www.cacole.ca/

International: HotPeachPages—worldwide directory of abuse hotlines, shelters, refuges, crisis centres and women's organizations, accessible in 110 languages
http://www.hotpeachpages.net/index.html

International: resources on domestic violence from New York lawyer and author Andrew Vachss
http://www.vachss.com/help_text/domestic_violence_intl.html

Europe: Women Against Violence Europe—network of women's groups active against domestic violence
http://www.wave-network.org/

UK: Women's Aid—resources on domestic violence
http://www.womensaid.org.uk/

France: INAVEM—resources and helpline from the National Institute for Victim Support and Mediation
http://www.inavem.org/

India: SNEHA—resources, legal support and free counselling
http://www.snehamumbai.org/our-work/domestic-violence.aspx

Australia: National Sexual Assault, Domestic Violence Counselling Service 1800-737-732
https://www.1800respect.org.au/

South Africa: People Opposing Women Abuse
http://www.powa.co.za/

HELPLINES

In case of injury or immediate danger, consider calling 911 (or the emergency number in your location). The following anonymous crisis and support lines can provide free information and help.

As noted in Appendix B, be aware that while these services are usually confidential, in many jurisdictions if a counsellor is concerned that you or someone else, particularly a child, is at risk of harm, they may be obliged to contact authorities and give them your contact information or, if you are using a chatline, your computer's Internet Protocol address (i.e. your computer's location). You may want to check the agency's privacy rules or clarify with the counsellor before deciding what to disclose.

U.S.: Chicago-based non-profit group Life Span's 24-hour crisis line for domestic violence survivors, including specialized support for police spouses
847-532-9540
http://life-span.org/

U.S.: National Domestic Violence Hotline—help 24-7 in English, Spanish and 170 other languages, chatline also available
1-800-799-SAFE (7233)
http://www.thehotline.org/

Ontario: Assaulted Women's Helpline—help 24-7, over 150 languages spoken
1-866-863-0511 or 416-863-0511
http://www.awhl.org/

Ontario: Fem'aide—ligne de soutien pour femmes touchées par la violence
1-877-336-2433
http://www.femaide.ca/

Quebec: Women Aware/Femmes Averties—domestic violence support by survivors in English and French
1-866-489-1110 or 514-489-1110
http://www.womenaware.ca/

Quebec: SOS Violence Conjugale—24-7 help in French and English
1-800-363-8010 or 514-873-9010
http://www.sosviolenceconjugale.ca/

British Columbia: Domestic Violence Helpline/VictimLink—help 24-7, multiple languages
1-800-563-0808
http://www.domesticviolencebc.ca/

Alberta: Family Violence Support and Services—help 24-7 in over 170 languages, chatline also available
1-800-310-1818 (Family Violence Info Line) or 1-800-387-5437 (Child Abuse Hotline)
http://humanservices.alberta.ca/abuse-bullying/14839.html

Canada: Kids' Help Line—24-7 help in English and French for kids and teens, chatline and online forums also available
1-800-668-6868
http://www.kidshelpphone.ca/
http://jeunessejecoute.ca/

UK: 24-Hour National Domestic Violence Freephone Helpline—in partnership with Women's Aid and Refuge
0808-2000-247
http://www.nationaldomesticviolencehelpline.org.uk/

France: national helpline of the INAVEM victim support group, operating seven days a week from 9 a.m. to 9 p.m.
08-842-846-37 (08VICTIMES)
http://www.inavem.org/index.php

India: list of domestic violence helplines
http://www.naaree.com/how-to-report-domestic-violence-in-india-call-these-helplines/

Australia: National Sexual Assault, Domestic and Family Violence Counselling Service—24-7 help by phone or online, including via interpreter
1800-737-732
https://www.1800respect.org.au/

Australia: Kids Helpline—phone, chat and email help for kids, teens and young adults
1800-551-800
http://www.kidshelp.com.au/

South Africa: People Opposing Women Abuse—phone and email help, shelters and legal support

011-642-4345/6

http://www.powa.co.za/

BOOKS AND OTHER PUBLICATIONS

A Blueprint for Canada's National Action Plan on Violence Against Women and Girls. Canadian Network of Women's Shelters & Transition Houses. February 18, 2015. Accessed August 10, 2015. http://endvaw.ca/sites/endvaw.ca/files/blueprint_for_canadas_nap_o n_vaw.pdf.

"Tacoma Confidential: Did Keeping Secrets Lead to Murder?" CBS News *48 Hours*. September 25, 2003. Accessed March 21, 2015. http://www.cbsnews.com/news/tacoma-confidential/. (See full broadcast here: http://www.cbsnews.com/videos/tacoma-confidential/.)

Bancroft, Lundy. *Daily Wisdom for "Why Does He Do That?": Encouragement for Women Involved With Angry and Controlling Men*. New York: The Penguin Group, 2015.

Bancroft, Lundy. *Why Does He Do That?: Inside the Minds of Angry and Controlling Men*. New York: The Penguin Group, 2002.

Beals, Judith E. *Understanding the Military Response to Domestic Violence: Tools for Civilian Advocates*. Battered Women's Justice Project, 2003. Updated by Patricia Erwin, 2007. Accessed April 26, 2015. http://www.bwjp.org/assets/understanding-military-response-domestic-violence.pdf.

Bogdanich, Walter and Glenn Silber. "Two Gunshots On a Summer Night; A Deputy's Pistol, a Dead Girlfriend, a Flawed Inquiry." *The New York Times*, November 23, 2013. Accessed March 21, 2015. http://www.nytimes.com/projects/2013/two-gunshots/.

Boulin Johnson, Leanor. "Police Officers and Spousal Violence: Work-Family Linkages." In *Continuing the War Against Domestic Violence*, 2nd ed., edited by Lee E. Ross, 189-210. Boca Raton, Florida: CRC Press, 2014.

Boulin Johnson, Leanor. Prepared statement before the U.S. House of Representatives Select Committee on Children, Youth and Families, Washington, D.C., May 20, 1991: 32-48. Accessed March 18, 2015. http://files.eric.ed.gov/fulltext/ED338997.pdf.

Boulin Johnson, Leanor et al. "Violence in Police Families: Work-Family Spillover." *Journal of Family Violence* 20, no. 1 (February 2005): 3-12.

Bouza, Anthony V. *The Police Mystique: An Insider's Look at Cops, Crime, and the Criminal Justice System*. New York: Plenum Press, 1990.

Bouza, Anthony V. *Police Unbound: Corruption, Abuse, and Heroism by the Boys in Blue*. Amherst, New York: Prometheus Books, 2001.

Boyd, Larry et al. "Domestic Assault Among Police: A Survey of Internal Affairs Policies." Southwestern Law Enforcement Institute and Arlington Police Department, 1995. Accessed March 18, 2015. http://www.cailaw.org/media/files/ILEA/Publications/domestic_99.pdf.

Brewster, Susan. *Helping Her Get Free: A Guide for Families and Friends of Abused Women*. Emeryville, California: Sea Press, 2006.

Canada. Department of Justice. *Abuse is Wrong*. Ottawa, 2009. Accessed April 14, 2015. http://www.justice.gc.ca/eng/rp-pr/cj-jp/fv-vf/aiw-mei/pdf/Abuse_is_Wrong.pdf.

Canada. Department of Justice. *La maltraitance est inacceptable*. Ottawa, 2009. Accessed April 14, 2015. http://www.justice.gc.ca/fra/pr-rp/jp-cj/vf-fv/mei-aiw/pdf/Abuse_is_Wrong_fr.pdf.

Cohen, Sarah, Rebecca R. Ruiz and Sarah Childress. "Departments Are Slow to Police Their Own Abusers." *The New York Times*, November 23, 2013. Accessed March 19, 2015. http://www.nytimes.com/projects/2013/police-domestic-abuse/.

Cross, Pamela. "It Shouldn't Be This Hard: A gender-based analysis of family law, family court and violence against women." Luke's Place Support & Resource Centre for Women & Children, September 2012. Accessed May 29, 2015. http://lukesplace.ca/pdf/It_Shouldnt_Be_This_Hard.pdf.

Dough, Jayne. *The Blue Abyss: A true story of a Domestic Violence Survivor within the executive law enforcement community.* CreateSpace, 2014.

Evans, Patricia. *The Verbally Abusive Relationship: How to Recognize It and How to Respond,* 3rd ed. Avon, Massachusetts: Adams Media, 2010.

Gallo, Gina. "A Family Affair." *Police: The Law Enforcement Magazine,* February 1, 2005. Accessed April 17, 2015. http://www.policemag.com/channel/patrol/articles/2005/02/a-family-affair.aspx.

Gallo, Gina. *Armed and Dangerous: Memoirs of a Chicago Policewoman.* New York: Tom Doherty Associates, 2001.

Gambacorta, David and Dana DiFilippo. *The Philadelphia Daily News,* September 11, 2014. Accessed August 16, 2015, https://web.archive.org/web/20160706140754/http://articles.philly.com/2014-09-11/news/53775430_1_police-officer-police-families-philadelphia-police-department.

Harrison, Deborah et al. "A research study on the wellbeing, family functioning and social development of adolescents in military families." 2008-2011. Accessed June 7, 2015. http://www2.unb.ca/youthwellbeing/.

Harrison, Deborah. *The First Casualty: Violence Against Women in Canadian Military Communities.* Toronto: James Lorimer & Company, 2002.

Harrison, Deborah et al. *Report on the Canadian Forces' Response to Woman Abuse in Military Families.* Submitted to the Minister of National Defence, Canada. 2000. Accessed March 19, 2015. http://www.unb.ca/fredericton/arts/centres/mmfc/_resources/pdfs/familyviolmilitaryreport.pdf.

Jacobson, Neil and John Gottman. *When Men Batter Women: New Insights into Ending Abusive Relationships.* New York: Simon & Schuster, 1998.

Kennedy Dugan, Meg and Roger R. Hock. *It's My Life Now: Starting Over After an Abusive Relationship or Domestic Violence*, Second Edition. New York: Routledge, 2006.

LaRosa, Paul. *Tacoma Confidential: A True Story of Murder, Suicide, and a Police Chief's Secret Life.* New York: Signet, 2006.

Law Enforcement Families Partnership. "Florida's Model Policy on Officer-Involved Domestic Violence." 2010. Accessed April 18, 2015. http://familyvio.csw.fsu.edu/wp-content/uploads/2010/05/FloridaModelPolicyonOfficerDV2010.pdf.

Lonsway, Kim et al. "Hiring & Retaining More Women: The Advantages to Law Enforcement Agencies." National Center for Women & Policing, Spring 2003. Accessed September 7, 2015. http://womenandpolicing.com/pdf/newadvantagesreport.pdf.

Lonsway, Kim et al. "Men, Women, and Police Excessive Force: A Tale of Two Genders." National Center for Women & Policing, April 2002. Accessed July 13, 2015. http://womenandpolicing.com/PDF/2002_Excessive_Force.pdf.

Macdonald, Nancy and Charlie Gillis. "Inside the RCMP's biggest crisis." *Maclean's.* February 27, 2015. Accessed May 5, 2015. http://www.macleans.ca/society/inside-the-rcmps-biggest-crisis/.

Mader, Katherine. *Domestic Violence in the Los Angeles Police Department: How well does the Los Angeles Police Department police its own? The Report of the Domestic Violence Task Force to the Board of Police Commissioners.* Office of the Inspector General, Los Angeles Police Department, July 22, 1997.

Merlo, Janet. *No One To Tell: Breaking My Silence on Life in the RCMP.* St. John's, Newfoundland: Breakwater Books, 2013.

National Domestic Violence Hotline. "What is Gaslighting?" May 29, 2014. Accessed April 16, 2015. http://www.thehotline.org/2014/05/what-is-gaslighting/.

Neidig, Peter H., Harold E. Russell and Albert F. Seng. "Interspousal Aggression in Law Enforcement Families: A Preliminary Investigation." *Police Studies* 15 (Spring 1992): 30-38.

Neidig, P. H., A. F. Seng and H. E. Russell. "Interspousal Aggression in Law Enforcement Personnel Attending the FOP Biennial Conference." *National FOP Journal*, Fall/Winter 1992: 25-28.

Nix, Jennifer. "To Protect and Abuse: An exploratory study discussing intimate partners of police as victims of domestic abuse." Paper presented to the Centre for the Study of Violence and Reconciliation, Johannesburg, South Africa, June 4, 1998. Accessed April 15, 2015. http://www.csvr.org.za/wits/papers/papnix.htm.

PBS *Frontline*. "A Death in St. Augustine." November 26, 2013. Accessed March 19, 2015. http://www.pbs.org/wgbh/pages/frontline/criminal-justice/death-in-st-augustine/transcript-53/.

Quindlen, Anna. *Black and Blue*. New York: Dell Publishing, 1998.

Rigakos, George S. "Situational Determinants of Police Responses to Civil and Criminal Injunctions for Battered Women." *Violence Against Women* 3, no. 2 (April 1997): 204-216.

Roslin, Alex. "Batterers in Blue." *The Georgia Straight*. July 24, 2003.

Roslin, Alex. "Black and Blue." *Saturday Night*. September 23, 2000.

Roslin, Alex. "Killer Cop." *This Magazine*. November/December 2004. Accessed March 18, 2015. http://albloggedup.blogspot.com/2007/09/police-family-violence-officer-involved-domestic-violence.html.

Roslin, Alex. "Police brutality at home: What happens when the cops must arrest one of their own for domestic violence." *The Montreal Gazette*, January 14, 2001, A1.

Roslin, Alex. "Violent Secrets; They're women in uniform married to cop husbands who beat them and get away with it." *NOW*, December 7, 2000. Accessed March 22, 2015. https://nowtoronto.com/news/violent-secrets/.

Russell, Jan. "Developing a Policy to Combat Officer-Involved Domestic Violence." 2011. Accessed April 18, 2015. http://www.ncdsv.org/images/Russell_DevelopingAPolicyToCombatOfficer-InvolvedDV_2011.pdf.

San Francisco Police Department. "Member-Involved Domestic Violence." Department General Order 6.20. October 8, 2014. Accessed April 18, 2015. http://www.sf-police.org/Modules/ShowDocument.aspx?documentID=27436.

Sheehan, Donald C., ed. *Domestic Violence by Police Officers*. Quantico, Virginia: Behavioral Science Unit, FBI Academy, 2000.

Sinha, Maire. *Family violence in Canada: A statistical profile, 2010*. Ottawa: Statistics Canada, May 22, 2012. Accessed March 18, 2015. http://www.statcan.gc.ca/pub/85-002-x/2012001/article/11643-eng.pdf.

Sonkin, Daniel Jay and Michael Durphy. *Learning to Live Without Violence: A Handbook for Men*. Volcano, California: Volcano Press, 1997.

Stinson, Philip M. and John Liederbach. "Fox in the Henhouse: A Study of Police Officers Arrested for Crimes Associated With Domestic and/or Family Violence." *Criminal Justice Police Review* 24 (2013). Accessed March 20, 2015. http://scholarworks.bgsu.edu/cgi/viewcontent.cgi?article=1005&context=crim_just_pub.

Stinson, Philip M. et al. "Police sexual misconduct: A national scale study of arrested officers." *Criminal Justice Policy Review*. Paper 30 (2014). Accessed July 14, 2015. http://scholarworks.bgsu.edu/cgi/viewcontent.cgi?article=1029&context=crim_just_pub.

Sutton, Danielle. "News Coverage of Officer-Invoved Domestic Violence (OIDV): A Comparative Content Analysis." A thesis presented to the University of Guelph in partial fulfillment of requirements for the degree of Master of Arts in Criminology and Criminal Justice Policy, Guelph, Ontario, August 2015. Accessed August 1, 2016. https://atrium.lib.uoguelph.ca/xmlui/bitstream/handle/10214/9099/Sutton_Danielle_201508_MA.pdf?sequence=1.

Ursel, Jane et al., eds. *What's Law Got to Do With It?: The Law, Specialized Courts and Domestic Violence in Canada*. Toronto: Cormorant Books, 2008.

U.S. Department of Justice. Civil Rights Division. *Investigation of the Puerto Rico Police Department*. September 5, 2011. Accessed May 21, 2015. http://www.justice.gov/crt/about/spl/documents/prpd_letter.pdf.

U.S. Department of Justice. Office of Justice Programs. National Institute of Justice. "Practical Implications of Current Domestic Violence Research: For Law Enforcement, Prosecutors and Judges." Washington, D.C., June 2009. Accessed May 28, 2015. https://www.ncjrs.gov/pdffiles1/nij/225722.pdf.

Violanti, John M. et al. "Life Expectancy in Police Officers: A Comparison with the U.S. General Population." *International Journal of Emergency Mental Health and Human Resilience* 15, no. 4 (2013): 217-228.

Walker, Samuel and Dawn Irlbeck. "Driving While Female: A National Problem in Police Misconduct." Police Professionalism Initiative, University of Nebraska at Omaha, March 2002. Accessed July 14, 2015. http://samuelwalker.net/wp-content/uploads/2010/06/dwf2002.pdf.

Walker, Samuel and Dawn Irlbeck. "Police Sexual Abuse of Teenage Girls: A 2003 Update on 'Driving While Female.'" Police Professionalism Initiative, University of Nebraska at Omaha, June 2003. Accessed July 14, 2015. http://samuelwalker.net/wp-content/uploads/2010/06/dwf2003.pdf.

Weiss, Elaine. *Surviving Domestic Violence: Stories of Women Who Broke Free*. Volcano, California: Volcano Press, 2004.

Wetendorf, Diane. "Annotated Safety Plan for OIDV Survivors." 2014. Accessed April 2, 2015.
http://www.abuseofpower.info/Tool_AnnotatedSafety.htm.

Wetendorf, Diane. "Police-Perpetrated Domestic Violence: An Advocate's Pessimistic Historical Perspective." *Domestic Violence Report* 19 no. 3 (February/March 2014). Accessed April 14, 2015.
http://www.abuseofpower.info/Wetendorf_Pessimist.pdf.

Wetendorf, Diane. "Safety Planning." Accessed April 14, 2015.
http://www.abuseofpower.info/Vict_Safety.htm.

Wetendorf, Diane. *Crossing the Threshold—Female Officers and Police-Perpetrated Domestic Violence.* 2006. Accessed April 14, 2015.
http://www.amazon.com/gp/product/B001FVEX8I.

Wetendorf, Diane. *Police Domestic Violence: A Handbook for Victims.* 2013. Accessed March 27, 2015.
http://www.abuseofpower.info/Book_Index.htm.

Wetendorf, Diane. *When the Batterer is a Law Enforcement Officer: A Guide for Advocates.* Battered Women's Justice Project, February 2004. Accessed July 14, 2015.
http://www.bwjp.org/assets/documents/pdfs/batterer_officer_guide_for_advocates.pdf.

Wetendorf, Diane and Dottie L. Davis. "Developing Policy on Officer-Involved Domestic Violence." 2015. Accessed April 17, 2015.
http://www.abuseofpower.info/Wetendorf_DevelopPolicy2015.pdf.

Wetendorf, Diane and Dottie L. Davis. "The Misuse of Police Powers in Officer-Involved Domestic Violence." 2015. Accessed May 3, 2015.
http://www.abuseofpower.info/Wetendorf_Misuse2015.pdf.

ACKNOWLEDGEMENTS

I am deeply grateful to Amy Morrison for sharing her story for this book and am honoured by her trust. I am also indebted to those who commented on drafts of this book's various editions and encouraged the project: Lane and Patty Judson, Amy Ramsay, Margaret Shorter, Dottie Davis, Leanor Johnson, Deborah Harrison, Albert "Bud" Seng, Michael Ryan, Joy Jones and my wife Rhonda Sherwood. (They are not responsible for any mistakes in the final result.) Thank you also to Diane Wetendorf for giving permission to reprint her annotated safety plan in Appendix B.

I'm especially grateful to my daughters for blessing our lives, for your kind, beautiful hearts and your unwavering sense of justice; to Sylvester, Pretzel and Saska for keeping me company many a late night; to my parents for your support; to my brothers for being my brothers; and to Rhonda for your wisdom, sense of humour and love. Thank you.

INDEX

Made in the USA
Columbia, SC
29 May 2018